RETHINKING FASHION

BLOOMSBURY VISUAL ARTS
Bloomsbury Publishing Plc
50 Bedford Square, London, WC1B 3DP, UK
1385 Broadway, New York, NY 10018, USA
29 Earlsfort Terrace, Dublin 2, Ireland

BLOOMSBURY, BLOOMSBURY VISUAL ARTS and the Diana logo
are trademarks of Bloomsbury Publishing Plc

First published in Great Britain 2021

A catalogue record for this book is available from the British Library.

Library of Congress Cataloging-in-Publication Data
Names: Cheang, Sarah, editor. | Takagi, Yoko, 1944– editor. | Greef, Erica de, editor.
Title: Rethinking fashion globalization / edited by Sarah Cheang, Erica de Greef and Yoko Takagi.
Description: London ; New York, NY : Bloomsbury Visual Arts, 2021. |
Includes bibliographical references and index.
Identifiers: LCCN 2020051637 (print) | LCCN 2020051638 (ebook) |
ISBN 9781350180062 (paperback) | ISBN 9781350180055 (hardback) |
ISBN 9781350180079 (pdf) | ISBN 9781350181304 (epub)
Subjects: LCSH: Fashion and globalization. | Fashion—Social aspects.
Classification: LCC GT525 .R484 2021 (print) | LCC GT525 (ebook) | DDC
391—dc23
LC record available at https://lccn.loc.gov/2020051637
LC ebook record available at https://lccn.loc.gov/2020051638

ISBN: HB: 978-1-3501-8005-5
       PB: 978-1-3501-8006-2
       ePDF: 978-1-3501-8007-9
       eBook: 978-1-3501-8130-4

Typeset by RefineCatch Limited, Bungay, Suffolk
Printed and bound in India

To find out more about our authors and books visit www.bloomsbury.com
and sign up for our newsletters.

RETHINKING FASHION GLOBALIZATION

Edited by Sarah CHEANG, Erica DE GREEF and TAKAGI Yoko

BLOOMSBURY VISUAL ARTS
LONDON • NEW YORK • OXFORD • NEW DELHI • SYDNEY

CONTENTS

Section III Global Design Practices

Introduction to Section III *TAKAGI Yoko*

ILLUSTRATIONS

Illustrations

NOTES ON CONTRIBUTORS

Sarah CHEANG is head of programme for the History of Design department at the Royal College of Art in London. Her research and teaching focuses on East Asian fashion history, gender and the body, with a special interest in fashion exchanges between China and Britain, and on fashion, race and cultural expression.

Hazel CLARK, is currently director of MA Fashion Studies, Parsons School of Design, The New School, New York. Her research and teaching reflect her residence in the UK, Europe, the US, Hong Kong and China, and her interests in fashion, design and culture, the everyday, slow, and fashion curating.

Daan van DARTEL is a museologist and anthropologist and curator of popular culture and fashion in the National Museum of World Cultures in the Netherlands. She is concerned with offering alternative views on ethnographic collections to bring multiple perspectives to broaden audiences' views on culture and cultural expressions, and to rethink fashion theory from a transcultural perspective.

Erica DE GREEF is a curator, academic and lecturer. She is the co-founder of the African Fashion Research Institute and curator at large: Fashion at the Zeitz Museum of Contemporary African Art in Cape Town. Her research focuses on African fashion, addressing absence and imaginaries that redress and rethink fashion histories for more sustainable futures.

Alla EIZENBERG teaches fashion design and theory at Parsons School of Design in New York, and is a doctoral candidate in the Department of Design, Aalto University in Helsinki. Her research focuses on the significance of the ordinary in the fashion practices of the early 21st century.

Osuanyi Quaicoo ESSEL teaches at the Fashion and Textiles Education unit in the Department of Art Education of the University of Education, Winneba. He is an African fashion and textiles historian, and a practising textiles artist. His research interest is in textiles and fashion history and Afrocentric beauty culture practices.

Courtney FU is a research fellow at the Faculty of Arts and Social Sciences, National University of Singapore. She is a historian of late imperial and modern China. Her current work aims to reconstruct fashion history of 20th century Singapore, focusing also on the transnational cultural circuits of transmission with Shanghai and Hong Kong.

Jenny HUGHES is a designer and senior lecturer in fashion/textiles at University of the Creative Arts. Research and studio teaching focuses on non-Western fashion perspectives, sustainability and biomimicry. These concerns also inform her own practice as a textile designer; she creates textiles for fashion/interior exploring memory trace and cultural history.

M. Angela JANSEN is a fashion anthropologist who has been working on fashion in Morocco for the last 20 years. In 2012, she created the Research Collective for Decolonizing Fashion (formerly known as the NonWesternFashionConference) as a critical platform to contest the ethnocentric claim of universality of dominant fashion discourse.

KOMA Kyoko (高馬京子) is Associate Professor of the School of Information and Communication at Meiji University in Tokyo. Her research and teaching focuses on Fashion, Gender and (Digital) Media Studies, with a special interest in trans-boundaries, representation, norms, cultural appropriation, stereotype, media discourse analysis, and comparative studies between France and Japan.

Malika KRAAMER is the Curator of the Africa Collection in MARKK, Museum am Rothenbaum, World Cultures and Arts, Hamburg, Germany. She worked at several museums and universities in the UK and the Netherlands. Her curatorial and research interests are in museums and decolonization, global dimensions of African fashion and textiles, and histories of Ghanaian cloth.

Elizabeth KRAMER is a Senior Lecturer of Design History at Northumbria University, Newcastle-upon-Tyne, UK. She is interested in how the materiality of garments can be used to understand cultural flows and transcultural identities, with a special interest in fashion and textile exchanges between Japan and Britain.

Abby LILLETHUN is Professor of Fashion History and Chairperson of the Department of Art and Design, Montclair State University, New Jersey. Abby's scholarship and teaching encompass social justice issues related to appearance and transcultural design exchange with a focus on Southeast Asia, the Arts and Crafts movement, and the Bronze Age Aegean.

Chepkemboi J. MANG'IRA is a journalist, fashion entrepreneur, decolonizing fashion activist and founder of OwnYourCulture based in Nairobi, Kenya. Her work focuses on showcasing the relevance of Kenyan heritage in fashion using mediums such as digital media, design, writing and events.

Harriette RICHARDS is Honorary Fellow in the School of Culture and Communication at the University of Melbourne, where she is co-founder of the Critical Fashion Studies research network. Her work considers questions of power and value within networks of labour and the decolonization of fashion in Aotearoa New Zealand and Australia.

TAKAGI Yoko （高木陽子） is Professor of the Graduate School of Fashion and Living Environment Studies at the Bunka Gakuen University, Tokyo. Focusing on Japonisme and the transboundary aspects of fashion and textiles from the field of Art Science, she has contributed to publications and curated exhibitions.

José TEUNISSEN is Dean of the School of Design and Technology at London College of Fashion, University of the Arts London as well as a Dutch fashion curator. Her research and curational practice focuses on fashion as a cultural phenomenon: an expression of the zeitgeist in which changing social and cultural developments are articulated.

Saskia THOELEN is Assistant-Professor at the graduate school of Fashion and Living Environment Studies at Bunka Gakuen University. Her research focuses on Mitsukoshi's departmentization and its kimono promotion during the Art Nouveau period. She is also interested in present-time kimono promotion and development, and *wasō* culture in Japan.

Linda WELTERS is Professor of Textiles, Fashion Merchandizing and Design at the University of Rhode Island where she teaches courses in the history of fashion. She directs the department's graduate program. Her research interests encompass Greek folk dress, archaeological textiles, American quilts, American fashion, and decolonizing fashion history.

ACKNOWLEDGEMENTS

The two-day seminar *(Re)Thinking Fashion Globalization* on February 15 and 16, 2019 at Bunka Gakuen University, Tokyo, co-organized by The Transboundary Fashion Seminar and the Research Collective for Decolonizing Fashion, was supported by JSPS KAKENHI Grant Number JP17K02382.

In addition to the contributors to this volume, we would like to thank Claudia Lucia Arana, Deirdre Clemente, Sheila Cliffe, Kawamura Yuniya, Katalin Medvedev, Toby Slade and Yoshimura Koka, who all played important roles in the shaping of this volume with us, through their generous participation and sharing of research and ideas in the wide-ranging and stimulating discussions in the seminar.

We would also like to thank Tanveer Ahmed, Magali Berthon, Hannah Heaf, Siviwe Siyabulela James, Celine Nguyen, Miriam Phelan, Teo Li-Xuan and Christin Yu. Their collective input and critical contribution has been invaluable in the selecting and arranging of terms for the index of this volume.

FOREWORD
M. Angela JANSEN

The edited volume before you is the result of a two-day seminar *(Re)Thinking Fashion Globalization* in February 2019 at Bunka Gakuen University, Tokyo, that was co-organized by The Transboundary Fashion Seminar and the Research Collective for Decolonizing Fashion. Fashion globalization has predominantly come to refer to Euromerican fashion, its theory, system and industry, spreading to the rest of the world due to processes of globalization in the last five decades, while mostly denying the large diversity of dress-fashion systems throughout the world, in their own right, through their own histories and their own global connectivities. The seminar's aim was to explore other interpretations of fashion globalization in an ongoing search for a diversity of meanings. Its ambition was to stimulate redrawing maps, rewriting narratives and rethinking fashion as diverse, multilingual and decentred.

The Transboundary Fashion Seminar was founded in 2014 by Takagi Yoko at Bunka Gakuen University in Tokyo, to research and formulate theory on transboundary contemporary Japanese fashion while promoting international collaboration. By assembling a variety of national and foreign experts, academics, designers, curators, journalists, industrial professionals and students, the TFS aims to stimulate a global research exchange. The Research Collective for Decolonizing Fashion (RCDF; formerly known as the Non-Western Fashion Conference), in its turn, was established in 2012 to disrupt Eurocentric underpinnings of dominant fashion discourse by acknowledging and valuing Other voices and narratives. The Collective critiques the denial, erasure and/or discrimination of Other dress-fashion systems due to unequal global power relations based on modern-colonial order, the Euro-American canon of normativity in regard to fashion and the exploitation and abuse of (Other) cultural heritages, human beings and natural resources by the dominant Euromerican fashion industry. The Collective aims to be a platform to connect, diversify and multiply the voices partaking in fashion discourse.

While fashion as a verb, e.g. the act of fashioning the body, is of all times and places, fashion as a noun has come to refer to a temporality (of contemporaneity), a system (of power) and an industry (of capitalism) that was conceived in Europe and exported to the rest of the world through European imperialism and globalization. There is an urgent need to decolonize and delink studies of fashion globalization when Other dress-fashion systems are predominantly considered and acknowledged through their (recent) relations and interactions with Euromerican fashion, either as producers or consumers, rather than in their own right, on their own terms and with their own definitions. With the recent 'discovery' of Other dress-fashion capitals in the context of fashion globalization, it is too often implied that these 'new' fashion capitals are the result of the introduction of Euromerican fashion, which perpetuates the denial and erasure of long, globally interconnected and dynamic dress-fashion histories outside the geographical and epistemological boundaries of Europe and North America.

A decolonial fashion globalization is one that does not set out to assimilate Other dress-fashion systems into the realm of modernity and erase difference, but one that acknowledges, values and celebrates the wide diversity of ways of fashioning the body throughout history and geography. Decolonizing fashion is not about 'taking the West out', but about correcting Euromodern fashion's claim to universality and reframing it in its historical and geographical context; about acknowledging that it is only one side of the (fashion) story. It is about humbling Euromerican fashion's discourse and listening to Other ways, aesthetics and senses in regard to fashioning the body. Most importantly, decolonial fashion discourse is not about the next fashionable theoretical framework, but about positionality and acknowledging what has been rendered invisible, denied, erased.

CHAPTER 1
INTRODUCTION
Sarah CHEANG, Erica DE GREEF and TAKAGI Yoko

This book explores the far-reaching cultural entanglements of 'global fashion' in terms of fashion's diverse, overlapping and hybrid contributions to crafting identities, negotiating change, developing technologies and making communities. But, more than this, it proposes a further area of entanglement: the study of 'global fashion' itself as an international academic activity which shapes understanding of what fashion is and the roles fashion plays within global flows of culture. This active and explicit *rethinking* of fashion and globalization calls for a wider range of perspectives and decolonial critiques that support and further develop ongoing attempts to write back against Eurocentricity.

The globalization of fashion is a notion that too often is understood as the global spread of Western fashion, and with it a hierarchy of Eurocentric fashion discourse over other fashion discourses, practices and systems. While the spread of Euro-American fashion styles and systems is undeniable and far-reaching, Western fashion systems are not the whole story.[1] As the image on the cover of this book shows, fashion and globalization can be considered from diverse perspectives, including positions that decentre the Western-centric notion of fashion, and foreground fashion histories that complicate matters of time and space. The kimono featured here was tailored in Japan in the 1980s from block-printed and resist dyed cotton made on the Coromandel coast of India during the 18th century.[2] Sarasa, also known as cotton calico or chintz, formed part of a significant Indian export industry that globalized Indian design in a flow of fashion textiles *from* the Indian subcontinent to Egypt and Indonesia in the 13th and 14th centuries or earlier, West Africa from the 15th century[3] and Europe from the 17th century.[4] Such a reading already involves a reimagining of matters of influence, and the need for 'linguistic and historical competence . . . far beyond the capacities of any single scholar'.[5]

Using the term 'sarasa' to describe this fabric already makes for a shift in thinking and speaking about global fashion. Sarasa is a Portuguese loan word 'saraça' for cotton calico, used in Japan from the late 1600s when Portuguese traders brought these fabrics from India to Edo Japan and they were copied by Japanese craftsmen to create Japanese garments.[6] The owner of this kimono, Kikuchi Nobuko (1925–2016), came across this particular example of sarasa in 1980 at an antique shop in Yurakucho, Tokyo.[7] She had it tailored into a kimono, and continued to purchase Javanese batik, Congolese kuba cloth and cashmere shawls to fashion garments and accessories for herself to wear.

During the 1980s, women in Japan were not wearing kimono as everyday wear, and the concept solidified of kimono as immutable tradition and thus national costume. Nobuko, on the other hand, developed her own way of wearing kimono, freely and as she liked, as an innovative style choice that would have been perceived as a connoisseur's deviation. For her, this was a rebellious act.[8] Frequent travel to Europe with her husband, a collector of Emile Gallé's Japanese-inspired art nouveau glass work, gave Nobuko awareness of international antiques markets, French fashion, and a view of kimono from outside of Japan. Her kimono collection was passed to her granddaughter Ere, a jazz dance instructor. Ere rarely wears kimono, but she occasionally wears her grandmother's in order to remember her. In Figure 1.1 she is pictured in her grandmother's garden reflecting Nobuko's own aesthetic choices. In this photograph, the 18th/20th century sarasa kimono has been teamed with an obi made from fabric dating from the early 19th century that was a Dutch copy of Indian calico.

In turn, Ere has also begun to craft Japanese fashion from antique transnational textiles, by reusing Nobuko's kimono collection as a source of textiles for her own fashion brand called 'ellection_ere', publicized through Instagram and Facebook. Since 2019 she has been recrafting her grandmother's kimono into new one-off pieces with an emphasis on the global circulation of fashion, such as the reinvented sukajan (souvenir jacket) depicted in Figure 1.2.[9] Embroidered flying cranes on a red silk ground, originally from an uchikake (outer-layer wedding kimono), are bordered by blue denim below and a fur collar above, combined with wide kimono sleeves of printed crepe with stream pattern, and styled with jeans and baseball cap in a street setting. In England, embroidered cranes also fly across the back pockets of the jeans worn with pride by youth cultures who prize the Japanese brand Evisu as something exclusive, that sets you apart and shows off your style know-how (Figure 1.3). In Europe, the desirability of Evisu products echoes William Gibson's novel *Zero History* that features unattainability, mystery and insider knowledge as driving forces of a Japanese 'secret' denim brand identity.[10] Those unable to afford to buy from Evisu's official retail outlets rely on second-hand markets and other internet selling.[11] These practices create much anxiety around fakes and have generated blogs teaching teenagers connoisseur knowledge about the history, materials and construction of Japanese denim.[12]

These complex histories of material and people cannot be understood with conventional histories of chintz as written by a dominant view of European fashion/technological advance and South Asian raw materials/hand-labour, or by studies of global fashion that see Americanization as a force that overwrites or displaces Japaneseness. They do not match accounts of Japanese fashion that separate kimono from fashion, and focus only on Harajuku streetstyle, cosplay and Japanese designers/brands such as Issey Miyake, Yohji Yamamoto, and Rei Kawakubo. They do not fit models of fashion globalization that are confined to the homogenizing spread of Euro-American culture or the 'glocalizing' activities of multi-national corporations seeking to capture local markets. Long-standing stories of garments and images passing through different places, sometimes repeatedly, lie beyond simple dichotomies. Indeed, this has been amply shown in the work of scholars of African fashion for several decades now, and countless studies of diasporic and postcolonial fashion cultures.[13] The appetite for Indian fabrics in the 17th century, or American garment types in the 20th century, and their appropriation into Japanese fashion, creates a rich tapestry of complex global

Figure 1.1 Kikuchi Ere wearing an ensemble that belonged to her grandmother, Kikuchi Nobuko Collection. Photograph: Murata Tatsuro. © Kikuchi Ere.

Figure 1.2 ellection_ere, Instagram © Kikuchi Ere.

interactions *within* Japanese fashion. And, in turn, these Japanese fashions return into Euro-American fashion circulations, in exhibitions or as cult objects of desire and status.[14]

This collection of essays does not attempt to represent all aspects relating to the global issues of fashion, or all fashion cultures globally. Neither does it aim to exclude Western fashion in search of 'non-Western' perspectives and experiences. Our starting point for 'rethinking fashion globalization' was a two-day meeting convened in Tokyo by the Transboundary Fashion Seminar (TFS) and the Research Collective for Decolonizing Fashion (RCDF), discussing the current challenges and key questions facing the globalization of fashion.[15] The structure and content of this event followed a joint ambition to explore global fashion and its forces through various lenses, with participants from Japan, the Netherlands, Belgium, the United States, the United Kingdom, Singapore, Australia, Ghana, Kenya and South Africa. It is important to note that the resulting volume, *Rethinking Fashion Globalization*, is not an overview of fashion histories, processes or practices from around the world. Rather, this collection of essays asks how fashion topics rooted *anywhere* could be approached in less Eurocentric ways. We seek to emphasize the power dynamics of cultural interconnectedness, and the transboundary nature of fashion objects over time, through a range of voices and perspectives, as well as the power dynamics of fashion writing, as a way of answering the decolonial charge to actively counter Eurocentrism in the study and spread of fashion. As a group of fashion academics, designers, activists and writers, we aim to reflect how the topic of the global is inflected within fashion studies at the present time. In the process, we have begun to rethink fashion discourse and globalization in ways that move away from the colonial project and towards decentred academic and aesthetic processes that challenge hierarchies and marginalization.

Figure 1.3 Evisu (Europe) jeans with embroidered flying cranes, owned and modelled by Lucian Duff. Photograph: Sarah Cheang.

Rethinking Fashion Studies

Writing about fashion in the spring and summer of 2020 – a time of COVID-19 pandemic, climate-change crisis, and the resurgence of Black Lives Matter protests in many parts of the world – underlines the importance of fostering a shared sense of the world and the interrelations of resources, people and ideas, now and in the past. Current health crises and racial tensions also highlight the many differences between and within nations, revealing inequalities of access to digital, material, and knowledge resources, and deep political and ideological divisions. Here, decolonizing debates are important because they offer a way to re-envision racist/colonial structures with a commitment to social justice. This could be seen in terms of a re-imagining and rewriting of the fashion system enforced by the various social, economic, cultural and economic impacts of the pandemic.[16] At the time of writing, serious, life-threatening contraventions of pandemic-related legislation in a garment factory in Leicester in the United Kingdom, a supplier of the fast fashion retailer Boohoo, have also exposed the multiple abuses of poor working conditions and pay.[17] This has prompted media exposés of 'modern day slavery' and renewed public interest in ethical fashion debates, as was also seen following the Rana Plaza factory disaster of 2013.[18] These discussions also respond to wider calls for 'rethinking' and 'remaking' the fashion system in ways that are kinder to the planet, across all forms of life.[19] This includes finding ways that replace the incredible violence enacted on the environment through fast fashion's demand for wood-pulp for viscose manufacturing, to water-demanding cotton, to chemical impacts on rivers, to overflowing landfills of non-composting, non-recyclable synthetic clothing, as well as the recognition of fashion cultures that might model more sustainable, slower, more ethical or kinder fashion systems.[20]

Decolonial thinking and postcolonial critique are part of the same struggle to write, speak and act back against colonialism and challenge racism. Key thinkers, working in the context of postcolonial India and Latin America, have shaped a field that identifies Eurocentricism as a crucial problem in knowledge production and cultural hierarchies.[21] Coloniality is understood as inseparable from modernity. Broadly speaking, where postcolonial interventions explore colonial power dynamics, challenging complicity with Western subject positions and the universalizing of Western intellectual frameworks, decolonial approaches centre on recognizing the presence of coloniality and colonial difference, and developing strategies for resisting structural racism and thinking habits that work to erase awareness of these colonial injustices. A decolonial approach therefore 'advances other ways of being, thinking, knowing, theorizing, analyzing, feeling, acting and living for us all'.[22] Decolonial thinking requires the terms of the debate or the encounter to be challenged, not just the content, through a focus on how we practice.

The need for decolonial fashion publications, platforms and projects is urgent. These forums aim to critique the denial and erasure of other fashion systems, recover genealogies and trajectories of clothing and fashion without automatically tracing back to Western fashion systems and histories, and contribute to decolonizing fashion media and fashion curricula.[23] The collective power of these kinds of decolonial fashion work seeks to re-frame the ideologies that support the economic and cultural power imbalances that have sustained a skewed Western fashion system through alternative relations to earth, to community, to language, to bodies, and to ourselves, and through alternative forms of worlding the world.[24]

This book was edited by scholars in the UK, South Africa, and Japan, and we have actively used our contrasting geographical locations of London, Cape Town, and Tokyo, our various academic fields, and our different ethnic origins to create awareness and challenge our own assumptions about 'world' events, identity politics and the writing of history. In seeking to challenge marginalization and address coloniality, we have tried to also build a wider, more global sensibility within fashion studies. Definitions of fashion/decolonizing/global that currently have purchase in Anglophone scholarship should not be applied in all fashion scholarship everywhere without careful deliberation. Instead, we have sought to feel into the ways that cultures have interacted, and how ideas feed each other, in order to understand how fashion and globalization can be discussed at a moment that demands a greater diversity of voices and perspectives, and a more careful listening to and learning from a wider reach of participants.

It is interesting to note that almost two decades after the publication of Sandra Niessen, Ann Marie Leshkowich and Carla Jones' *Re-Orienting Fashion: The Globalization of Asian Dress* (2003), many of the key issues of colonialism/orientalism/racism, cultural appropriation and exoticization raised in that text are still prevalent, and have since become even more urgent to address. Other recent studies of global fashion have also shown great awareness of the importance of diversity as a way of drawing attention to and countering Eurocentricity.[25] Building on these foundations, this volume aims to do more than show multiple fashion contexts, but to think through the implications of this approach to confronting ongoing hegemony in Western fashion studies, and to argue for more inclusive futures by highlighting both conceptual approaches and multiple perspectives, voices and disciplinary positions on fashion.

It is crucial to adopt models of fashion, globalization and modernity that avoid the perpetuation of the exact problems that decolonial approaches seek to redress. If fashion is defined as a function of Western mercantile capitalism, and if globalization is seen as the spread of this Western-centric model of fashion, then fashion studies will re-inscribe and maintain European-derived concepts and world-views. As a starting point, this volume argues that working with dichotomies – like fashion versus dress, modernity versus tradition, West versus non-West and global versus local – is itself a persistence of imperialist thinking that protects boundaries, and discriminates, discredits and excludes many cultures from dominant fashion discourse. Taken as a whole, this volume uses the term 'fashion' to mean style choices that create a sense of now, and a sense of self, embedded within wider social structures – fashion systems – that support, supply and give social meaning to those style choices. Fashion is a process of change whose social structures vary from culture to culture.[26] Fashion systems are therefore understood to be multiple and interrelated, closely intertwined with questions of modernity and selfhood that are themselves multiple and interrelated. This does not mean that we dismiss the existence or the relevance of dominant notions of Western 'modernity', or that the term 'fashion' is used to mean all style changes regardless of their context and nature. It is to more subtly counter perceptions of fashion as a Western invention, while recognizing the effects of unequal economic and power relations.

Developing a Decolonial Framework for Rethinking

The contributors to this edited volume were selected not necessarily because their work is decolonial, but because individually and collectively they present a range of approaches and practices that can contribute to developing a more decolonial fashion studies. This is not the same as claiming that this book is a decolonial text, or that it succeeds in decolonizing fashion studies or fashion discourse. The 'productive' nature of this book lies partly in a choice to work with potential tension or friction created by bringing together a more complex, nuanced and culturally diverse set of values, aesthetics, practices, and histories into thinking about fashion, its definitions and circulations/movements through time and across place. In allowing space for misunderstandings and competing meanings, we invite editors, authors and readers to become involved in 'negotiating more or less recognized differences in the goals, objects and strategies of the cause. The point of understanding this is not to homogenize perspectives but rather to appreciate how we can use diversity as well as possible'.[27] Following on the heels of work on African fashion, recent work on East Asian fashion has emphasized how fluidity and ambivalence are crucial concepts for understanding global flow.[28] Taken as a whole, this volume adds to those debates in the ways that its structure and content are not pinned down to a particular geographical place or form of cultural identity, instead mapping transboundary movements that disrupt singular geographies. While we began with a collaborative event held in Tokyo, facilitating the inclusion of many Japanese voices, this project did not actively seek to produce an Asia-specific dialogue. Decolonizing work, however, argues strongly that Asia needs to be de-orientalized, especially the understanding that 'Asia' is not one.[29] While we have allowed decolonial debates to remain an open question with respect to East Asia, there is a clear necessity for further studies that critique the complexity of East Asian intra-regional colonial histories when working with wider decolonial themes and approaches in contemporary fashion studies.

A core concern within decolonial approaches is the rethinking of structures of knowledge and attempts to delink from colonial pedagogies and ontologies. For this collection of essays, developed and completed over a 15 month period from our initial meeting in Tokyo, a central issue has been a keen awareness of what it means to be writing on global fashion in English, for publication by an academic press. While English is often used as the lingua franca of international meetings of scholars, authors who are not writing in their first language have the additional burden of translation.[30] As editors, we have tried to remain sensitive to how we might enable the clear communication of ideas without losing the 'voice' of the writer, and matters of house style came into conflict with our sense of decolonial principles. Checking in with authors about uses of terminology, being open to dialogue, being aware of and researching nuances in language, all takes time, and this is a small indication of the extra labour of thinking decolonially for authors, editors, readers and publishers. This is also revealing of the ways in which decolonial intentions can easily be lost where time is a precious resource, or for example where funding is not evenly distributed, because of the fundamental requirement to challenge existing systems and assumptions.

There are three decisions that were made in order to arrive at a more equal and inclusive approach to producing an edited collection. The first was not to italicize 'foreign' words. Publishing conventions normally dictate that, when writing in English, all non-English words that have not been adopted into the English language (for example, that do not appear in a dictionary of English) must be italicized. For this volume, engaged with many different fashion cultures past and present, this would have involved the italicization of all fashion-related terms that are not English fashion terms. This clearly has the result of marking out non-Euro-American fashion terms as unfamiliar and exotic, at one remove from the reader and their assumed vocabulary. Writing from many perspectives, and inviting readers from many perspectives, we have chosen not to use this method of italicization. Furthermore, we encouraged the authors' own preference for either US or UK English spelling (for example 'globalization' or 'globalization') within each chapter, rather than adhering to a single spelling system across the book as a whole.

Second, we considered the order in which people's names are represented in English. While the standard practice in English-language writing is to place the family name last, in many cultures, for example in China, Japan and Korea, the family name comes first, followed by the given name. When working cross-culturally, East Asian authors are often forced to alter their accustomed name order, which can result in feelings of alienation, and also leads to further confusion as readers attempt to work out which name-order convention has been used in any given instance. In this volume, we have sought to address this issue by using capitalization to indicate an author's family name, rather than the naming order. Within the content lists of this book, authors have used their preferred name order, indicating their family name with capitalization. In the general text of each chapter, name order is also according to common usage rather than English-language conventions, but capitalization has not been employed in order to not disrupt the flow of reading.

Lastly, as this collection encompasses work by academics, educators, curators and fashion industry professionals, we have not sought to produce content that is highly standardized in terms of chapter length or writing style. While intellectual rigour has been consistently paramount, and most chapters do take the form of an academic essay, we have actively encouraged the inclusion of some other styles and formats, responding to strategies that question whose knowledge counts.[31] It is our intention that working across borders involves a degree of polyvocality, increasing the potential for 'dialogic interaction between differently socially situated subjects that helps to expand the epistemic worlds inhabited by both practitioners and readers'.[32] How we read and interpret the contents of this book should be part of an active process of reflection with much to teach us about the global and its entangled relations of meaning and power.

We have divided this book into three sections, each with its own short introductory remarks. The first section, *Disruptions in Time and Space*, explores non-Eurocentric approaches to transnational flows of fashion, contests the prevailing idea that other fashion systems have only recently emerged following the global spread of Western fashion, and argues for an urgent remapping of fashion (and its histories) by moving away from a unidirectional hierarchy of fashion towards new multi-directionalities. The second section, *Nationalism, Transnationalism and Fashion*, expands upon the entanglement and importance of identity and place via the production of both national and transnational fashions resulting from multi-directional movements in identity constructs and politics. The third section, *Global Design Practices*, provides examples of fashion designers of mixed backgrounds and geographical roots, who are not bound to Western design, production and consumption practices, or who are using non-Eurocentric approaches both in response to, and creatively prompting a rethinking of, global fashion.

In exploring this book, we invite readers to be part of a more decolonial framework, by engaging with the variety of ways that global themes are presented, and reflecting on the multitudinous ways coloniality and globalization project forward and back in time, affecting what we remember, how we remember it, and how we construct our world(s).

Notes

1. For example, a key contributor to the spread, and therefore globalization, of Western fashion as an economic and global project was the role of religion as central to the colonizing mission between the 15th and 20th centuries, with Christian concepts of dress used to signify the adoption of civilized manners, and the symbolized conversion of the colonized. See Jean Comaroff, 'Fashioning the Colonial Subject: The Empire's Old Clothes'. In Louise Lamphere, Helena Ragoné and Patricia Zavella, Eds. *Situated Lives: Gender and Culture in Everyday Life* (London and New York: Routledge, 1997) 400–419.

2. Kimono and obi from Kikuchi Nobuko Collection. Kimono: Cotton, mordant and resist dyeing. Coromandel Coast, India, 1700–1800; tailored in Japan, 1980–1990.
   Obi: Cotton, mordant and resist dyeing and block printing. Probably Dutch, 1800–1825; tailored in Japan, 1980–1990.

3. See Lola Sharon Davidson, 'Woven Webs: Trading Textiles around the Indian Ocean'. *PORTAL Journal of Multidisciplinary International Studies: Indian Ocean Traffic Special Issue*, guest edited by Lola Sharon Davidson and Stephen Muecke (2012) 9: 1.

4. Beverly Lemire, *Cotton* (Oxford: Berg, 2011).

5. Prasannan Parthasarathi and Giorgio Riello, 'Introduction: Cotton Textiles and Global History'. In Giorgio Riello and Prasannan Parthasarathi, Eds. *The Spinning World: A Global History of Cotton Textiles, 1200–1850* (Oxford: Oxford University Press, 2009) 12.

6. Rosemary Crill, 'Local and Global: Patronage and Use'. In Rosemary Crill, Ed. *The Fabric of India* (London: V&A Publishing, 2015) 176–178.

7. Kohka Yoshimura, 'Kikuchi Nobuko: Stylish Rebellion'. In Anna Jackson, ed. *Kimono: Kyoto to Catwalk* (London: V&A Publishing, 2020) 263.

8. Yoshimura, 'Kikuchi Nobuko', p.263.

9. Ere uses Instagram and Facebook as a showcase for garments which are crafted in her atelier as a series of unique pieces, made in response to individual requests through social media. As Nobuko's kimono fabric came from overseas, so Ere seeks to connect with global citizens and circulate her work worldwide. Personal interview, Kikuchi Ere, 4 January 2021.

10. William Gibson, *Zero History* (London: Penguin, 2010).

11. Personal interview, Lucian Duff, 12 July 2020.

12. Kojoe, 'How to Spot Fake Evisu Fake Evisu Guide', http://evisu-guides.blogspot.com/2010/01/how-to-spot-fake-evisu-jeans.html (accessed 12 July 2020); Keezy TV 'EVISU real VS fake/Replica & Authentication Comparison', www.youtube.com/watch?v=8_hewkHUxNI (accessed 12 July 2020).

13. Jean Allman, Ed. *Fashioning Africa: Power and the Politics of Dress* (Bloomington and Indianapolis, IN: Indiana University Press, 2004); Marie Brown, *Khartoum at Night: Fashion and Body Politics in Imperial Sudan* (Stanford, CA: Stanford University Press, 2017); Victoria Rovine, *African Fashion, Global Style: Histories, Innovations and Ideas You Can Wear* (Bloomington, IN: Indiana University, 2014).

14. For example, 'Kimono: Kyoto to Catwalk', Victorian and Albert Museum, 27 February-25 October 2020; 'Kimono Refashioned', Asian Art Museum, San Francisco 8 February – 5 May 2019.

15. '(Re)thinking Fashion Globalization', February 15–16, 2018 at Bunka Gakuen University, Tokyo. https://transboundaryfashion.files.wordpress.com/2018/11/booklet.pdf (accessed 12 July 2020).

16. See Imran Amed and Achim Berg, 'The State of Fashion 2020: Coronavirus Update – It's Time to Rewire the Fashion Industry', *Business of Fashion* (2020) www.businessoffashion.com/articles/intelligence/the-state-of-fashion-2020-coronavirus-update-bof-mckinsey-report-release-download (accessed 12 July 2020); Marcus Fairs, 'Coronavirus offers "a blank page for a new beginning" says Li Edelkoort', *Dezeen* (2020) www.dezeen.com/2020/03/09/li-edelkoort-coronavirus-reset/ (accessed 4 June 2020); Sandra Niessen, 'Connecting the Dots – or Why I eschew the term "Garment Workers"', *Research Collective* for Decolonizing Fashion. http://rcdfashion.com/ (accessed 20 July 2020).

17. Ellie Violet Bramley, 'Seven Ways to Help Garment Workers', *The Guardian Online*, 9 July 2020, www.theguardian.com/fashion/2020/jul/09/seven-ways-to-help-garment-workers (accessed 9 July 2020). The Leicester abuses were first highlighted by the group Labour Behind the Label, who campaign for garment workers' worldwide; https://labourbehindthelabel.org/ (accessed 9 July 2020).

18. Lauren Bravo, 'The Fast Fashion Fix: 20 Ways to Stop Buying New Clothes Forever', *The Guardian Online*, 14 July 2020, www.theguardian.com/fashion/2020/jul/14/fast-fashion-20-ways-stop-buying-new-clothes-fair-wage-wardrobes (accessed 14 July 2020). Fashion Revolution week happens every year in the week coinciding with 24 April, the anniversary of the Rana Plaza disaster in Bangladesh, see Fashion Revolution, 'We are a Global Movement', *Fashion Revolution* (n/d) http://www.fashionrevolution.org/about/ (accessed 12 July 2020).

19. Kate Fletcher and Mathilda Tham, *Earth Logic: Fashion Action Research Plan* (London : The JJ Charitable Trust, 2019). Authors Kate Fletcher and Mathilda Tham argue for earth before profit.

20. Rolando Vazquez, 'Precedence, Earth and the Anthropocene: Decolonizing Design', *Design Philosophy Papers*, 15 (1): Design and the Global South (2017) 1–15.

21. For example, Gayatri Chakravorty Spivak, 'Can the Subaltern Speak?' In Cary Nelson and Lawrence Grossberg, Eds. *Marxism and the Interpretation of Culture* (University of Illinois Press, 1988) 271–313; Homi Bhabha, *The Location of Culture* (New York: Routledge, 1994);

Walter D. Mignolo, *Local Histories/Global Designs: Coloniality, Subaltern Knowledges and Border Thinking* (Princeton, NJ: Princeton University Press, 2000); Aníbal Quijano, 'Coloniality and Modernity/Rationality', *Cultural Studies*, 21 (2) (2007) 168–178.

22. Walter Mignolo and Catherine Walsh, *On Decoloniality/Concepts Analytics Praxis* (Durham, NC: Duke University Press, 2018) 10.

23. A special issue of *Fashion Theory* 24 (6) (2020) on 'Decoloniality and Fashion' draws on the work of the steering committee members of the Research Collective for Decolonizing Fashion (RCDF), established in 2012 (originally as the Non-Western Fashion Conference). This Special Issue results from the sustained conversations and efforts to bring attention to more inclusive, other and diverse fashion systems, with *Decolonial Fashion Discourse* evolving as a new and growing sub field of fashion studies. The Canadian Fashion Scholars is a platform led by Kat Sark and designed for individuals working on fashion-related topics in universities, museums, and the creative industries in Canada. It aims to bring together fashion scholars and professionals, and to facilitate collaborations on fashion-related projects in Canada and beyond. See https://fashionscholars.wixsite.com/home (accessed 20 July 2020). The African Fashion Research Institute (AFRI) founded by Erica de Greef and Lesiba Mabitsela stems from an interest in decolonizing, and drive to decolonize, fashion; to rethink and reframe knowledge about African fashion; and to create dynamic platforms for engagement around African fashion that can be disruptive, productive and generative (website forthcoming). Kimberley Jenkins has launched an online platform, *The Fashion and Race Database*, with the support of Ryerson University, designed to provide teachers, students and anyone interested in learning with open-source tools that 'expand the narrative of fashion history and challenge mis-representation within the fashion system'. See Dhani Mau, 'Kimberly Jenkins Wants To Help Decolonize Our Understanding Of Fashion', *Fashionista* (2020) https://fashionista.com/2020/07/kimberly-jenkins-fashion-and-race-database (accessed 12 July 2020).

24. Angela Jansen, for example, cites the work of decolonial thinker Rolando Vazquez. Angela Jansen 'Fashion and the Phantasmagoria of Modernity: An Introduction to Decolonial Fashion Discourse' *Fashion Theory* 24 (6) (2020) 815–838.

25. Eugenia Paulicelli and Hazel Clark, Eds. *The Fabric of Cultures: Fashion, Identity, and Globalization* (London: Routledge, 2009); Giorgio Riello and Peter McNeil, Eds. *The Fashion History Reader: Global Perspectives* (London: Routledge, 2010); Linda Welters and Abby Lillethun, *Fashion History: A Global View* (London: Bloomsbury, 2018).

26. See Leslie W. Rabine, *The Global Circulation of African Fashion* (Oxford: Berg, 2002); Jennifer Craik, *The Face of Fashion: Cultural Studies in Fashion* (London: Routledge, 1993); and Suzanne Baizerman, Joanne B. Eicher, and Catherine Cerny, 'Eurocentrism in the Study of Ethnic Dress'. In Joanne B. Eicher, Sandra Lee Evenson, and Hazel A. Lutz, Eds. *The Visible Self: Global Perspectives on Dress, Culture and Society*, 3rd edn (New York: Fairchild, 2008).

27. Anna Lowenhaupt Tsing, *Friction: An Ethnography of Global Connection* (Princeton, NJ: Princeton University Press, 2005) x.

28. Rovine, *African Fashion*; Rabine, *The Global Circulation of African Fashion*; Sarah Cheang and Elizabeth Kramer, 'Fashion and East Asia: Cultural Translations and East Asian Perspectives', *International Journal of Fashion Studies*, 4 (2) (2017): 145–155; Wessie Ling, Mariella Lorusso and Simona Reinach, 'Critical Studies in Global Fashion', *ZoneModa Journal*, 9 (2) (2019); Wessie Ling and Simona Reinach, Eds. *Fashion in Multiple Chinas: Chinese Styles in the Transglobal Landscape* (London: I.B. Tauris, 2018).

29. hong an truong, Nayoung Aimee Kwon and Guo-Juin Hong, 'What/Where is Decolonial Asia?' *Social Text* (15 July 2013) https://socialtextjournal.org/periscope_article/whatwhere-is-decolonial-asia/ (accessed 7 June 2020).

30. Emanuela Mora, Agnès Rocamora, Paolo Volonte, 'The Internationalization of Fashion Studies: Rethinking the Peer-Reviewing Process', *International Journal of Fashion Studies*, 1 (1) (2014) 3–17. One author poignantly said to us during an editorial meeting for this book that we could change the words she had written because, if she wants to be read, she has to accept that she will always be translated.

31. An excellent example of this approach is Lipi Begum, Rohit K. Dasgupta and Reina Lewis, *Styling South Asian Youth Cultures: Fashion, Media & Society* (London: I.B. Tauris, 2018).

32. Patricia Derocher, *Transnational Testimonios: The Politics of Collective Knowledge Production* (Seattle, WA: University of Washington Press, 2018) xi.

SECTION I
DISRUPTIONS IN TIME AND SPACE

INTRODUCTION TO SECTION I
Sarah CHEANG

Fashion moves ideas, images, and material objects around the world and within societies, and has been doing so for millennia. In the process, fashion transcends and disrupts many boundaries while reaffirming new delineations of 'us' and 'them', 'me' and 'you'. Relationships between past and present are also played with, as designers, consumers and makers create references to history and heritage, and replicate or recycle old clothing in order to make tangible their sense of the present. Fashion therefore enables boundaries of space and time to leap and shift. The borders between national and international, yesterday and tomorrow, can be blurry and in constant flux because fashion is constantly remade each day as people dress in response to the place and the hour *as they perceive and live it*, not as it might appear on a map or by the calendar. This destabilizes ideas of centre and periphery, re-maps where fashion happens (and has been happening), and helps to take into account how movements, migration and memories have impacted fashion evolutions and definitions over time.

This section brings together four new studies of fashion and its border-crossings. They explore what some of the main referents might be if we want to take a less Eurocentric approach to fashion globalization, and suggest ways that fashion studies can engage with colonial contexts and decolonial debates. Takagi Yoko and Saskia Thoelen examine the spread of waso (cultures of kimono wearing), showing how debates around globalization can be centred on Japan, even when Europe and America are the objects of study. Sarah Cheang and Elizabeth Kramer focus on embroidered shawls and sukajan (jackets), which have played a key role in the global spread of Chinese and Japanese motifs and materials, to demonstrate how historians can tackle multi-centred and multidirectional stories of fashion transmission that are full of ambiguity and contradiction. Daan van Dartel sketches out the development of the Afro-Surinamese kotomisi (creole dress in Suriname) to stimulate new ideas on both fashion and cultural heritage, and with it to remove supposed agency from the colonizer and reinstall the personal and communal activism of the colonized. The final chapter of this section seeks to redraw the map by rescripting the narrative of two globally ubiquitous garment types – coats and trousers. By examining a number of 'origin' stories, Abby Lillethun and Linda Welters challenge the tendency for global fashion stories to become a linear narrative culminating in European experience.

The chapters in this section make no claims as to where coats and trousers, kotomisi, shawls and sukajan really come from or who owns them, nor who should dictate kimono-wearing. They point instead to the impossibility of such claims and the futility of constructing neat and singular global fashion narratives. In order to understand the significance and driving forces of fashion and globalization, it is important to allow alternative, messy and even contradictory narratives of cultural assignation to exist side by side. These chapters also show that the presence of decolonial debates has pushed fashion studies to start to think harder and differently about histories that imply European cultural domination, opening up cracks in colonial narratives of time and place.

CHAPTER 2
KIMONO MIGRATING ACROSS BORDERS: WASO CULTURE OUTSIDE OF JAPAN[1]
TAKAGI Yoko and Saskia THOELEN

Introduction

The kimono is an iconic image of Japan. It is a garment for wrapping the body, and therefore it requires a technique when wearing it. The term waso consists of wa (Japanese) and so (way of wearing). This chapter focuses on how people wear kimono, more than on the kimono itself. The research for this paper was conducted during March 2018, as part of the larger 和装のグローバル研究拠点形成のための基礎的研究 (A Fundamental Study for the Establishment of a Global Hub of Kimono Research – the Kimono Research Network) project. This research team came from different fields and regional backgrounds: two Japanese (Takagi Yoko, an art historian interested in the transboundary aspects of fashion and Japonisme, and Yoshimura Kohka, a curator specializing in fashion and clothing history); and two foreign kimono researchers and wearers in Japan (Sheila Cliffe, a British social scientist focusing on kimono culture, and Saskia Thoelen, a Belgian art historian and Japanologist researching historical kimono promotion and design).[2]

Even though the kimono was worn on a daily basis up until World War II, the garment disappeared gradually as an everyday wear and fashion item in Japanese society from the end of World War II onward. The large-scale adoption of Western styles of dress resulted in the Japanese losing their everyday practice of wearing kimono. Aiming to counter this phenomenon, kimono shops tried to increase their customer base through offering expensive kimono for special occasions, and codifying its wearing rules during the 1970s and 1980s, turning the kimono into a kind of costume. Hairdressers took on the role of dressing kimono for special occasions and kimono dressing schools popped up. However, as a result of these codifications, the kimono industry instead suffered a further major downturn during the 1990s.[3] Today, the majority of Japanese do not know how to wear kimono, nor how to express themselves through kimono fashion.

However, Japan has also recently seen a modest increase in the wearing of kimono as everyday fashion, which is being interpreted as the development of a contemporary kimono renaissance.[4] The large-scale appearance of second-hand kimono shops and shops selling new kimono for relatively cheap prices has renewed interest in the garment in Japan, and this has in turn sparked interest overseas. Since the start of the 'Kimono de Ginza' group in 1999, in which people gathered to enjoy wearing kimono together, many kimono wearing groups have been established.[5] These groups offer a forum for the exchange of kimono information, teaching kimono wearing in a democratic format unlike the established kimono dressing schools, which have a strong vertical structure.

One of these groups is the Kimono de Jack movement (hijacking urban space by kimono wearers), which has gained popularity both within and outside of Japan. The first overseas Kimono de Jack group was established by Lyuba Johnson in the UK in 2010.[6] Following that, Kimono de Jack groups were established in many other countries around the world, most notably in Europe and in North America, in a short span of time.

Since the opening up of Japan in the late 19th century, Japanese arts, crafts, and aesthetics have had a major impact on European styles, taste, and art. This period is referred to as the period of Japonisme.[7] Recent scholarship on Japonisme has started to interpret the Japanese influence ranging from high art to interior design and kimono as 'fashion'.[8] During the early stages of the Japonisme period, Japonaiserie, or objects from Japan, were filtered through a Western lens, and appropriated for use in European or American settings. Within an oriental paradigm, there was little consideration given to many of these items' original contexts. In the case of kimono, they were used as dressing gowns, props for erotic paintings, or sewn into embroidered gowns for wealthy socialites. Foreigners came to Japan and took Japonaiserie back home with them, while Japanese (and foreign) private businessmen actively started to work as mediators in this process. The exchange of goods and information mostly occurred through private enterprise with lagged support from the Japanese government. In a later stage, following the increase of information exchange during the second half of the 19th century, this fervent collection of objects developed into a serious study of Japan's culture and art, and the entire period of Japan's influence would be referred to as Japonisme.[9]

More than a century after the peak of the Japonisme movement, communication technologies and the global distribution of objects have changed dramatically with the rise of the internet. However, the current situation still bears many similarities to the Japonisme period, as with the spread of the internet, goods and information are still spread privately, with the Japanese government only functioning to further promote (through 'Cool Japan') an already existing network.

On the other hand, when focusing specifically on kimono, it becomes clear that both in Japan and in the West, a different orientalist paradigm continues to operate, which is the idea that fashion is something that originated in the West. The kimono is still often considered as traditional Japanese dress,[10] and the Japanese themselves today tend to fall into the trap of fashion self-orientalism. This chapter aims to challenge this dominant belief that fashion is a Western system, and that kimono are ethnic dress rather than fashion.

Terry Satsuki Milhaupt, one of the first researchers who considered kimono as a fashion item, has paved the way for discussions on the transfer of kimono across space and time from the 19th century until the present. In her 2005 chapter 'Second Hand Silk Kimono Migrating Across Borders', she discussed three distinct paths in which kimono move across borders, and in doing so change their meaning.[11] She stated that the kimono's simple shape has facilitated these moves, and that the kimono's border crossings are both generational (passed from mother to daughter) and geographical. It is used, reused, fragmented and reconfigured, exchanged and sold. In *Kimono: a Modern History*, she further developed this idea, stating that kimono fluctuate between different interpretations as art and fashion. By doing so, Milhaupt paved the way for more historical research focusing on the fashion aspects of kimono.[12] However, her work focused on the kimono as an object, and did not analyze the act of wearing itself, nor the agency that is involved in the re-interpretation of objects.

This chapter focuses on the current state of kimono, diffused globally through the internet, and appropriated as a fashion item in various regions. We will clarify the way in which kimono and waso are currently crossing geographical boundaries, and analyze how kimono are being used and are creating new meanings for their users in locations outside of Japan. We use a Japonisme framework to research this movement and the adaptation of objects and information from Japan to other countries. We differentiate our Japonisme framework from post-colonial frameworks, because we follow the Japan-oriented point of view that aligns with the idea that Japan was a non-Euro-American country that was not colonized, and therefore occupied a special position amongst other Asian countries that were colonized.[13] Scholarship in Japan often goes against the idea that the Meiji reform and the subsequent introduction of Western culture was something that was simply imposed on Japan, and focuses on Japan's agency in the development of its relations with Western countries.[14]

Furthermore, Japanese art and aesthetics were evaluated higher than the West's at the time.[15] Even though part of the Japan craze during the 19th century was defined by the collection of Japonaiserie (art) objects within wider orientalist points of view, Japonisme scholarship and the reinterpretations and adaptations that developed from it were rooted in a different kind of interest and study of Japan, its culture, and its aesthetics.[16] The ideas that are presented in this chapter are therefore rooted in Japonisme as a valid framework that enables us to research and analyze the transnational transfer of information and objects from Japan to other countries in the 21st century. Through this lens, we aim to contribute to the contemporary debate on fashion globalization and decolonization.

The purpose of this research is to examine the processes through which waso[17] is re-interpreted in different settings outside Japan. We have therefore also taken an art historical and material culture approach, recognizing the fact that we can learn a lot about human behaviour from the objects that we make and choose to surround ourselves with, interpret and appropriate for personal style. Concepts of agency provide a lens to clarify the role that kimono play within this process, and to retrace how the kimono is actively re-interpreted and adapted outside of its original context.[18]

Our fieldwork in Paris, Amsterdam, New York and Philadelphia[19] consisted of a combination of surveys and individual interviews, conducted during March 2018.[20] The surveys covered general demographic information and basic questions concerning the acquisition and wearing of kimono. Brief personal histories were also collected from Kimono de Jack participants. Interviews were conducted with people (Kimono de Jack members and non-Kimono de Jack members) who were considered to be 'key players', people involved either directly or indirectly with the setting up or running of the Kimono de Jack groups or in the participation thereof, or people who are in some form or other promoting Japanese culture in these locations through the use of waso. The interviews asked about the past, present and future of waso in these locations. Interviewees included

Japanese and non-Japanese who wore kimono to parties and special events, who dressed people in kimono, who were involved in setting up exhibitions of kimono, or who sold Japanese clothing in their shops. We also conducted visits to stores where Japanese goods, in particular waso items, were on sale in order to see how Japan is represented. In some cases, we were able to talk with staff members who sold Japanese goods. The consulted group presented a balanced variety of members belonging to one or more of the above-mentioned groups. It will become clear that the character of these regions, their cultural background and history have a strong influence on the way in which goods from other countries are absorbed and used within each culture.

Analysis of Waso Outside of Japan

Socio-Historical Background

The relationship between the Netherlands and Japan is longstanding, dating back to the Dutch arrival in Japan in 1609. The two countries' early relationship is signified by the Netherlands' unique position as the only Western country that was allowed to trade with Japan during its period of isolation (1639–1854), through the island of Dejima. Remnants of this exchange in cultural goods and interest in Japanese culture are still visible today, including an active interest in kimono in the country. Amsterdam hosts a few kimono specialty stores such as Van Hier tot Tokio, a small antique shop known for its kimono, and Episode, a used clothing store selling kimono next to other second-hand clothes. Furthermore, Amsterdam hosts one of the most active branches of the Kimono de Jack groups, Kimono de Jack NL. The open Facebook community has over seven hundred followers. The group is active, meeting about once a month. There is a great diversity of age (ranging from 2 to 60 years old), and a diversity of ethnicity in the group.

In France, on the other hand, the development of the Japonisme movement in the 1860s represents France's major link with Japan and its culture. Through Siegfried Bing's publication *Le Japon Artistique* (published in French, English and German), information on Japanese art and culture was spread from Paris to the rest of Europe and the United States. During this period, kimono were adopted as theatre costumes and gowns within the home. Later, they became an important source of inspiration for designers such as Paul Poiret and Madeleine Vionnet, who actively made use of exotic influences. On the other hand, Paris became one of the main destination of international study for Japanese scholars, and its art and design formed the basis of Japanese concepts of modern art. From the 20th century onward, Paris became known as the center of fashion, and many well-known Japanese designers gained fame through their shows at Paris Fashion Week. Today, Paris holds one of the biggest events of Japanese popular culture outside of Japan, namely Japan Expo, which attracts more than two million people over the course of three days, presenting Japanese traditional culture, cosplay, manga, martial arts, video games, J-POP, food, etc. During this event, the kimono is introduced as a mix of traditional culture, cosplay, and fashion. However, other than at these venues, kimono are rarely seen on the streets in France, as until the present, there exists no Kimono de Jack group in the country.

Finally, the relationship between the United States of America and Japan was first marked by the arrival of commodore Matthew C. Perry in Japan in 1853, which led the country to open itself up after more than two hundred years of isolation. However, it was through the Philadelphia Centennial Exposition of 1876 that the American public at large was introduced to Japan, its culture, and kimono.[21] At the time, the city of Philadelphia acted as a gateway through which Japanese culture could expand. Bing's publication of *Le Japon Artistique* in English was of major influence in the USA, and the spread of Japanese culture led to the development of Japonisme and other art movements inspired by Japanese culture in North America. Currently, even though Philadelphia actively promotes Japanese culture through the Japan America Society of Greater Philadelphia, the city does not host any shops selling kimono. The city is home to a significant community of Japanese Americans, but events organized by the association focus more on the general culture of Japan, rather than on the kimono itself. New York, on the other hand, hosts one of the most active Kimono de Jack groups (Kimono de Jack NY) on the East coast, as well as a few kimono shops and kimono consulting centers, such as Kimono House and Kaede Kimonos. In addition, Globus Washitsu, organized by Stephen Globus, acts as a hub for the spread of Japanese culture, with a strong focus on the exhibition and promotion of kimono culture.

The Role of IT and Social Media

Online platforms have had a major influence on the development of the current international kimono boom. Analyzing Kimono de Jack groups' activities in each of these regions, we see that the movement relies largely on the internet as an educational medium. Apart from the older members of the groups, almost all members used YouTube videos to learn how to dress in kimono. In addition to this, some of the Kimono de Jack members have put up their own tutorials on YouTube, explaining how to buy, fold, wear and walk in kimono, including obi-tying tutorials. YouTube videos uploaded by kimono enthusiasts worldwide also include detailed explanations on the making of kimono. Some of these tutorial videos focus on how to solve 'problems' in the wearing of kimono, for example what to do when one cannot fold a hashori.[22] Making use of the YouTube platform, they provide an alternative open source for the closed and unavailable knowledge of kimono dressing schools located in Japan and overseas. In doing so, they show that they are agents, playing an active role in the worldwide spread of interest and knowledge concerning kimono for others who do not have the means to access it. In opening up closed knowledge concerning kimono, they break with established ways of wearing kimono controlled by the kimono schools in the same ways as kimono enthusiasts in Japan do.

However, this is not the only use of the internet by the Kimono de Jack groups. Members are dependent on the internet in other ways too, for example for shopping. Online platforms such as Ichiroya or Rakuten play a major role in providing many members of Kimono de Jack a platform for most or all of their kimono shopping. The number of kimono outlets in Amsterdam and New York is small, with limited stock, which means that there is little choice available locally. Furthermore, these platforms offer extra conveniences, such as detailed information on the garment (its year of production, fabric, length, current condition) with pictures (including close-ups), services in English (next to Japanese), or the postal services of other shops. We see that thanks to the development of these online platforms there has also been a gradual evolution in the wider process of finding and buying kimono overseas. Kimono specialty stores in Amsterdam, Paris and New York have developed, gradually working together with online platforms such as Ichiroya to expand their stock.

The internet is also used as a method of communication. Facebook has been the chosen way through which kimono wearers in Amsterdam and New York communicate with each other, and Facebook events are created for planned meetings. After the meetings, the day's photographs are uploaded and further sharing is encouraged through introductions to related businesses, organizations and events on these Kimono de Jack event pages. Finally, platforms such as Instagram show enthusiasts how their peers (both in Japan and overseas) play with existing kimono styles and waso rules to provide inspiration for new interpretations.[23]

It is due to the existence of YouTube and other online platforms that the current kimono boom has been able to evolve. Thanks to the spread of open-source knowledge concerning the garment and its culture, both newcomers and veterans were able to familiarize themselves with kimono in new ways. Where they were at first mainly adopting a culture that was brought to them, now they have the opportunity to actively spread the knowledge and culture concerning kimono as cultural agents themselves. They are able to share their experiences, connect with fellow kimono enthusiasts, and invite new enthusiasts to the group. Furthermore, in doing so, they are able to connect with other groups, unlimited by geography. On these final points of community development, we will elaborate in a later section.

Thanks to these online visual resources, the wearing of kimono has gradually started to be seen as less rule-bound and more open to free interpretation. In other words, waso has become more liberalized, and the Kimono de Jack groups are a fitting example to illustrate this 'liberalization of kimono' process in practice.

In what follows, we will present a few examples of the liberalization process in kimono, in which non-Japanese Kimono de Jack wearers show their personal creative adaptations in the wearing of their kimono, even though most of them are well aware of the establishment rules to which kimono wearing is supposed to abide.[24] Furthermore, the rule-breaking nature of the groups, inherent to the concept of hijacking urban space with kimono appearances, allows room for freer interpretations of how kimono should and could be worn.

Figure 2.1 shows the example of Kate (pseudonym), in Amsterdam, who was wearing a dark green ro[25] summer kimono in early spring. Through doing this, she decided to ignore the waso rule which prescribes that certain textiles and materials can only be worn during certain seasons. The choice was aesthetic, as Kate felt that this colour of

Figure 2.1 Ignoring the seasonal rules: wearing a summer kimono in early spring. Photographs: Takagi Yoko.

kimono was the best option to go with her black and white cat obi. In Figure 2.2, Sophie (pseudonym) shows us a type of waso that is usually used for men. Sophie, who identifies as a woman, sees it as an opportunity to wear kimono that are on the short side, without having to worry about the hashori. Combining the outfit with ballerina shoes, she provides a feminine touch to the ensemble. Figure 2.3 shows David (pseudonym), who wore a red-white kimono with dark blue obi combination that is reminiscent of the Dutch flag. Finishing the outfit with orange sneakers, the Dutch image is completed.

Other examples of kimono play were as follows. One participant of the Kimono de Jack NL group decided to combine her traditional furisode[26] outfit with an obiage[27] that was made from a pink gingham cloth – a pattern that is typical for Dutch cloth – in order to insert a small eclectic element bringing together Japan and the Netherlands. In contrast, one participant in the Kimono de Jack NY group joined one of the meetings in a complete Taisho period (1912–1926) style outfit, wearing a Taishō kimono, integrated with a 1920s headpiece and vintage bag to finish off the ensemble. Finally, Marina (the current leader of Kimono de Jack NY) decided to wear an obidome[28] with the logo of the group instead of a regular obidome, to show that she was the group's organizer.

It is clear that there are varying degrees in how much the wearing of kimono is liberalized and can have a playful character. While some participants go so far as to break gender rules, others add small touches, showing that they are not completely bound by

Figure 2.2 Ignoring gender rules: wearing men's kimono while identifying as a woman. Photographs: Takagi Yoko.

Figure 2.3 Free style kimono: combining the colours of the Dutch flag with the Dutch 'orange' image. Photographs: Takagi Yoko.

waso rules. As most of the Kimono de Jack members do know the rules of waso, the small areas of play and slight breaking of the rules reflect an intentional effort: these wearers know exactly what they are doing and how far they are taking this game. The stance of the wearers is that they are not there merely to abide but also to disrupt. It is a game to see how far they can go. However, it needs to be noted that Kimono de Jack participants realize that they are able to break the rules more freely exactly because they are not in Japan, and this stance was confirmed in the personal-history-focused interviews that were conducted. In these open-ended interviews, we specifically focused on the wearing experience of the Kimono de Jack members. While having them talk about the kimono outfits they wore that day, we asked for their opinions about kitsuke rules (kimono dressing rules). Multiple interviewees stressed their intentional breaking of the rules, and some of the Kimono de Jack NY participants echoed this statement: 'I like to assemble the components in the way that a kimono is supposed to look, but making it mine. So play with it a little bit, but not too much'.

Marina, the leader of Kimono de Jack NY, focused on the fact that seasonality works differently in Japan, which leads to limitations, but also opportunities of play: 'It's sometimes difficult to match to Japanese seasonality because of the weather, and also the blooming schedule is different in New York, so sometimes I fudge it . . . That's something you have to take into account, 'cause you can't really follow the Japanese schedule so strictly when you're not in Japan, unless you're in the same exact kind of climate'.

Kimono de Jack interviewees in New York also stressed their liberal position in breaking the rules exactly because they don't reside in Japan, where they feel there would be a higher social pressure to abide by these rules: 'It might not be pristine or appropriate when I'm in Japan, but I'm not in Japan, and there are some alterations that I can make'.

Some of them also linked their liberal position to the fact that they are foreigners, as they feel that, from a Japanese perspective, it is more accepted for foreigners to break some of the rules. Kimono de Jack participants feel that they are in a more liberal situation to begin with when they play around with kimono rules, and this enhances their creativity in wearing kimono.

Interpretation of Kimono by Non-Japanese Waso Wearers

The migration of cultural elements from one cultural zone to another involves adaptation, as the cultural elements need to be re-interpreted to fit into the new context they are being introduced into, with processes of reinterpretation, rethinking and re-signification.

From the surveys and interviews of both individuals and Kimono de Jack members, it was clear that there were both geographical differences and similarities in the interpretation and appropriation of kimono. First, regarding the question of whether the kimono was felt to be more fashionable or more traditional, the majority of non-Japanese interviewees perceived kimono as more fashionable, while the majority of Japanese interviewees perceived kimono as more traditional. Furthermore, a significant number of the non-Japanese interviewees interpreted the kimono as being both traditional and fashionable, stressing that it depended on the situation.

Second, among the non-Japanese interviewees, there were four major ways through which kimono were interpreted and used. First, the kimono was regarded as a fashion item. Especially in New York and Philadelphia, the kimono was mainly promoted by kimono experts, enthusiasts and vendors as a fashion statement, different from the little black dress. Second, a significant number of interviewees interpreted kimono as a cosplay item. They would wear a full kimono outfit, or integrate waso items such as obi into their cosplay costumes (Figure 2.4). Several members of the Kimono de Jack NY and Kimono de Jack NL groups, as well as respondents in Paris, reported the use of kimono for cosplay purposes. Also, in New York, kimono were perceived as either cosplay or fashion garments, depending on the event in which wearers participated. This was in contrast to France, where kimono were mainly interpreted as cosplay. Therefore, cosplay was a significant part of non-Japanese wearers' waso experience in the sample interviewed, especially in France, where unspoken cultural rules prohibited people from wearing full kimono outfits on the street. We saw that one French kimono enthusiast avoided these cultural rules by travelling four hours to the more liberal Netherlands to wear kimono as part of the Kimono de Jack NL group. She too, interpreted kimono as a kind of cosplay.

Third, the kimono was interpreted as a medium for understanding Japanese culture/cultural activities. A significant number of the interviewees noted that they wore kimono

Figure 2.4 1920s/steampunk and wa-gothic cosplay by Kimono de Jack NY members. Photograph: Kimono de Jack NY participants.

as part of their identity as a tea ceremony practitioner. This tendency was strongly felt in Paris, where enthusiasts would participate in kimono classes or other classes on Japanese traditional culture. However, the wearing of kimono was limited to these spaces, and they would not wear kimono in the street like their peers in Amsterdam or the East Coast. If kimono were worn, they would be adapted to fit the French taste, reflecting the idea of 'Traditional Japanese elegance meets Parisien Chic', as expressed by the store Ikian.[29] They would be worn with belts, or even backwards, and haori (a kimono jacket) would be worn on top of everyday wear as outerwear. Shop staff in Ikian did not consider that Parisian people would have any desire to learn to wear kimono as garments in the original Japanese way. It is thought to be too complex and impractical for French women. The adaptation of waso in Paris can be explained in different ways. One is that Paris sees itself as the heart of high fashion, and therefore it must make fashion goods. The kimono is seen as traditional, and cannot be a part of fashion unless it is somehow re-fashioned into another item or form. Another reason could be that the kimono is still seen as an oriental item, to be appropriated and refashioned according to the aesthetics of the French fashion sense. This could be framed as a continuation of the Japonisme movement.

Finally, a large number of the interviewees interpreted kimono as a collector's item. When asked about the kimono they owned, they often referred to them as part of a collection they had gathered over the years. To some of these collectors, kimono were also seen as works of art, treasured for the craftsmanship they reflect. These enthusiasts did not only collect kimono for themselves to wear, but collected all kinds of kimono, such as kimono for the opposite sex, or children's kimono.

The above-mentioned attitudes show that kimono are interpreted in several ways, some of which are linked to a certain geographic area or certain historical past. It is clear that processes of re-interpretation, rethinking and re-signification have occurred in order for the kimono to be integrated in these new societies. Some of these interpretations are relatively modern (such as cosplay), while others (kimono as a means to understand Japanese culture) date back to the 19th century kimono introduction in Europe and the United States. This re-interpretation of the kimono can also be linked to the above-mentioned process of liberalization of the kimono, in which not only the garment's image but also its practical approaches are re-interpreted to fit new cultural environments and needs.

The Development of Community

From the interviews and observations conducted, it became clear that kimono-wearing or waso plays an active role in connecting people into groups and even extended communities. It is through the kimono that people get together, starting from an individual experience and leading to experiences in a group.

Especially in the case of non-Japanese kimono wearers overseas, the first encounter with kimono is an individual experience in which wearers mainly come into contact with kimono through a variety of popular culture encounters such as cosplay, anime, movies depicting Japan, conventions and Japan-related events; or through more traditional encounters, such as tea ceremonies, traditional dance, Zen, etc.

Berber Oostenbrug, former leader of the group Kimono de Jack NL, bought her first kimono from the Japanese goods shop the Japan Center in Antwerp. After she realized that her first kimono was a very formal one, she decided to purchase another kimono from Ichiroya in 2001. After a relatively long period of personal kimono engagement, in 2010 Oostenburg decided to form a kimono group that would later grow to be Kimono de Jack NL. Support for the group in the form of an online Facebook presence was offered by other fellow kimono enthusiasts in the area, and this online presence allowed the group to expand quickly.

In our interview with Marina, current leader of the Kimono de Jack NY group, she mentioned that her encounter with kimono happened in 2006, when she bought an obi for cosplay purposes, and after that quickly started to collect other things to go with it. However, it was a while before she joined Kimono de Jack NY. Before joining Kimono de Jack NY, Marina created the Kimono NYC group in around 2015. After that, she joined the Kimono de Jack NY group, and merged the two groups when she became the leader in 2017.

Whether it is through family, friends or alone, for Kimono de Jack members, the initial encounter with kimono is a personal one, in which the wearer 'discovers' kimono, before getting in touch with fellow kimono enthusiasts, participating in group events, and joining a Kimono de Jack group. Among the interviewed individual waso enthusiasts, we observed a similar tendency. Even though some interviewees did not have the ability to join a Kimono de Jack group due to geography, they would participate in online groups such as fora, and others would go to events held by Japan-related organizations such as the Japan America Society of Greater Philadelphia in order to meet fellow enthusiasts.

Therefore, within the sample that was interviewed for this research, it is clear that as time passes, the kimono enthusiast becomes part of a community centered around kimono. When this happens, the kimono experience is not a singular experience anymore, but an experience shared with fellow enthusiasts.

Once groups are created, participation increases thanks to online presence and word of mouth, allowing the groups to get into contact with other groups, to plan joint activities or to even merge. Also in Europe, it is clear that different groups are becoming closer: several Kimono de Jack groups have organized joint meetings. There was even a global meeting in Japan in 2011, gathering all existing Kimono de Jack groups in one place.

Especially in New York, the joint activities of kimono-related groups in the area have led to an interesting phenomenon of cooperation between the groups. New York has a well-developed kimono scene with non-profit groups like Kimono de Jack, and profit organizations like Kaede Kimonos, Kimono Hiromi and Kimono House. As New York's kimono customer base is limited, one would think that the sense of competition between the profit organizations would be strong, and even though Kimono House – the longest existing member – expressed some rivalry, Kaede Kimonos explicitly stated that they see other groups as mentors or allies with a similar vision. They didn't want to create competition precisely because the kimono scene is small. Instead, they want to cooperate with other groups to create a pool, a community to introduce more people to kimono and to teach them about kimono.

Stephen Globus operates Globus Washitsu,[30] a privately owned event space open to the public, active in the spread of Japanese culture through events such as tea ceremonies or Japanese film screenings, and the promotion of kimono through bi-annual exhibitions interpreting kimono both as works of art and as fashion items. Globus specifically facilitates cooperation between kimono groups in New York, as his kimono related events and exhibitions bring them together. Globus' VIP parties and exhibitions focus on physically bringing together all the local kimono interest parties, for example Kimono de Jack organizes group visits to Globus' exhibitions, and stores like Kaede Kimonos and Kimono House provide kimono rentals for Globus' VIP parties. During our participant observations in March 2018 at one of Globus' VIP parties and exhibitions, Globus' central role in the formation of an extended kimono community became very clear.

However, this strong sense of community across groups was something that was unique to New York. In Philadelphia, the Japan America Society of Greater Philadelphia acts as a central organization where events organized by the society will bring together several kimono enthusiasts in the area. However, as their activities do not focus on kimono explicitly, and the kimono scene in Philadelphia is far less developed than in New York, the cooperation between several interest groups is not as explicit. The same can be said for the kimono scene in Amsterdam. Even though Kimono de Jack NL brings together people not only limited to the Netherlands but also from Belgium and France, the communication with other interest groups in the area is not as extensive as in New York. It needs to be noted that this is mainly due to the fact that existing Kimono de Jack groups and other kimono interest groups/individuals in Europe are more spread out geographically, and are limited by socio-historical and linguistic differences, which can prevent the gathering of individual groups into a larger active community.

It is clear that kimono groups are being formed, and many of these groups reach out to other groups for cooperation. The chance that these communities will become further intertwined in the future is high. The New York kimono scene definitely hints at further intertwinement and connections with new groups in new areas along the East Coast.

Within these evolving networks we see that even though there are central players who facilitate the connections between people and groups, in the end it is the kimono and waso that function as the central object and practice that connect people. The members of the Kimono de Jack groups are so diverse in age and background[31] that it would be difficult to see the commonalities that hold such people together. It is however the kimono that functions as a central agent that enables social relations, learning, sharing of information and experiences in a non-threatening environment. Members visit gardens, exhibitions, talks on Japan, festivals and other events, but also discuss experiences in

Japan, their kimono problems, purchases, and their obi tying triumphs and failures. It is the kimono around which people act, and around which communities are formed and extended. Just as Kimono de Jack NL former leader Linda Kentie stresses: 'kimono is a language in itself, it's like a virus, people get hooked'.

Conclusion

Examining the processes through which waso is re-interpreted and is given meaning in different settings outside of Japan, we have stressed the active role of both the kimono and kimono enthusiasts in the re-interpretation of waso and the formation of waso-centered communities. Furthermore, we have clarified some discrepancies in attitudes towards waso between Paris, Amsterdam, New York and Philadelphia.

The analysis shows there are different kinds of agentic powers visible in the re-interpretation process of kimono across borders. It is an understanding of all these factors that enables kimono enthusiasts to actively re-interpret the kimono in their own cultural settings as agents. Within this reinterpretation process, one can actively attribute new meanings to the garment (i.e. kimono as cosplay, kimono as a collection item, etc.), or approach the garment in original ways (i.e. playfully). However, we need to acknowledge that there are systems and structures in each place that enable or disable agency. This explains the difference in approach between Paris on one hand, and Amsterdam, New York, and Philadelphia on the other.

The kimono is the object that is being appropriated within this process, together with the act of waso, playing a central role in bringing people together into communities. This is crucial for the development and sustainability of waso-centered communities outside of Japan, which are playing a major role in the blossoming kimono renaissance globally.

Through our research, we have discovered that non-Japanese waso practitioners outside of Japan perceive kimono in a more playful and less restrictive way than their Japanese counterparts, who consider kimono to be a Japanese tradition that solidifies their identity, although waso was only codified recently in the 1970s. It may therefore be the non-Japanese kimono lovers living abroad who will help overcome persistent remnants of fashion self-orientalism and who will open up new perspectives for waso culture as a fashion culture.

Finally, even though Japan was not a colony of Western empires, actively integrating research focusing on Japan can help in the development of a relative perspective for fashion research conducted from a decolonized lens. The Japonisme framework is argued here to be a valid framework for analyzing fashion in contemporary Japan, as it focuses on the ways objects and information have been reinterpreted based on serious interest and study towards the country's culture, art, and aesthetics. It provides insights into how persistent orientalist frameworks can be overcome through processes of meaning-making and reinterpretation. However, Japonisme is not a universally applicable framework. It is therefore important within decolonized fashion research to adopt other frameworks that, like Japonisme, are rooted in each country's history, and can provide a different perspective going beyond the post-colonization viewpoint, allowing for a new framework to develop.

Notes

1. This work was supported by JSPS KAKENHI Grant Number JP17K02382 and Bunka Gakuen University 和装共同研究資金.

2. Sheila Cliffe is a certified kimono dresser and specialist. She has researched the social history of kimono, has lectured at conferences, museums and events in Japan, England, Hawaii and Korea. Yoshimura Kohka has worked as curator at the Bunka Gakuen Costume Museum for 27 years, and has researched sarasa (batik) kimono. Both researchers have played an active role in the exhibition 'Kimono: Kyoto to Catwalk', held at the Victoria and Albert Museum in 2020. Sheila Cliffe, 'Kimono Revolution'. In Victoria and Albert Museum, Ed. *Kimono: Kyoto to Catwalk* (London: V&A Publishing, 2020) 291–303; Yoshimura Kohka, 'Kikuchi Nobuko: Stylish Rebellion'. In Victoria and Albert Museum, Ed. *Kimono: Kyoto to Catwalk* (London: V&A Publishing, 2020) 263–269.

3. Koyama Noriko and Kubo Masayoshi (小山典子と久保雅義), 'Kimono Būmu to Raifusutairu he no Eikyō', 「きものブームとライフスタイルへの影響」 *Nihon Dezain Gakkai Kenkyū Happyō Taikai Gaiyōshū* 『日本デザイン学会研究発表大会概要集』53 (2006) 141–141.

4. Adachi Toshiki (足立敏樹), 'Hōsei/Apareru Kimono no Fukkatsu ha Honmono ka', 「縫製/アパレル　着物の復活は本物か」 *Seni Torendo* 『繊維トレンド』113 (2015) 58–72; Koyama Noriko and Kubo Masayoshi (小山典子と久保雅義), 'Kimono Būmu to Raifusutairu he no Eikyō', 「きものブームとライフスタイルへの影響」 *Nihon Dezain Gakkai Kenkyū Happyō Taikai Gaiyōshū* 『日本デザイン学会研究発表大会概要集』53 (2006) 141–141.

5. Sheila Cliffe, *The Social Life of Kimono* (London: Bloomsbury, 2018).

6. Ibid., 191.

7. Takagi Yoko, *Japonisme in Fin de Siècle Art in Belgium* (Pandora: Antwerp, 2002).

8. Miyazaki Katsumi (宮崎克己), *Japonisumu Ryūkō Toshite no 'Nihon'* 『ジャポニスム　流行としての「日本」』 (Kōdansha 講談社, 2018).

9. Society for the Study of Japonisme, Ed. (ジャポニスム学会編), *Japonisumu Nyūmon* 『ジャポニスム入門』 (Shibunkaku Shuppan 思文閣出版, 2000).

10. Carlo Marco Belfanti, 'Was Fashion a European Invention?' *Journal of Global History*, 3 (3) (2008) 419–443; Toby Slade, *Japanese Fashion: A Cultural History* (Oxford: Berg, 2009).

11. Terry Satsuki Milhaupt, 'Second Hand Silk Kimono Migrating Across Borders'. In Hazel Clark and Alexandra Palmer, Eds. *Old Clothes, New Looks: Second-Hand Fashion* (Oxford: Berg, 2005) 67–83.

12. Terry Satsuki Milhaupt, *Kimono: A Modern History* (London: Reaktion Books, 2014).

13. Andrew Gordon, *Postwar Japan as History* (Berkeley, CA: University of California Press, 1993).

14. Kuwabara Takeo (桑原武夫), *Meiji Ishin to Kindaika: Gendai Nihon wo Umidashita Mono* 『明治維新と近代化：現代日本を産みだしたもの』 (Shōgakukan 小学館, 1984); Jung-Sun N. Han, *An Imperial Path to Modernity: Yoshino Sakuzō and a New Liberal Order in*

East Asia, 1905–1937 (Cambridge, MA: Harvard University Asia Center, 2012); Karube Tadashi (苅部直), *'Ishin Kakumei' he no Michi: 'Bunmei' wo Motometa Jūkyū Seiki Nihon* 『「維新革命」への道: 「文明」を求めた十九世紀日本』 (Shinchōsha 新潮社, 2017); William M. Steele *Meiji Ishin to Kindai Nihon no Atarashii Mikata* 『明治維新と近代日本の新しい見方』 (Tōkyōdō 東京堂出版, 2019).

15. Ernest Chesneau, 'Exposition universelle. Le Japon à Paris', *Gazette des Beaux-Arts* (September 1, November 1, 1878); Louis Gonse, 'L'Art japonais et son influence sur le goût européen', *Revue des Arts Décoratifs* (April 1898).

16. Takashina Shūji (高階秀爾), 'Jo • Japonisumu to ha', 「序・ジャポニスムとは」 in *Japonisumu Nyūmon* 『ジャポニスム入門』 Ed. Society for the Study of Japonisme (ジャポニスム学会編) (Shibunkaku Shuppan 思文閣出版, 2000) 3–10.

17. When this paper refers to waso, it refers concretely to the kimono outfit comprising kimono, obi, and other accessories that complete it.

18. Anthony Giddens, *Profiles of Critiques in Social Theory* (London: Macmillan, 1982); Anthony Giddens, *The Constitution of Society* (Cambridge/Malden: Polity Press, 1984).

19. Fieldwork in these cities was conducted by all four participants of the waso research project in the following way: Amsterdam: Takagi and Cliffe; Paris: Takagi, Cliffe, and Yoshimura; New York and Philadelphia: Thoelen. The gathered fieldwork data was discussed by all four researchers. For this contribution, it was further developed from a Japonisme/decolonized framework by Takagi and Thoelen.

20. The interviewees presented in this paper are all introduced under a pseudonym, unless explicitly stated by the person in question that they wanted their name to be listed. In that case, the real name of the interviewee is used.

21. Anette Lynch and Mitchell D. Strauss, *Ethnic Dress in the United States: A Cultural Encyclopedia* (Lanham: Rowman & Littlefield, 2014) 180.

22. A hashori refers to the fold that is made when women wear kimono to adjust the length to their own size. For example, the following videos show some tips on kimono wearing: www.youtube.com/watch?v=7ZfDH18THpA (accessed 28 August 2019); www.youtube.com/watch?v=zr_sLYj8bvk (accessed 28 August 2019); www.youtube.com/watch?v–XG-Zjb0BhE (accessed 28 August 2019).

23. For example, see note 22 above.

24. A few examples of standard kimono rules are as follows: lined kimono are to be worn between October and May, while unlined kimono are to be worn between June and September; women wearing kimono have to make sure they have a hashori fold that gathers up the extra length of kimono, men wear their kimono without a hashori fold; the space between the back of the collar and the neck for women should be one fist and a half length; young women are allowed to wear bright and vivid colours, whereas older women wear more subdued colours; prints on kimono are strongly linked to the seasons and seasonal flowers are generally not worn out of season (e.g. cherry blossom print in autumn), etc.

25. Ro is an example of a textile that is worn for summer kimono. The textile is loosely woven from very fine silk threads, creating sheer, airy, kimono perfect for summer.

26. Furisode refers to a type of kimono that is usually worn by unmarried women during formal occasions. It is characterized by its long sleeves.

27. Obiage refers to a long piece of cloth that assists in folding the obi and holding it in place.

28. Obidome refers to a decoration that is placed on top of the obijime chord that assists in holding the obi in place.

29. Ikian, www.ikian.fr/en/ (accessed 28 August 2019).

30. Globus Washitsu, www.nycwashitsu.com/ (accessed 28 August 2019).

31. Participants' age varied from people in their late teens to people in their sixties. Various backgrounds included designers, coaches, students, data analysis consultants, developers, IT security workers, etc.

CHAPTER 3

GLOBAL CONNECTIONS AND FASHION HISTORIES: EAST ASIAN EMBROIDERED GARMENTS[1]

Sarah CHEANG and Elizabeth KRAMER

Introduction

This chapter explores Asian/American/European fashion interactions across the 19th, 20th and 21st centuries. It seeks to avoid a simplistic narrative of 'exotic' components in European fashion, or interpreting fashion globalization in broad strokes as the adoption of European dress styles by non-European societies in cultural flows from 'the West' to 'the Rest'. Instead, it focuses on the complex fluidity of two particular garment types within global movements of fashion that have created multi-centred and multi-directional stories: the sukajan, also known as the souvenir or tour jacket, and the embroidered shawl (Figures 3.1 and 3.2).

Sukajan were originally created by the Japanese as souvenirs for American troops serving in Occupied Japan (1945–52). As their popularity grew, sukajan became available at military bases around the world to commemorate further tours of duty in both peace and wartime. From the 1960s onward, its use in subculture and celebrity style, both in Japan and outside of Japan, ensured its longstanding popularity as a fashionable garment.[2] These developments, coupled with a shifting production base, demonstrate the ways in which the garment's production, marketing and consumption are embedded in global flows between (but not limited to) Japan, Korea, China, Vietnam, North America and the United Kingdom. This results in a multiplicity of agents in the garment's fashionability, including wearers and entrepreneurs across many State and counter-cultural agendas.

Such complex transnational lives for East Asian embroideries are far from unique, for fashion stimulates the mixing of cultures, links local and global, and has allowed travelling objects to be many things at once. In 1920s Britain and North America, large colourful shawls with silk tassel fringes became highly fashionable for women. Made of silk crepe, and covered in Chinese embroidery motifs, especially flowers, these shawls were sometimes called Spanish, and sometimes called Chinese, according to fashion. Depending on the place and time, this type of shawl was termed a mantón de Manila, a Spanish shawl, a Flamenco shawl, a Mexican shawl, a Chinese shawl, and a piano shawl.[3] With a history of trade linking Europe, China, the Americas and the Philippines, these shawls draw our attention to ambivalence in the ways that fashion exploits ethnic identities and colonial encounters.

Figure 3.1 Tailor Toyo sukajan gifted to Elizabeth Kramer by TOYO Enterprise in 2019. Photograph by Elizabeth Kramer.

Figure 3.2 Silk crepe shawl with silk embroideries showing flowers, birds, insects, and animals, made in China for European markets c.1870–1920. 170.8cm x 167cm (excluding fringes). Victoria and Albert Museum T.316-1960. © Victoria and Albert Museum, London.

Definitions of fashion that are rooted in a European framework are also rooted in European constructions of modernity. That modernity, its ideological and social frameworks, subjectivities and effects in the material world, has been formed in and through conditions of coloniality. Whether the term 'modern' is taken to mean the world since the 15th century when Europeans began to build empires in the Americas, the world since the Enlightenment of the 17th and 18th centuries, or the world since the Industrial Revolution, these are Eurocentric models of what it is to be modern, and world-views that were conditioned by coloniality. Decolonial thinkers have therefore highlighted the way that modernity/coloniality are not just intertwined or inseparable terms, but a confluence; modernity and coloniality are one.[4] Thinking decolonially therefore implies certain shifts in thinking about fashion and the assumptions that are made about concepts of modernity, newness and identity. Questions such as 'when is fashion?' or 'what is fashion?' seek to pin down the conditions under which a culture's clothing can or cannot be defined as fashion. But these questions are posed because of the inseparability of modernity/coloniality which makes 'modernity' and 'tradition' into opposing terms.[5] As scholars of African fashion have made clear for some time now, studies of dominant, capitalist mass-market fashion networks have failed to grasp a much bigger global picture of transnational culture, for which a greater investment in the logic of contradiction and blurred meanings is essential.[6] Part of the work of this chapter is to explore the degree to which the study of fashion enables historians to pursue a decolonial agenda of delinking from Eurocentric structures of knowledge, or whether thinking about fashion merely exposes the contradictory and conflicted nature of the colonial condition. We ask if Chinese embroidered shawls and Japanese souvenir jackets require fashion scholars to think differently about the ways that fashions achieve 'global' significance. We hold the colonial and the fashionable in a 'single analytical phrase', as we explore the impossibility of grasping and defining globalization, and the ambivalent and contradictory values that fashion exploits.[7]

Creating the Chinese/Spanish Shawl

Embroidered garments have certainly played a key role in the global spread of Japanese and Chinese fashions in which the Japanese kimono and the Chinese robe have had global influence as distinctive garment forms crossing over into many cultures.[8] There is, however, an important flexibility about embroidery as a locally rooted practice that can be applied to any garment or set of motifs, and as a technique that can be moved or transmitted from culture to culture and respond to technological changes.[9]

Embroidered shawls were not part of fashion cultures in China before the 20th century. This places the 'Chinese shawl' firmly within the context of Chinese export industries that created objects to fulfil foreign requirements. Chinese motifs, cultural references, materials and making techniques were used to create goods, such as painted wallpapers, that had no use within China, but that could be sold abroad.[10] From the late 16th century, the Spanish were trading Chinese goods through the Philippines after they had invaded the archipelago and established colonies and fortifications. In the 18th century, Spanish traders ordered shawls in Canton, and they were traded via Manila in the Philippines to the Pacific coast of Mexico, where the China trade was integral to the development of the sea port of Acapulco in what the colonizers called New Spain.[11] From there, the shawls were imported into the south of Spain through the port of Seville. This linked Chinese production to Latin American colonial cultures, and European garments and aesthetics to Chinese motifs, materials and manufacturing techniques.

During the 19th century, Chinese shawls were highly prized on the Spanish market, products of the Canton export embroidery industry which was characterized by vivid colours, compact stitches and pictorial content. They spread from the elites to become a more widely fashionable garment for women, but were especially identified with the south of Spain and the Flamenco dance, even though they featured Chinese bats, butterflies, flowers and even Buddhist symbols and pagodas. The Spanish silk making and silk embroidery industries were well established by the 18th century, and in order to compete with the Chinese imports coming into Southern Spain, they copied the Chinese motifs (Figure 3.3). In 1898, Spain ceded the Philippines, Guam and Puerto Rico to the United States. This final dwindling away of the Spanish Empire created a crisis of Spanish identity. With the loss of Manila, a new 20th-century emphasis on local shawl making in the Seville region created Andalusian traditions out of former Chinese designs, and Spanish-made Chinese shawls became a focus of Spanish national pride.[12]

Another set of colonial/trade relations were those between China and Britain. At the Great Exhibition held in London in 1851, embroidered and plain Chinese crepe shawls

Figure 3.3 Detail of a Spanish shawl. According to family stories, this shawl was acquired sometime between 1899 and 1920 by John Swan Tindale while on business in the dockyards of Barcelona. Tindale brought the shawl back to his wife in Lancashire, England, and it has now been worn by several generations of the family. Reproduced by permission of the Newell family. Photograph: Sarah Cheang.

were displayed alongside handkerchiefs and scarves as examples of the goods that China could provide the British people. Significantly for their encoding as Chinese in this time and place, they were shown in the China section, but not in the section representing Spain.[13] Both the 1851 Exhibition and the South Kensington museum collections that were founded as a result were an inextricable part of the workings of empire, from the presentation/control/possession of colonial lands, their products and the labour of their peoples, to reforms in design education that aimed to increase the power and reach of British manufacturing industries across the globe.[14] The Exhibition occurred in the midst of a series of Sino-British military conflicts in China known collectively as the 'Opium Wars' (1839–1842 and 1856–1860), which were won by allied Franco-British forces. China was forced to allow foreign missionaries, businesses and travellers to travel in China, and was made to grant extra-territorial rights to certain Western nations at key diplomatic and trading cities, as well as the ceding of Hong Kong to the British. This began a semi-colonial status for China in European and American eyes.[15] Though invited to participate in the Exhibition, in the midst of this armed struggle against undisguised British imperial aggression, the conditions of Chinese self-representation within a celebration of British industrial pre-eminence were clearly impossible. The Chinese government therefore refused to take part, and the Chinese section was instead organized by a group of British importers who created 'China' within the Exhibition's empire of things.[16]

It is claimed that one of the Chinese shawls in the collections of the South Kensington Museum, now the Victoria and Albert Museum, came from the Exhibition of 1851, giving an indication of the styles that were being promoted to mid-Victorian consumers in Britain (Figure 3.4).[17] The large size, around 2 metres along each side, matched a mid-century trend for Kashmiri and Paisley shawls that often used fringing and were folded and worn on the diagonal to create an expanse of colour and pattern that covered the shoulders, back and most of the crinoline-enhanced skirt, finishing in an attractive point.[18] The colours and decoration – white embroidered flowers on cream crêpe silk ground – show the uses of whitework (white on white embroidery) that was part of Chinese export production alongside pastels for the European palette, as well as the brighter colours more associated with the Chinese domestic market.

The shawls displayed at the Exhibition occupied a middle ground between the everyday and the spectacular. Chinese silks such as Shantung Pongee and Shanghai silk were raw textile imports that were used to create a wide range of familiar clothing, such as dresses and undergarments.[19] At the other extreme, the looting and immense social upheaval in the course of the Opium Wars, Taiping Rebellion (1850–1864/71), Boxer Uprising (1899–1901), and the fall of the Qing dynasty (1911), each created new opportunities for foreigners to obtain second-hand or stolen Chinese embroidered robes, skirts, jackets and hangings. These lavish and colourful Chinese embroidered garments and hangings were often cut up to provide trimmings and decorative details for British clothing and interior design schemes.[20]

The British department store of Liberty & Co were advertising Chinese-made shawls from the 1880s onwards. These came in a range of shapes, sizes and price points depending on the amount of embroidery, and were marketed as fashionable accessories

Figure 3.4 Detail of white silk shawl made in China for European markets in the early 19th century. 213cm x 213cm (approx.). Victoria and Albert Museum T.105-1921. © Victoria and Albert Museum, London.

of artistic distinction.[21] The Chinese origin of the shawls was constantly highlighted in the Liberty catalogue, and other UK importers also emphasized the Chinese origin of the shawls with wording such as '. . . shawls from Canton . . . beautifully embroidered by skilled Chinese workmen . . . just landed', which implies that these shawls came directly from the hands of Chinese craftsmen to the shores of the UK.[22]

Liberty were also a likely conduit for Chinese shawls to be consumed within elite fashion cultures in the United States. During the first two decades of the 1900s, delicately coloured embroidery on a white ground and deep ten-inch fringes were considered a 'distinct novelty' in the pages of American *Vogue* magazine, although pink and blue Chinese shawls were also promoted as 'unusual, and pretty' and selling better than ever. Readers were instructed to seek them at Liberty's or other 'oriental importers'. [23] The largest shawls with floral designs were recommended as evening wraps, and these were sold alongside other adaptations to fashion, such as Chinese shoulder wraps with turned over collars and box-pleating with tassels, Shantung silk robes in pale colours, and Chinese batiste (fine cotton or linen) robes, all richly embroidered.[24]

Another notable trend was the recycling of Paisley wool shawls. Seen as heirloom pieces, a lively trade in second-hand shawls is evidenced in the 'Sale and Exchange' advertisements placed in *Vogue* magazine by its readers, where Chinese embroidered shawls were being sold as antiques alongside Paisley and 'Indian' shawls, to be worn as they were, or as material to be cut and sewn into new garments.[25] These show how the value of the Chinese shawl within Western fashion cultures cannot be understood without reference to its earlier histories, the semantic flexibility of the 'orient', and the material flexibility of textile objects. A 1916 feature on the return to fashionability of the Paisley shawl for American women of all ages provides a visual and textual manifestation of this context. The article reserved the highest praise for 'heirlooms' that had been remodelled into 'something more suitable to the age', showing a design in which a Paisley shawl had been transformed into a 'Chinese cap', cape, muff and bag ensemble, all completed with dangling silk tassels.[26] Further possibilities are offered by a reader's advertisement in the previous issue of *Vogue* which offered an 'Indian crepe shawl, two yards square, very handsome fringe'.[27] While the references to crepe and fringes could make this item a misidentified Chinese export shawl, it is also possible that it was a Parsi shawl.

Chinese shawls were collected by members of the Parsi Zorastrian community living in Gujarat province, as Chinese-style embroideries were part of Parsi women's distinctive clothing.[28] Parsi merchants were trading in Canton from the 1700s, as a result of close ties with the British East India Company and their extensive interests in China. In the 19th century, affluent Parsis owned fleets of cargo ships and partnered with British firms in the opium trade with China.[29] Some Parsis also had businesses and homes in England and were likely also aware of British chinoiserie trends. Saris made from Chinese silk, fully embroidered with Chinese motifs (the gara) were worn by Parsi women, but not by other Indian communities involved in the China trade such as the Sindhis or the Ismailis.[30] In the early to mid-20th century, Chinese itinerant pedlars visited Parsi communities in India, selling embroidered goods and also teaching Chinese embroidery techniques, and it is also believed that Chinese embroidery workshops were established in the town of Surat in Western India to directly supply the Parsi market (Figure 3.5).[31]

In this network of Chinese/Parsi/British trade, colonial and intra-Indian relations, it is clear that the story of Parsi traders in Canton is an inter-cultural history that not only chronologically parallels the Spanish and British shawl trade, but can also be considered a part of it. For scholars of Indian textiles, the Chinese export embroideries consumed by Parsi women are known as Parsi embroideries, not Chinese embroideries, in the same way that the Chinese export shawls were also known as Spanish shawls, named for their users rather than their makers. In addition to the web of interactions arising from the spread of the motifs, flexibility of materials and movement of techniques and people, in order to rethink fashion globalization, fashion scholars need to attend to the ways that certain areas of that history, especially those outside of dominant, White Euro-American

Figure 3.5 Detail of silk embroidery tunic made in China for the Indian Parsi community, 19th century. Victoria and Albert Museum T.87-1925. © Victoria and Albert Museum, London.

cultures, have been ignored.[32] A focus on the history of Parsi embroidery motifs and techniques would also link 10th century Zoroastrian migration with the Tang and Song dynasties (618–1279 CE), Chinese trading networks, and intercultural exchanges between India, Persia and China pre-dating European imperialism.[33]

Fashion, Cultures and Categorization

Museums are forced by their cataloguing systems to select a culture of origin for every object, causing the elision of many histories. Culturally hybrid objects may be relegated to storage if they are too difficult to place within galleries arranged around geographical, ethnic or national groupings. Often, however, they can be used to tell stories of colonial contact, making transnational histories a useful area of focus for decolonial curation, because they require the questioning of many structures of knowledge. It can sometimes appear that this work has already been done by the wearers and makers of global fashion; the ways in which materials, garments and trends travel make fashion the quintessence of the transnational. Yet, we should be wary of the idea that fashion's global flows make it decolonial to any degree; the semantic flexibility and ephemerality that are a core part of fashion's cultural dynamics are used as much to serve as to oppose the power structures encoded in racial/colonial hierarchies. Beyond fashion and cultural appropriation debates that pitch problematic claims of inspiration and respect against deeply felt and important accusations of theft, racism and disrespect, fashion's material and symbolic flexibility, global flows and fast-paced changes are sadly often used as a means to defend offensive fashion imagery.[34]

The geographical looseness of the Chinese shawl was used as a licence for fashion creativity with respect to symbolic meaning. In a 1921 report on how Europe's elite style leaders were wearing Spanish shawls, *Vogue* informed readers that the shawls were coming from Venice, Spain, Persia and the Philippines. China was not mentioned, even though, 20 years earlier, importers of Chinese goods and travellers to China had been key sources for the shawls. This is also surprising because the 1910s had seen a marked resurgence in Euro-American Chinese-inspired fashions across clothing, interior design, furniture and even trends in Chinese pet dogs.[35] By the 1920s, dragons motifs, 'Mandarin' sleeves, pagoda shapes, and the British chinoiserie Willow Pattern print were recurring features in fashion, as well as the wearing of Chinese embroidered garments as evening coats. This likely stimulated Liberty to begin producing full page catalogue images of the shawls, maintaining their Chinese-ness while skirting round their place and time of manufacture by describing them as: 'clever reproductions' of antique Canton Shawls: 'Correct both in colour and needlework.'[36] Paradoxically though, Liberty also began offering these shawls in a colour called 'tango', making a direct reference to the wearing of these same garments in dance performances connected with Spanish and Latin American identity, and parallel fashions for Spanish themes (Figure 3.6).

The overwhelming evidence of film and print media is that Chinese shawls provided a vehicle for simultaneous fantasies of oriental and Latin excess through concurrent fashions for chinoiserie, the tango and Spanish dancing. Furthermore, the shawl's iconography in the 1920s came to include tight wrapping around the naked female body, creating a highly sensual long-fringed dress. By 1921, British and American fashion articles were advising on the 'Spanish fashion' that was being seen in three key areas of fashion practice: the latest designs of Paris fashion houses that featured fringing, tassels, shawl-like shapes and asymmetric hemlines; Spanish-themed social events such as charity balls; and the widespread wearing of embroidered, long-fringed shawls as fashionable garments in their own right (Figure 3.7).[37]

In literature of the period, descriptions of fashionable parties featured both 'Spanish' and 'Chinese' shawls equally. Virginia Woolf makes multiple references to Spanish shawls being worn by elite fashionable women in *Mrs Dalloway* (1925), set in London in 1923, while in F. Scott Fitzgerald's *Great Gatsby* (1925), Spanish shawls had a presence amidst the garish hedonism of American modernity: 'the cars from New York are parked five deep in the drive, and already the halls and salons and verandas are gaudy with primary colors, and hair shorn in strange new ways, and shawls beyond the dreams of Castile.'[38] Whereas, in Patricia Wentworth's novel *The Chinese Shawl*, the high class fashionability of a 1920s heroine was communicated in her decision to wear a Chinese shawl and Chinese jade pendant to go dancing.[39] *Vogue* reported that Spanish influence could be

Figure 3.6 Dancer Beth Beri aka Elizabeth Kislingbury, who was performing in cabaret at the Piccadilly Hotel, London. *Illustrated Sporting & Dramatic News*, 4 July 1925. © Illustrated London News Ltd/Mary Evans.

characterized by a 'square of Canton crêpe . . . lined with jade'.[40] This lays bare the close, carefree interchangeability of Spanish and Chinese references within interwar shawl fashion, and more accurately captures the cultural in-betweenness of the shawls than any museum catalogue.

Such geographical fluidity was also rich with colonial anxiety. The threat that was posed by shawl trading networks that further reinforced the in-between is seen in a British cartoon published in the *Bystander* in 1924. It satirises tourism at Colon, an Atlantic coast port in Panama that was established in 1850 and became an important stopping off point for cruises.[41] A local population, descended mainly from Black and Spanish labourers who dug the canal, are depicted as 'pirates' and 'modern coloured gentlemen of fortune from the Indies and the China seas'.[42] They are shown preying on

Figure 3.7 Front cover illustration showing a fashionable woman wrapped in a shawl inspired by Chinese embroidery, *Judge*, 2 October 1926. Mary Evans Picture Library.

unsuspecting White female tourists from a cruise ship by offering shoddy East Asian embroidered silk garments as souvenirs, which the cartoon typifies as Chinese/Spanish shawls and kimono-like garments. The dislocations in space produced by such tourism are here used to construct the fashion consumers as disempowered dupes, who place themselves at the mercy of unscrupulous men of colour because the tourists are shopping outside of the authenticating safety zones of elite Euro-American fashion institutions.

The ability for these shawls to be simultaneously Spanish and Chinese, and belong in many places (for example Venice, Argentina, Panama and London), and at the same time in no place, affords a valuable unknowability; it creates space for something that is neither universal/global nor authentic/local, *and* both universal/global *and* authentic/local. This quality of both/and is crucial for understanding how fashion cultures unfix the meanings attached to textiles and garments, with the potential to challenge structures of race and confuse dichotomies such as East/West or modernity/tradition.[43] However, it should be stressed that there is nothing decolonial about the ways that magazines like *Vogue* or the *Bystander* and retailers such as Liberty used and redefined a multiplicity of cultural identities and imperial histories. The global sensibilities that the shawls engendered – whether as heirloom, latest fashion purchase or touristic souvenir – were underpinned by a power to define that ultimately reaffirmed the dominance of European coloniality and models of modernity; they constituted another kind of colonial violence. Pursuing and working into the further complexities of hybrid global products such as the Chinese/Spanish shawl, and recognizing how colonial power relations have generated and shaped the currents of global fashion by both exploiting cultural ambiguity and simultaneously shutting down multiple or ambiguous fashion pathways, can be the first step towards a decolonial rejection of an entire apparatus of thinking around fashion and its histories. But these power relations of fashion should not be discussed without a more direct consideration of the role of violence in the generation and circulation of transnational East Asian culture.

Fashion and Military Expansionism

Sukajan embroidery provides an example of the ways in which Japanese and Chinese cultural elements have been globally circulated between cultures and incorporated into sartorial expression in and outside of East Asia in parallel with militaristic ventures. Born out of military conflict following the Second World War, the feature embroideries on these garments allowed their wearers to 'bring back into ordinary experience something of the quality of an extraordinary experience'[44] – active military service or time spent in a culture different from their own. The flamboyant garment loudly reports unrepeatable experiences.[45] And yet while Susan Stewart has argued that this 'narrative of interiority and authenticity . . . is not a narrative of the object; it is a narrative of the possessor',[46] the materiality of the garment and the circumstances under which it was made and by whom tell other narratives. These multidirectional stories demonstrate the ways in which imperial expansionism and militarization, business ventures and fashion are entangled on a global scale, in ways that complicate how scholars such as Stewart have conceptualized souvenirs as an 'exotic' in relation to modernism.

Souvenirs have long played an important role in travel, and while sometimes these were purchased in trade ports or gifted, at other times they were taken as the result of plundering or pillaging.[47] These types of acquisition need to be examined with regard to the context of colonization from which they often arose. There is an established history of embroidered souvenir production aimed at military personnel as they travelled in East Asia.[48] There is also evidence of military personnel acquiring unauthorized embroidered additions to personalize their uniforms for sartorial expression. For example, when uniforms were custom-made by civilian tailors[49] for U.S. sailors, personalized details such as hidden pockets and embroidery were sometimes added to the garments. Such embellishments included 'liberty cuffs', enabling a sailor to roll back his sleeves to reveal when he was off-duty, or 'at liberty'.[50] Since the late 19th century, liberty cuffs were formed through the addition of non-regulation embroidered patches sewn inside the garment, as demonstrated by the colourful dragons embroidered on the inside of the cuffs of the naval jumper belonging to an officer aboard the USS Austin (commissioned in 1965) (Figure 3.8). While liberty cuffs were made available all over the fleet, including from tailors based in the United States, they were most commonly made in Asian ports, and associated with China in particular,[51] indicating an established history of off-duty sartorial expression on a global scale. Similar designs, such as embroidered motifs depicting sinuous dragons or those in medallions and their placement on the contrasting fabric of the sleeve cuffs, are apparent in sukajan produced during the immediate post-war period. These designs suggest Chinese inspiration, if not direct intervention, in the early production of souvenir jackets in the form of a US military issue field jacket (Figure 3.9). This is further demonstrated in the bright colouring or regular use of lustrous materials such as silk or rayon in the construction of early sukajan that calls to mind embroidered Chinese robes or other souvenirs.

In Japan, sukajan expanded upon a broad range of embroidered souvenirs offered to military men such as embroidered kimono purposely designed for the souvenir market that had long served as popular gifts to bring home to wives, daughters or other female relatives or friends after completing tours of duty.[52] Export kimono featured elaborate embroidered designs across the upper back such as flowers associated with Japan including wisteria, chrysanthemums and cherry blossoms, a padded hemline, gussets to resemble a skirt and an embroidered and fringed or tasselled tie. These were popular with markets in America and Europe from the early 20th century.[53] Sukajan likewise featured stunning embroidered motifs applied to the very masculine shape of the bomber or baseball jacket (Figure 3.1). Initially tailored and embroidered ad hoc by private commission for soldiers, the Japanese fabric import/export company Kosho & Co (later TOYO Enterprise) devised a jacket featuring embroidered motifs and arranged for these garments to be manufactured on a larger scale in Kiryu and Ashikaga near Tokyo by craftspeople formally engaged in the kimono industry, which had been severely disrupted during the war.[54] As the sukajan became a popular souvenir among the US soldiers

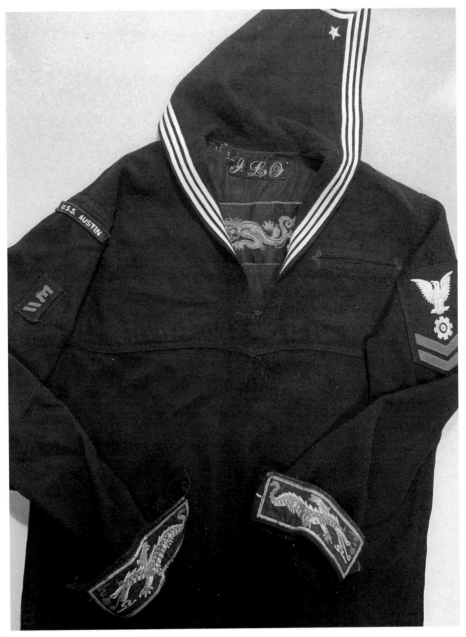

Figure 3.8 US navy jumper with embroidered liberty cuffs, mid-20th century, collection of Elizabeth Kramer. Photograph: Allison Hedstrom.

Figure 3.9 Sukajan depicting 'Dragon and Japan Map' (late 1940s), collection of TOYO Enterprise Company Ltd. Reproduced by kind permission of TOYO Enterprise Company Ltd.

stationed in Japan, Kosho & Co., the leading supplier of souvenir jackets, expanded their operation through distribution to Post Exchanges.[55]

The sukajan's sartorial use demonstrates a bi-directional rather than unidirectional stylistic dialogue between Japan and the United States. This is important to note because globalization is often associated with a worldwide unidirectional spread of American culture.[56] While the military occupation of Japan between 1945 and 1952 was intended to Americanize Japan by radically transforming its government, economy, educational system, press, and social institutions, and '"educat[ing]" Japanese citizens about "freedom", "democracy", and other American cultural sensibilities',[57] a close study of the sukajan allows us to unpick how, through fashion, aesthetic influence and other value systems might move back and forth between nations in unexpected ways, despite very visible, unequal power distributions.

The term sukajan draws upon two words: Yokosuka, the location of a Japanese (and then later American) naval base; and the Japanese word for jumper, ジャンパー (jyanpa). Notably jyanpa is written in katakana, a writing script used for foreign words adopted and transformed into the Japanese language. The base at Yokosuka served an important role in the maintenance and repair of the US fleets during the Korean and Vietnam Wars. It remains the largest strategic naval installation in the Western Pacific and continues to serve as an important recreational site for US military personnel in the region. Several sukajan specialty shops still operate along Dobuita Street in Yokosuka, popular for souvenir shopping and nightlife, just minutes from the American base, as they have done since Occupation, providing US servicemen in peace and wartime with opportunities to purchase sukajan.

Although the sukajan is an off-duty garment, in addition to the elaborately embroidered scheme across the back, embroidery is a notable feature on the shoulder sleeves and breast pockets, zones usually reserved for service patches in uniform design. Object analysis of sukajan further demonstrates the global-facing nature of this garment. According to company history, an employee of the leading postwar producer of sukajan, Kosho & Co., suggested that these garments should be constructed in the form of an American varsity or baseball jacket.[58] The motifs embroidered on postwar sukajan draw on a diverse iconography referencing an 'orient' or Japan, including dragons, tigers, koi, sakura blossoms or trees, maiko or geisha, as well as maps of Japan. This strategy of self-orientalism[59] reinforced and circulated particular stereotypes of Japan and demonstrates an awareness of the marketability in, and hoped-for profitability from, such references in the desperate economic climes of postwar Japan. At the same time, such motifs were also used in combination with, or replaced by, American military phraseology and iconography such as eagles, fighter planes or Native American motifs that had long been appropriated in expressions of national identity of the United States.[60] Tailor Toyo demonstrated financial acumen and moved beyond self-orientalism by supplying tour jackets to Post Exchanges beyond that of the US Fleet activities based at Yokosuka. These jackets are also a testament to the military expansionism of the United States and related conflicts. The motifs embroidered on sukajan during this time are therefore emblematic of the other nations in which US military presence spread in the late-19th and 20th centuries. In 1898 the United States replaced Spanish colonizers in the Philippines and established a further presence in Greenland during World War II and Panama following this war, to name but a few examples.

Sukajan can be reversible, featuring alternative colour and embroidery schemes on each side of the garment (Figure 3.10). This is not dissimilar to the hidden embroidery associated with liberty cuffs, as well as a phenomenon in Japanese menswear where haori (the coat worn over kimono), can be quite reserved in design but when turned inside out reveal an intricate design on the inner lining that can relate very personally to its wearer, for example to his love of poetry or political leanings. When analyzing the reversible nature of post-war sukajan in TOYO Enterprise's garment archive, it was pointed out that reversible garments offered increased variety and were thus more profitable.[61] These innovations in the design of the sukajan – its reversibility and similarity in form to American military and sport garments – demonstrate Japanese initiative to create a profitable market, which was additionally increased by adapting and transplanting further foreign motifs through local embroidery.

Figure 3.10 Reverse of Tailor Toyo sukajan gifted to Elizabeth Kramer by TOYO Enterprise in 2019. Photograph: Elizabeth Kramer.

In the souvenir jacket celebrating the Alaska Highway (Figure 3.11), the military connection at first may not be apparent. Construction on the 1523-mile highway (commenced in 1942) aimed to connect Alaska to the west coast of the United States through Canada at a time when Japanese invasion seemed a distinct possibility.[62] TOYO Enterprise produced souvenir jackets commemorating the highway, to which US servicemen provided much of the labour, in the mid- to late-1950s. On the illustrated example, the embroidered motifs are focused on conjuring a stereotypical view of a subarctic North American landscape through its wildlife and Indigenous people. A couple in fluffy parkas with hoods drawn can be found embroidered on the breast of the garment while a large moose head features on the reverse. The former motif counts among the images that objectified the dispossessed and unfairly treated Indigenous people of the Americas. These highly romanticized images became prolific at the end of the 19th century when Native populations had reached their lowest.[63] Within a decade of the first sukajan being sold to US occupying forces, TOYO Enterprise was producing souvenir jackets in a wide range of designs corresponding to the region in which they were being sold, adding an additional layer of complexity to the matters of US settler colonialism, cultural appropriation and racial stereotyping. When a Japanese company portrayed Indigenous peoples of the west coast of North America to appeal to US

Figure 3.11 'Alaska Highway' sukajan (mid to late 1950s), collection of TOYO Enterprise Company Ltd. Reproduced by kind permission of TOYO Enterprise Company Ltd.

customers, Japanese constructions of race, nation and Otherness, and their entanglement with wider constructions of difference circulating in East Asia, Europe *and* America, brought Japanese embroideries directly into the wider use of ethnic stereotypes within global systems.[64]

Souvenir to Global Fashion

As souvenir jackets became ubiquitous with tours of duty, the production of souvenir jackets spread to other centres. For example, while TOYO Enterprise continued to produce sukajan two decades later for American military personnel on shore leave in Japan during the Vietnam War, souvenir jackets also began to be made in Vietnam. During the 1960s, confidence in the United States' military intervention in Vietnam waned, and the character of these jackets transformed dynamically. Documentary footage from Ken Burns and Lynn Novik's *The Vietnam War* (2017) captures a naval officer bidding a fond farewell to his family before departing for Vietnam. His little boy is dressed in a brightly coloured embroidered sukajan perhaps purchased for him by his father while on a previous tour of duty (Figure 3.12).

The boy's jacket contrasts sharply with those produced in Vietnam during the War. The Vietnam souvenir jackets still performed commemoration and were rather formulaic

Figure 3.12 'The Vietnam War' directed by Ken Burns and Lynn Novick © Florentine Films and WETA 2017. All rights reserved.

in featuring battle maps relating to tours of duty and motifs related to military prowess or stereotypes of Asia such as tigers and dragons, but they also differed notably from the earlier Japanese examples. The colourful, sumptuous rayon of the sukajan was replaced with the utilitarian fabric of field uniforms. Military or South Vietnamese tailors directly embroidered battle maps upon used garments as well as the specific details of where and when the wearer served. Mottos such as 'When I die I'll go to heaven because I've served my time in hell', communicated a less triumphant stance, as seen in the jacket that heavy truck driver Joseph Monroe had custom made before departing Vietnam in 1968 following his tour of duty (Figure 3.13).

Further meanings were folded into the garment when sukajan were adopted by Japanese youth cultures. In the 1960s a working-class fashion movement called sukaman (Yokosuka Mambo) rejected the popular post-war Ivy look, inspired by college dress at Ivy League institutions in the United States and precursor to the preppy look.[65] Sukaman instead imitated the dress of Japanese gangsters and American soldiers, patronizing the very shops that dealt souvenirs to the Americans.[66] This style was brought to popular attention in Japan through Shohei Imamura's 1961 film *Buta to gunkan* (*Battleships and Pigs*), set in the red light district and docks near the American naval base in Yokosuka in which the ineffective, wanna-be yakuza character Kinta dons two such jackets. The jacket's association with deviant behaviour has continued to be reinforced through international film and television. Both its military and subcultural associations made it an attractive garment outside of military circles and subcultural groups to consumers hoping to draw on these associations, as well as fashion labels hoping to capitalize on them. The contradictory reading of military garments as both highly ordered and subversive lends to their irresistible fashion appeal.[67] Likewise, the 'most common narrative about subcultures

Figure 3.13 Souvenir jacket belonging to Specialist Fourth Class Joseph 'Joe' E. Monroe (1969), Collection #MHI 2014.22.01, US Army Heritage & Education Center, Carlisle, PA.

is one that casts them as non-conformist ... different, dissenting',[68] adding further to the desirability of the garment.[69] The appeal of the sukajan has been enhanced by celebrities who donned the jacket, from Mick Jagger in the 1960s to Kayne West in 2016. While the garment now has little to do with class, political struggle, or criminality, the 'badass' exchange value of the jacket is promised to global audiences through such associations in fashion blogs and advertising and reinforced through film and TV.[70] Indeed, in the mid-2010s the souvenir jacket became a 'must-buy piece'[71] in mainstream fashion. However, while its relationship to violence gives the sukajan its fashionable edge, the depoliticization of the garment through popular and celebrity culture obscures its history. The potent impact of politics and the military on the everyday in post-war Japan – desperation, injury and death, sexual exploitation and rape[72] – has been lost in fashionable translation.

In an oversaturated market, fashion brands have increasingly turned to storytelling to capture attention and connect emotionally with the consumer. Fashion blogs and product descriptions during the 2010s trend latched onto the origin story of the sukajan, emphasizing the pleasures and excitement of its militaristic and subculture associations without looking too deeply at the related violence and trauma.[73] For example the Japanese distributor SUKAJACK, which sells upmarket sukajan, emphasizes such connections in its blog; it recommends the brands Tailor Toyo as the first and continuous line of sukajan since the 1950s, Alpha-One Industries as an established producer of military wear since 1959, and Houston as another manufacturer of military wear since 1947 and responsible for the first flight jacket in Japan.[74] These sanitised heritage narratives are key to the garment's sartorial appeal as markers of authenticity, but the omitted stories of sukajan are also crucial in that they enable a new reading of culture and power displays that can help us rethink global fashion flows.

Sukajan continue to be available for purchase as souvenirs in Japan. However, fieldwork analysis of the sukajan available at speciality shops in Tokyo and Kyoto in 2019 revealed that most of these garments emblematic of Japan are now manufactured in China.[75] The Japanese textile and fashion industry experienced dramatic heights, dizzying falls and recovery either side of the Second World War, most recently succumbing to import competition from more newly industrialized economies.[76] When we asked at BSC Gallery in Kyoto why most of the sukajan featured in their specialty shop were manufactured in China, we were handed a bilingual, laminated sign explaining this was due to financial hardships that the Japanese textile industry underwent in 2000 but to rest assured that Japanese apparel companies built garment factories in China resulting in 'high-quality works by cutting-edge technologies' so 'please don't worry about it'. The nonchalance with which this sign dismisses a shift in the production base for sukajan demonstrates both the geographical fluidity of fashion due to economic imperatives and also how fashion retailing seeks to minimize this in order to capitalize on more historic cultural capital.

Conclusion

Global flows of fashion have enabled the presence of paradoxical hybridities within codes of national identity, and underline the ways in which both international trade and national subjectivities have formed up in conditions of colonialism. Writing a history of the Chinese embroidered shawl in Britain and America has involved consideration of transformation and transmission between China, the Philippines, Latin America, Spain, the United States, Britain, France, Italy and India. The sukajan offers material evidence of distinct transnational narratives through local sewing cultures and personal and public narratives of travel across a similarly wide range of locations. Multicultural roots resulting in an ambivalence and multiplicity of meanings and overlapping resonances have given these garments their fashionable edge at particular moments in time and in many places. These are accretions of the local and the transnational. They create localized fashion phenomena that in turn create distinctive styles associated with particular times, places and people that are then appropriated and acquire wider commercial uses. They show that fashion cultures traverse continents in response to business ventures bound up in narratives of imperialistic expansionism. Rather than repulsing consumers, these stories of militaristic prowess attract them. However, histories of Americanization/ globalization and American history making are also turned inside out when the fashion acts of American soldiers are appropriated by Japanese 'bad boys' too.

Many discussions of the globalization of fashion, including notions of internet 'fashionscapes', are still based on overall definitions of fashion, modernity and postmodernity created within the modern/coloniality frame, focused mainly on the late 20th and 21st century, and most often reflecting a White Euro-American perspective.[77] Attempts to write back – by arguing from the perspective of the local, the indigenous, the colonized, the margins – risk re-inscribing categories of oppression, confirming their validity and reproducing colonial power relations.[78] Shawls and sukajan are two examples in transnational fashion research that have the capacity to catalyse other ways of discussing East Asian fashion histories as globally connected, but without recourse to positions of Otherness. Decolonial debates require a re-envisioning of the dynamics of globalization. The word 'global' often masks specific transnational interactions, with specific power relations and histories of conflict. Through our work on embroidered things, we have sought to underline both the specificity and imprecision of global flows of fashion. Bringing attention to bear on these relationships and journeys involves holding lightly the idea that cultural assignations can be made at all. This enables us to pay attention to the in-between and the transformation and transplantations that 'globalization' implies and that fashion makes an everyday, material experience. Exploring how the paradoxical nature of fashion is driven by ideas of distinction and difference creates a particular set of dynamics around travelling objects and allows us to think differently about how globalization works, and how fashion has exploited colonial activities and legacies. This does not enable fashion scholars to create neat narratives, geographically or in time. Indeed, any attempt to reduce fashion globalization to something simple would be to miss the presence of narratives with decolonial potential.

Notes

1. The authors would like to thank Tom Tanaka and Tatsuro Matsuyama at TOYO Enterprise, and Kaleb Dissinger, Keiko Suzuki, Rie Mori, Helen Persson, Susan Newell and Tara Zanardi for their invaluable assistance in the research conducted for this chapter. This chapter is part of a larger ongoing project on transnational fashion histories, colonial power relations and East Asian embroidered garments that builds on the AHRC Research Network Fashion and Translation: Britain, Japan, China, Korea.

2. Elizabeth Kramer, 'New Vintage -New History? The *Sukajan* and its Fashionable Reproduction', *International Journal of Fashion Studies* 7, no.1 (2020): 24–47.

3. Mei Mei Rado '中國外銷披肩與西方時尚 Chinese Export Shawls and Western Fashion'. In Cai Qin, Ed. *Far-Reaching Elegance and Magnificent: Chinese Export Silk Collection of China National Silk Museum* (Hangzhou: China National Silk Museum, 2014).

4. Walter D. Mignolo, *Local Histories/Global Designs: Coloniality, Subaltern Knowledges and Border Thinking* (Princeton, NJ: Princeton University Press, 2000); Aníbal Quijano, 'Coloniality and Modernity/Rationality', *Cultural Studies*, 21 (2) (2007) 168–178.

5. Three contrasting approaches to these debates are: M. Angela Jansen and Jennifer Craik, 'Introduction'. In M. Angela Jansen and Jennifer Craik, Eds. *Modern Fashion Traditions: Negotiating Tradition and Modernity through Fashion* (London: Bloomsbury, 2016); Joanne Entwistle, *The Fashioned Body: Fashion, Dress and Modern Social Theory*, 2nd edn

(Cambridge: Polity, 2015) xv–xxi; Joanne B. Eicher, 'Introduction: The Fashion of Dress'. In ed. C. Newman, *National Geographic Fashion* (Washington, DC: National Geographic, 2001) 17–23.

6. Leslie Rabine, *The Global Circulation of African Fashion* (Oxford: Berg, 2002); Victoria Rovine, *African Fashion, Global Style: Histories, Innovations, and Ideas You Can Wear* (Bloomington, IN: Indiana University Press, 2015).

7. Catherine Hall, *Civilizing Subjects: Metropole and Colony in the English Imagination, 1834–1867* (Cambridge: Cambridge University Press, 2002); Justin Rosenberg, *The Follies of Globalization Theory* (London: Verso, 2001) 17–43; Françoise Lionnet and Shu-mei Shih, 'Thinking Through the Minor, Transnationally'. In Françoise Lionnet and Shu-mei Shih, Eds. *Minor Transnationalism* (Durham, NC: Duke University Press, 2005) 1–23; Prasannan Parthasarathi and Georgio Riello, 'Introduction: Cotton Textiles and Global History'. In P. Parthasarathi and G. Riello, Eds. *The Spinning World: A Global History of Cotton Textiles 1200–1850* (Oxford: Oxford University Press, 2009) 1–13.

8. See Anna Jackson, Ed. *Kimono: Kyoto to Catwalk* (London: V&A Publications, 2020); Yuki Morishima and Rie Nii, Eds. *Kimono Refashioned: Japan's Impact on International Fashion* (San Francisco, CA: Asian Art Museum, 2018); Terry Satsuki Milhaupt, *Kimono: A Modern History* (London: Reaktion, 2014); Verity Wilson, 'Studio and Soirée: Chinese Textiles in Europe and America, 1850 to the Present'. In Ruth B. Phillips and Christopher B. Steiner, Eds. *Unpacking Culture: Art and Commodity in Colonial and Postcolonial Worlds* (Berkeley, CA: University of California Press, 1999) 229–242; Mei Mei Rado, 'The Hybrid Orient: Japonism and Nationalism of the Takashimaya Mandarin Robes', Fashion Theory, 19 (5) (2015) 583–616; Peter Lee, 'Dressing Badly in the Ports: Experimental Hybrid Fashion.' In Peter Lee, Leonard Y. Andaya, Barbara Watson Andaya, Gael Newton and Alan Chong, *Port Cities: Multicultural Emporiums of Asia, 1500-1900* (Singapore: Asian Civilizations Museum, 2018) 64–79.

9. Rovine, *African Fashion*, 47–67; Hazel Lutz, 'Cultural Authentication and Fashion in the Global Factory: A Panel of Four Papers'. In *Textile Society of America Symposium Proceedings* (2004), Paper 438.

10. Anna Wu, 'Chinese Wallpaper, Global Histories and Material Culture' (PhD Thesis, Royal College of Art, 2018).

11. Tara Zanardi, 'From Global Traveller to Costumbrista Motif: The Manton de Manila and the Appropriation of the Exotic'. In Tara Zanardi and Lynda Klitch, Eds. *Visual Typologies from the Early Modern to the Contemporary: Local Contexts and Global Practice*s (New York: Routledge, 2019).

12. Tara Zanardi, 'Fabricating the "Manton de Manila" as National Dress' unpublished conference paper, Beyond Chinoiserie: Artistic Exchanges between China and the West during the late Qing Dynasty (c.1795–1911), Seton Hall University, 30–31 October 2015.

13. *Official Catalogue of the Great Exhibition of the Works of Industry of All Nations, 1851* (London: Spicer Brothers, 1851) 209, 297–301.

14. Jeffrey Auerbach, *The Great Exhibition of 1851: A Nation on Display* (New Haven, CT: Yale University Press, 1999); Lara Kriegel, 'Narrating the Subcontinent in 1851: India at the Crystal Palace'. In Louise Purbrick, *The Great Exhibition of 1851: New Interdisciplinary Essays* (Manchester: Manchester University Press, 2001) 146–178.

15. Robert Bickers, *Britain in China* (Manchester: Manchester University Press, 1999). On the terminology and cultural politics of studying semi-coloniality, see Dipesh Chakrabarty, 'Foreword: The Names and Repetitions of Postcolonial History'. In Rachel V. Harrison and Peter A. Jackson, Eds. *The Ambiguous Allure of the West: Traces of the Colonial in Thailand* (Hong Kong: Hong Kong University Press, 2010) vii–xviii.

16. Judith Green, 'Britain's Chinese Collections, 1842–1943: Private Collecting and the Invention of Chinese Art' (PhD thesis, University of Sussex, 2002) 40–46.

17. V&A FE.532-1992.

18. Andrea Gayatri Hoffman, 'Unwrapping the "Spanish" Shawl's Chinese Past', *Helen Louise Allen Textile Centre Newsletter* (Fall 2001) 12–13.

19. Shuye Zhang, 'Chinese Silk in Late Victorian Britain 1870–1901: Textile Trade, Consumption and Cultural Identity' (MA dissertation, Royal College of Art, 2018).

20. Sarah Cheang, 'Dragons in the Drawing Room: Chinese Embroideries in British Homes, 1860–1949', *Textile History*, 39 (2) (2008) 223–249.

21. *Catalogue of Eastern Art Manufactures and Decorative Objects* (London: Liberty, c.1881); *'Liberty' Yule-Tide Gifts* (1898) 55–56; *Liberty & Co's Yule-Tide Gifts* (London: Liberty, 1909) 45.

22. Advert for John Burton, importer, Falmouth 1885, cited in Zhang 'Chinese Silk', 110.

23. 'Seen in the Shops', *Vogue* (New York) 6 August 1903, vii.

24. 'What She Wears', *Vogue* (New York) 15 Oct 1908, 604.

25. Advertisement, 'Sales and Exchanges: Wearing Apparel', *Vogue* (New York) 15 Mar 1914, 23; Advertisement, 'Sales and exchanges: Wearing apparel', *Vogue* (New York) 1 June 1914, 4; Advertisement 'Sales and Exchanges: Wearing apparel', *Vogue* (New York) 1 Nov 1914, 18.

26. 'Paisley Shawls Are Back', *Vogue* (New York) 1 Dec 1916, 126.

27. Advertisement, 'Sales and Exchanges: Wearing Apparel', *Vogue* (New York) 15 Nov 1916, 14.

28. Yuah-Siang Chang, 'Exported Exotic: Embroidered Silks of China'. In Shilpa Shah and Tulsi Vatsi, Eds. *Peonies and Pagodas: Embroidered Parsi Textiles: Tapi Collection* (Surat: Garden Mills Ltd, 2010) 110–117.

29. Tulsi Varsal, 'The China Connection'. In Shilpa Shah and Tulsi Vatsi, Eds. *Peonies and Pagodas: Embroidered Parsi Textiles: Tapi Collection* (Surat: Garden Mills Ltd, 2010) 17–24.

30. Tulsi Varsal, 'Looking West, Buying East'. In Shilpa Shah and Tulsi Vatsi, Eds. *Peonies and Pagodas: Embroidered Parsi Textiles: Tapi Collection* (Surat: Garden Mills Ltd, 2010) 98–103.

31. Chang, 'Exported Exotic' 114; Madhavi Thampi, 'Chinese Communities in India'. In Shilpa Shah and Tulsi Vatsi, Eds. *Peonies and Pagodas: Embroidered Parsi Textiles: Tapi Collection* (Surat: Garden Mills Ltd, 2010) 186–187.

32. Rolando Vázquez, 'The Museum, Decoloniality and the End of the Contemporary'. In Thijs Lijster, Eds. *The Future of the New: Artistic Innovation in Times of Social Acceleration* (Amsterdam: Valiz, 2018) 181–195; Gayatri Chakravorty Spivak, 'Can the Subaltern Speak?' In Cary Nelson and Lawrence Grossberg, Eds. *Marxism and the Interpretation of Culture* (Champaign, IL: University of Illinois Press, 1988); Catherine Grant and Nancy Price, 'Decolonizing Art History', *Art History*, 43 (1) (2020): 8–66.

33. Shernaz Cama, 'Parsi Embroidery: An Intercultural Amalgam'. In Marie-Louise Nosch, Zhao Feng and Lotika Varadarajan, Eds. *Global Textile Encounters* (Oxford: Oxbow Books, 2014) 263–274.

34. Susan Kaiser, *Fashion and Cultural Studies* (London: Routledge, 2012) 48; Minh-Ha T. Pham, 'Fashion's Cultural Appropriation Debate: Pointless', *The Atlantic*, 15 May 2014, www.theatlantic.com/entertainment/archive/2014/05/cultural-appropriation-in-fashion-stop-talking-about-it/370826/ (accessed 12 July 2019).

35. Sarah Cheang, 'What's in a Chinese Room? 20th Century Chinoiserie, Modernity and Femininity'. In David Beevers, Ed. *Chinese Whispers: Chinoiserie in Britain 1650–1930* (Brighton: The Royal Pavilion & Museums, 2008) 74–81; Sarah Cheang, 'Women, Pets and

Imperialism: The British Pekingese Dog and Nostalgia for Old China', *Journal of British Studies*, 45 (2) (2006) 359–387.

36. *Liberty Yule-Tide Gifts 1920–1921* (London: Liberty, 1920) 9.

37. 'Essence of Spain – à l'anglaise', *The Bystander*, 5 March 1924, 550.

38. Virginia Woolf, *Mrs Dalloway* [1923] (Ware: Wordsworth Classics, 1996) 119, 121, 130; F. Scott Fitzgerald, *The Great Gatsby* [1926] (Penguin Books, 1950) 46.

39. Patricia Wentworth, *The Chinese Shawl* [1943] (London: Hodder, 1969).

40. 'Seen in the Shops', *Vogue* (New York) 1 July 1921, 82.

41. 'The Modern Pirates of Panama', *The Bystander*, 30 January 1924, 245.

42. Stephen Frenkel, 'Geographical Representations of the "Other": The Landscape of the Panama Canal Zone', *Journal of Historical Geography*, 28 (1) (2002) 85–99.

43. Homi Bhabha, *Location of Culture* (London: Routledge, 1994); Marjorie Garber, *Vested Interests: Cross-Dressing and Cultural Anxiety* (London: Penguin, 1992).

44. Beverly Gordon, 'The Souvenir: Messenger of the Extraordinary', *Journal of Popular Culture*, 20 (3) (1986) 135.

45. Susan Stewart, *On Longing: Narratives of the Miniature, the Gigantic, the Souvenir, the Collection* (Durham, NC: Duke University Press, 1992) 135.

46. Stewart, *On Longing*, 136.

47. Kristen K. Swanson and Dallen J. Timothy, 'Souvenirs: Icons of Meaning, Commercialization and Commoditization', *Tourism Management*, 33 (2012) 489.

48. See for example George Schwartz, 'In Memory of Our Famous Cruises Around the World'. In H. T. McDermott and C. Pollard, Eds. *Threads of Silk and Gold: Ornamental Textiles from Meiji Japan* (Oxford: The Ashmolean Museum, 2012) 74–81, which discusses a range of embroidered items produced from the 1880s onward by the George Washington Company in Yokohama for sailors.

49. As uniforms are essential to the military apparatus, in addition to state manufacturers and commissioned agents, private entrepreneurs could also be turned to for uniforms. See Kjeld Galster and Marie-Louise Nosch, 'Textile History and the Military: An Introduction', *Textile History*, 4 (Supp.1) (2010): 1. The latter could be found at any port and were no doubt the freest to make illicit alterations.

50. Douglas Gunn and Roy Lockett, *The Vintage Showroom: An Archive of Menswear* (London: Laurence King, 2015) 136.

51. Daniel D. Smith (2006–17), 'Navy Dress Blues, "Tailor-Mades" and "Liberty Cuffs"', http://navycollector.com/Navy_Traditions.htm (accessed 12 July 2019).

52. Keiko Suzuki, 'Kimono Culture in Twentieth-Century Global Circulation'. In Miki Sugiura, Ed. *Linking Cloth-Clothing Globally: Transformations of Use and Value c1700–2000* (Tokyo: ICES, 2019) 272–298. A tour of duty is here defined as a specified period of time during which a member of the armed forces is deployed to engage in operational duties (such as combat or patrol). This service is often undertaken in a foreign country.

53. Akiko Savas, 'Dilute to Taste – Kimonos for the British Market at the Beginning of the Twentieth Century', *International Journal of Fashion Studies*, 4 (2) (2017) 157–181; Allie Yamaguchi, 'Kimonos for Foreigners: Orientalism in Kimonos Made for the Western Market, 1900–1920', *The Journal of Dress History*, 1 (2) (2017) 100–111.

54. *TOYO Enterprise Company Ltd* (Tokyo: TOYO Enterprise Company Ltd, 2015) 6–7; Keiko Suzuki, 'Kimono Culture in Twentieth-Century Global Circulation', 289.

55. A Post Exchange or PX is a type of retail store operating at a US Army post.

56. Peter L. Berger, 'The Cultural Dynamics of Globalization'. In Peter L. Berger and Samuel P. Huntington, Eds. *Many Globalizations: Cultural Diversity in the Contemporary World* (Oxford: Oxford University Press, 2002) 1–16.

57. Malia McAndrew (2014), 'Beauty, Soft Power, and the Politics of Womanhood During the US Occupation of Japan, 1945–1952', *Journal of Women's History*, 26 (4) (2014) 83–107.

58. TOYO Enterprise Co., 'Story' (2018), www.toyo-enterprise.co.jp/tailor_toyo/about_001.htm (accessed 12 July 2019).

59. Sandra Niessen, Ann Marie Leshkowich and Carla Jones, *Re-Orienting Fashion: The Globalization of Asian Dress* (London: Bloomsbury, 2003); Grace Yan and Carla Amieda Santos, '"CHINA FOREVER": Tourism Discourse and Self-Orientalism', *Annals of Tourism Research*, 36 (2) (2009) 295–315.

60. Cécile R. Ganteaume, Colin G. Calloway and Paul Chaat Smith, *Officially Indian: Symbols that Define the United States* (Washington, DC: Smithsonian Institution, 2017).

61. We thank Tom Tanaka and Tatsuro Matsuyama at TOYO Enterprise for sharing this information.

62. For a detailed history of the highway, see Ken Coates, *North to Alaska: Fifty Years on the World's Most Remarkable Highway* (Toronto: McClelland and Stewart, 1992).

63. Colin G. Calloway, 'Forward'. In Cécile R. Ganteaume, Colin G. Calloway and Paul Chaat Smith, Eds. *Officially Indian: Symbols that Define the United States* (Washington DC: Smithsonian Institution, 2017) 12.

64. Louise Young, 'Rethinking Race for Manchukuo: Self and Other in the Colonial Context'. In Frank Dikötter, Ed. *The Construction of Racial Identities in China and Japan* (London: Hurst, 1997) 158–176; Stefan Tanaka, *Japan's Orient: Rendering Pasts into History* (Berkeley, CA: University of California Press, 1993); Ganteaume, Calloway and Chaat Smith, *Officially Indian*.

65. Ikuya Sato, *Kamikaze Biker* (Chicago, IL and London: University of Chicago Press, 1998).

66. W. David Marx, *Ametora: How Japan Saved American Style* (New York: Basic Books, 2015).

67. Jennifer Craik, *Uniforms Exposed: From Conformity to Transgression* (Oxford and New York: Berg, 2005).

68. Ken Gelder, *Subcultures: Cultural Histories and Social Practice* (London: Routledge, 2007) 3.

69. Ted Polhemus, *Street Style* [1995] (London: PYMCA, 2010).

70. Kramer, 'New Vintage – New History?' 33.

71. Warren Beckett, 'Everything You Need to Know about Souvenir Jackets', *Fashionbeans*, 3 March 2016, www.fashionbeans.com/2016/what-to-know-about-souvenir-jackets/ (accessed 12 July 2019).

72. See for example Shunya Yoshimi and David Buist, '"America" as Desire and Violence: Americanization in Postwar Japan and Asia During the Cold War', *Inter-Asia Cultural Studies*, 4 (3) (2003) 433–450; and Rumi Sakamoto, 'Pan-Pan Girls: Humiliating Liberation in Postwar Japanese Literature', *Journal of Multidisciplinary International Studies*, 7 (2) (2010) 1–15.

73. Jane Tynan, 'Military Chic: Fashioning Civilian Bodies for War'. In K. McSorley, *War and the Body: Militarization, Practice and Experience* (Abingdon: Routledge, 2013) 78–89; and Paul Achter, '"Military Chic" and the Rhetorical Production of the Uniformed Body', *Western Journal of Communication*, 83 (3) (2013) 265–285.

74. SUKAJACK, 'What is Vietnam Souvenir Jacket?' 2 May 2017, https://sukajack.com/blogs/article/what-is-vietnam-souvenir-jacket (accessed 12 July 2019).

75. The authors visited a range of sukajan speciality shops and tourist shops that included sukajan amongst souvenirs available for purchase in February 2019.

76. Chiang Hsieh, 'Post-War Developments in the Japanese Textile Industry', *International Labour Review*, 62 (1950) 364–388; and Young-Il Park and Kym Anderson, 'The Rise and Demise of Textiles and Clothing in Economic Development: The Case of Japan', *Economic Development and Cultural Change*, 39 (3) (1991) 531–548.

77. For example, Adam Geczy and Vicki Karaminas, *The End of Fashion: Clothing and Dress in the Age of Globalization* (London: Bloomsbury, 2019).

78. Rey Chow, *Ethics After Idealism: Theory-Culture-Ethnicity-Reading* (Bloomington, IN: Indiana University Press, 1998) 101–103; Pham, 'Fashion's Cultural Appropriation Debate'.

CHAPTER 4
AFRO-SURINAMESE KOTOMISI: FASHION AND THE ETHNOGRAPHY MUSEUM
Daan van DARTEL

Introduction

The non-verbal communication of two unidentified young Afro-Surinamese women in local fashion style in a photograph from the beginning of the 20th century (Figure 4.1), immediately caught my attention when searching the photography collection of the National Museum of World Cultures (Nationaal Museum van Wereldculturen, NMVW) where I am employed as the Curator of Popular Culture and Fashion. They wear kotomisi – koto means skirt and misi means miss – probably following the latest fashionable trends in fabric they could attain, which by then could come from all over the world. They are also wearing the accompanying angisa – a head cloth that could change shape every time it was folded – that today is one of the most important material cultural heritage objects for Afro-Surinamese people in Suriname and its diaspora.[1]

Laura Ann Stoler describes a method of reading images along (and against) the grain, and my reading of this photograph developed while I was attempting to grow my understanding of the effect of wearing koto on self-awareness, or its performativity.[2] To me, a White curator of world cultures trying to come to terms with the colonial past, the way the women look straight into the camera communicates a strong-will, and almost slight contempt or irritation at having to pose. The woman on the left takes a seemingly self-confident stance, as if inviting a discussion with me through her posture and expression. Both women expressed to me what fashion, or fashions, meant in colonial times; it was not only imposed, or influenced by European fashion, as is often presumed, but it also functioned as a tool of bricolage, resistance and survival. In this photograph and in this chapter I will explore how creolization did not mean the abandonment of African customs, but led to new, uniquely Caribbean creations, strongly influenced by African aesthetics. Creolization prevented European dress from taking over the whole, and in that way it was subversive. In Steeve Buckridge's words, 'the preservation of cultural identity was essential to survival, and dress a means to that end' – as methods of accommodation they were a form of resistance.[3]

When seeking out global fashion histories, the colonial collections of the NMVW abound with garments that embody the inherent dynamism of cultural production and global entanglement. Many of the approximately 26,000 textile dress items in the collection evidence intricate and transcultural origins. In the so-called West, globalization was often seen as starting with European imperialism, excluding the rest of the world as

Figure 4.1 Two young women in kotomisi. First quarter 20th century. TM-10019360. Collection Nationaal Museum Van Wereldculturen.

Figure 4.2 Liesbeth Accord wearing contemporary koto, 2017. Photographer: Misja Beijers.

people without history.[4] The fashioning of self and Other during the colonial era is a very powerful example of the hegemony of Europe in fashion theory, meaning that all developments in fashion were, and often still are, mainly attributed to European agency.[5] However, during the period of colonialism, exploited people were as much agents of change as their oppressors, though they had to be much more creative than the colonizers, often moving within tight frameworks of colonial hierarchies to exert influence or resistance.

This chapter looks at how dress collections from ethnography museums can be researched as part of fashion and globalization narratives, and offer new readings of both global fashion and the premise that ethnographic museum collections 'verify' the view that 'fashion is Western'. It is an attempt to use fashion thinking as a new lens for a thus far neglected aspect of many ethnographic textile collections in order to provide new, alternative readings of the collections, as well as an opportunity to use ethnographic collections to rethink the hegemony of fashion thinking.[6] Throughout this chapter I will be working with three terms, namely dress, fashion and style. 'Dress' is primarily defined as the assemblage of modifications to the body and/or supplements to the body.[7] 'Fashion' however refers to a wider, context-dependent and socially constructed system around dress, including ways of production, distribution and consumption, and depends on many external factors such as purposeful change and expert knowledge.[8] This definition of fashion implies there may be different, concomitant fashion systems operating in the world. 'Style', lastly, is a combination of items into a recognizable whole that defines identity.[9]

In this chapter, I will track changes in the social construction of Afro-Surinamese kotomisi, next to its origins in slave society as it traversed from 'fashion' to 'dress' to heritage 'costume' to national symbol and back to 'fashion' again between the second half of the 19th century and the present day. By doing so, the chapter tries to illuminate the changeability not so much of fashion itself, but of ideas of what and when fashion is, while simultaneously helping to remap and undo the concept of fashion as primarily located in the West and followed by the rest.

Fashion and the Ethnographic Museum

'Fashion' objects are found in all sorts of museums except for the ethnographic; fashion collections and exhibitions are encountered in municipal, art, history and design museums, as well as specialist fashion museums. Since a large reorganization and subsequent merger of three ethnographic museums in 2014, the NMVW is using several ideas of fashion and fashion theory to renew its vision of its 'ethnographic' textile and clothing collections. I purposefully do not use the word 'dress' here, as the term 'dress' in an ethnographic context contains perceived colonial implications of tradition, of remaining frozen in the past, and of never changing, supporting the belief that in so-called non-Western cultures, there is no fashion *over there*.[10] Textile departments of anthropology museums are filled with beautiful, skilfully made clothing items, we all know that, but are they considered as fashion? The general consensus is that they are not. Ethnographic objects belong to the realm of the Other. This idea of the Other has been indelibly shaped by the colonial project (and its afterlife).[11] Underpinned by colonial ideologies, both the study of fashion and museums have primarily been Eurocentric in their knowledge construction, and the concept of fashion as Western can be seen as a form of epistemic violence.[12]

When using concepts of fashion theory as a lens to look at ethnographic collections, the most ubiquitous criteria when defining fashion are the notion of change and its relation to identity construction. This suggests that all clothes are in fact fashion.[13] For museum professionals, Ingrid Loschek offers a different view, arguing that objects are not fashion in themselves and that fashion is not an inalienable aspect of one type of clothing, but that objects can or cannot be fashion when looked at from different perspectives.[14] For anthropology museums that hold large textile and clothing collections, this question of *when an object is fashion* is particularly important. Museum institutions rely on strict categorization needing structured and demarcated identities of objects to be able to register and document them. Fashion however, cannot be categorized so easily because of its contextual nature.[15] By accepting that objects can be fashionable within specific contexts, but are not necessarily part of a contemporary, or complex political, social and economic system that we call fashion, we can avoid the understandable inclination to call all clothing fashion. We can then have fashionable items (i.e. innovative and of the moment), which do not have to be part of a larger or more dominant fashion system.[16]

The Nationaal Museum van Wereldculturen and Koto

The NMVW is an overarching foundation of three formerly separate museums which were merged in 2014, and comprises the Tropenmuseum in Amsterdam, Museum Volkenkunde (Ethnology) in Leiden, and the Afrika Museum in Berg en Dal. Since 2018 the municipal Wereldmuseum Rotterdam also resides under its umbrella. The merging of the collections offers us fresh insight into Dutch museum collecting discourse of 'other cultures' and the development of anthropology and ideas of the Other in the Netherlands.

The NMVW takes care of a total collection of over 750,000 objects, including 310,000 photographs. The museum holds 26,000 textile dress items. According to the logic of its collecting history (firmly located within the framework of Dutch colonialism) many of these objects come from, or are images of, former Dutch colonies, mainly Indonesia and Suriname and to a lesser extent the Dutch Caribbean. Some 24,000 objects pertain to Suriname, with objects from different cultural groups including Hindustani, Afro-Surinamese Creole and Maroon, and Asian-Surinamese. Nearly 3,000 of these are categorized as clothing, of which around five-hundred can be considered kotomisi-related objects, including dress as well as kotomisi dolls, prints, photographs and painted calabashes with representations of kotomisi. Interestingly, the number of angisa headcloths (indispensable within kotomisi fashion) totals almost 450 across the merged collections, while complete koto ensembles, often also called 'kotomisi costumes', are relatively few.

The kotos in the museum were collected over several distinct periods since the end of the 19th century. The collectors were mostly Dutch or Afro-Surinamese who were born in Suriname or who had worked there and returned to the Netherlands in later life. Only 36 complete kotomisi ensembles were collected across the four museums that historically collected Surinamese objects in the Netherlands, which appears little for such an important national emblem of Afro-Surinamese identity. This may be attributed to a gender-specific history of collecting – most collectors were men who had less access to, or were perhaps less interested, in local female fashion in Suriname. However, when looking at the NMVW collection, the Surinamese collections are far smaller than Indonesian collections, as the Netherlands considered Indonesia a more important colony, and Indonesian textiles and clothing are one of the largest NMVW collections – batik dress objects amount to over 2500 in number alone. Furthermore, Surinamese dress objects that are better represented in the collection relate to people whose perceived 'Otherness' was clearer, namely Maroons and Indigenous people who mostly wore uncut cotton or beaded loin and shoulder cloths, rather than those of the koto-wearing city dwellers.

As kotos were mostly made from European and industrially produced and printed cloth, perhaps these objects were not 'Other' enough? Yet the angisa, acting as a sign (unknown to outsiders) and a visible signifier of its origins across different African cultures and perpetuated in slave societies,[17] was perceived as more 'authentic', and collected more numerously. The koto has also been perceived by some Afro-Surinamese people as an imposed European style of dressing, whereas the angisa is considered as more African in nature.[18] In addition, many Afro-Surinamese women collect and keep kotos in their homes; these objects just did not end up in museum collections. Significantly though, members of the Dutch Surinamese community – some of whom still make kotos to order for special occasions – hope that these kotos may one day be collected by museums.[19] These women also give classes in the techniques involved in tying angisas, such as starching and folding. It is their hope that younger generations will continue preserving the kotomisi tradition, supported by an increased cultural awareness and pride.

The Creation of Koto

The koto consists of several items, with the most emblematic being the skirt (koto), after which the outfit is named. On top a jacket or yaki is worn.[20] If these are of similar cloth and colour, it is called (h)eristel. There are also many styles in which jacket, skirt and/or angisa differ in material. Underneath both is a slip dress (ondro empi), sometimes with embroidery at its hem which peeks out under the skirt. Depending on the occasion and wealth of the owner, there can be additional layers, such as cotton underwear trousers, a pangi (a sort of sarong) and several underskirts creating the desired voluminous effect. The silhouette or shape is key in this fashion look, with as much volume as possible created by starching, folding, shaping and supporting materials.

In the public imagination of the Netherlands (and among some people in Suriname), the koto is strongly linked to the period of slavery, and often thought of as originating in the period of the slave trade, slave plantations, and slave labour. Enslaved men, women and children of African descent were owned by colonizers from the mid-17th century to the second half of the 19th century.[21] In discussions on the afterlife of slavery (currently an important topic of public debate in the Netherlands and the rest of the world), there appears a difference in thinking among Afro-Surinamese people about the koto and its relationship to slavery.[22] Some celebrate their history and use the koto as a material expression of pride and Afro-Surinamese identity. Yet, in their collective memory, where slavery and the role of European ideas on modesty in the development of the koto greatly influences current ideas about the value of the koto, some Afro-Surinamese feel the koto is not something to remember and celebrate.[23] The following section looks into the development of kotomisi fashion more closely, exploring the importance of this style as a tool of resistance and sign of creativity, and not of defeat or shame.

Complicating 'Slave Cloth'

Enslaved Africans in colonized Caribbean lands and South America were needed, and bought, by land owners of sugar, coffee, cotton, cacao, and tobacco plantations. Upon arrival, most enslaved people wore a short or long loin cloth made from either locally worn African cotton textiles, or imported European woven cloth including also natural fibres such as flax or linen and wool which was scarcely distributed among them.[24] A further, limited provision of clothing by enslavers became habitual in plantation life.[25] Archival records and 18th century publications make mention of the distribution of cloth by plantation owners once or sometimes several times a year. These were often raw or grey Osnaburgs, blue Osnaburgs[26] and Harlem or Frieze Bont, the latter two referring to materials with stripe or checked patterns called madras, originally from India, that became staple objects of exchange and trade.[27] After increasing European industrialization in the 18th and 19th centuries, textile factories in Europe took over the originally handmade production of local European wool or linen and Indian madras textiles, and exported many of these to their colonies. Historical Maroon clothing in museum collections show that these checkered and striped textiles were available in the colony.[28]

Archival plantations records indicate that mostly raw cloth was exported to the Dutch Caribbean, with some records mentioning the additional purchase of tens of boezeroentjes, the cotton or linen work-wear of Dutch seamen and labourers.[29] In general though, enslaved women had to make their own clothing, or barter or pay for clothing made by others.[30] However, wealthier slave owners liked to dress their enslaved women and girls in the best apparel they could afford, often in the latest fashions, as this would raise their status as owners.[31] Enslaved women (and men) could earn their own money in different ways, and this could be spent on textiles and jewellery, as there were possibilities of wearing expensive clothing and jewellery, sometimes to the alarm of

Figure 4.3 Doll in kotomisi, 1824. Height: 49cm. TM-A-6195b. Collection Nationaal Museum van Wereldculturen.

European men.[32] They shopped in the capital of the colony, Paramaribo, where small shops and larger retailers sold clothes and textiles.

Enslaved women thus wore both simple dresses or more intricate styles. Europe was a great influence on the development of clothing styles in the Caribbean and other colonies. J. D. Herlein, for example, mentions the bobbelap, a striped square cloth folded into a triangle and worn across the breast, that references the influence of European fashion and Christian morality.[33] There are no museum examples of these early clothes of enslaved people. What was collected by museums are large textile sample books as several Dutch cities became successful textile producers exporting to the colonies in the late 18th century.[34] It is however unknown where the late 19th century koto textiles in the NMVW's collection were produced.

A number of dolls dressed in koto style dating from the early 19th century are also in the NMVW collection.[35] Research suggests that the dolls were made both as toys and as

Figure 4.4 Japanese Inspired sample from a sample book by Kralingsche Katoen Maatschappij (1891–1901), collection Museum Rotterdam. Inventory Number Museum Rotterdam 20983.

examples of Surinamese dress styles to educate people in the Netherlands, and inform cloth printers and merchants.[36] During the late 19th century, Japan became a cotton producer and exporter, yet before this, Dutch factories had been producing Japanese prints for koto textiles, as can be seen in one kotomisi doll from around the 1830s, along with a similar pattern in a Kralingsche Katoen Maatschappij sample book (Figures 4.3 and 4.4). Textile printing factories such as this cotton-printing factory in Rotterdam produced textiles for the colonies from the end of the 18th century and well into the 1900s, where merchants would deliver cotton cloth to the factory and order popular patterns chosen from sample books such as this (Figure 4.4).

Shape, Silhouette and Status

The global history and provenance of textiles used for clothes in the slave society of Suriname gives insight into the transculturality of colonial objects. Koto, as worn today during important festivities, remain a visually impressive way of dressing, or rather, presenting the self (Figure 4.2). The look's volume is its most striking feature. There are different techniques for enhancing the volume, such as starching the cloth, layering with underskirts, and using a supportive tool, known as a koi or famiri to enlarge the back of the dress.[37] All these elements are present in both contemporary expressions of koto and the historical koto objects in the NMVW collections.

Historical drawings and prints are also informative in terms of the development of the kotomisi. The work of military servicemen, such as captain John Gabriel Stedman (1744–1797), navy lieutenant commander Hendrik Huygens (1810–1867), and officer G. P. H. Zimmermann (1839–1928), as well as Belgian artist and ship captain P. J. Benoit

(1782–1854) and plantation owner Theodore Bray (1818–1887), offer us multiple views into Surinamese colonial society and its sartorial developments.[38]

It is evident from these images that Surinamese colonial society was (as is Suriname today) a racially and culturally diverse one, clearly expressed in what people wore. From what people wear in these representations, we can largely deduce the occupation and status of people within Surinamese society where evidence of enslavement is often expressed through the material. Men working on plantations wore linen trousers and shirts, whereas women often were bare breasted with only a large skirt, or sometimes two, drawn high on their waist. In drawings by P. J. Benoit, fish vendors and sellers of land produce wear shorter skirts, similar to the hip cloths (pangi) in West-Africa at that time.[39] In his writings, Benoit states: 'Many [women in Suriname] even wear skirts or dresses that are open in the front, with underneath a piece of cloth or linen in bright colours, called paigsen or loin cloth. They fall halfway the legs, which are decorated with coral bands, as are arms, neck and feet ... when they get together, they often dress up with jewellery and finery ... they are not used to adapting, or even wearing adapted [European] clothes' (my translation), this last point implying poverty to him.[40]

Images from the late 18th and 19th century also depict enslaved women of a higher status, working in plantation houses as cooks or housekeepers, wearing wide blouse-like tops, with bare shoulders on a voluminous skirt, often consisting of more than one layer.[41] Shoulder cloths were used to cover the upper body or to carry goods or children. The many drawings and prints in museum collections show that there were different fashions at one time in Suriname, and this depended on both social status and race. Around 1830, Benoit writes: 'Although the way of dressing is relatively simple and shows hardly any influence of fashion, [all women] love to look fabulous. At any price, they will purchase the latest fads or *mooi sanis* (beautiful things)'.[42] As such, what was perceived as fashion – namely Western modernity – both locally and by Europeans, was a way to move upward in social and racial hierarchies.

In using the above quotations from Benoit's writing, I am questioning how he discusses two different fashion systems functioning within a single geographical space. When he says that there is hardly any influence of fashion, he refers to the impact and evidence of the external influence of European ideas of what fashion is at the time, relating to ideas of modernity; and, on the other hand, he states that women would purchase the latest fads, indicating there is another idea of fashion, or system, at work at the local level.

A famous example of a higher status expressed through fashion is Elisabeth Samson, a wealthy freeborn woman who was the first Black woman to marry a Dutch White man in 1767.[43] She wore the latest possible fashions from Europe, as far as White or free women of mixed descent could access them. Luxurious textiles such as silk, velvet and lace, as well as accessories, would be ordered from Europe and worn in the colony by those who could afford it. Samson could do this due to plantation inheritances from her mother and brother, and a relationship with a Dutch merchant who left her his possessions, including enslaved men and women. Samson was a good businesswoman, making profit and expanding her business. She is a well-known example of the mobility and agency of people within slave-based societies. The role of fashion in the performance of such multiple identities is evident too.[44]

Benoit concludes on Surinamese fashions:

> ... in a town where so much luxury and finery is available, and the women are not inferior to European ladies in indulgence, the number of 'modistes' [dressmakers], mostly female negroes, is rather large. Many saleswomen have their goods transported from Paris or London; still I am convinced that ladies from these two cities would look down on hats and caps that are worn here, on which ... beauty has been lost. It also seems that Surinam does not receive the most fashionable or elegant from these cities. However, one is satisfied because there is no comparison and a [mistress] or even a rich Creole woman walks with as much pride as a queen, adorned with what the bourgeoisie of Brussels or The Hague would refuse.[45]

Figure 4.5, a print of drawings by Benoit from around the 1830s, shows different ways of dressing by enslaved women. The upper image shows a dancing woman dressed in a wide skirt with nothing on top. It was only in the late 1870s, after the abolition of slavery and the additional ten years tenure track, that this 'African way' of dressing without upper garments was prohibited by law.[46] The lower image shows that enslaved women also wore upper garments in the style of later kotomisi, long before topless dressing was banned. In this picture, a plantation director or owner with his wife and their enslaved staff are going to church, all dressed differently according to their function and possibilities within the range of choices for their status. The enslaved women – identifiable by their bare feet – are all dressed in a look that resembles the koto with a skirt (koto), a jacket (yaki) and a headcloth (angisa). Again, different fashion systems are functioning simultaneously; the Black women are dressed in local fashion styles, whereas the White woman is dressed in a style that adheres to a European fashion system.

The NMVW also has several dioramas on display and in storage by the early 19th century Surinamese artist Gerrit Schouten that provide information on dress and fashion in Suriname.[47] The dioramas show different aspects of Surinamese people and culture, and are often used as reference sources on slavery. In the diorama in Figure 4.6, enslaved people hold a special celebration, called du or dou, that was held once or twice a year. Permitted by plantation owners (in an effort to prevent dissatisfaction and resistance) these celebrations offered an opportunity to forget, or at least momentarily ignore, as well as to feast, drink and dance, and sometimes gather and talk to people from other plantations. As Laddy van Putten and Janny Zantinge have explored, early 19th century accounts describe how landowners and their wives loved the looks of their well-dressed enslaved women at these special occasions.[48] Exuberantly dressed in their best clothes, the enslaved participants would however sometimes mock planter society in satirical performances.[49]

Figure 4.5 Drawing by P. J. Benoit (Antwerp 1782 – Brussels 1854). Lithograph by Jean Baptiste Madou (Brussels 1796 – Sint-Joost-ten-Node 1877), 1828–1839. TM-3728-377. Collection Nationaal Museum van Wereldculturen.

Figure 4.6 Diorama of a du feast by Gerrit Schouten, 1819. TM-A-6371c. Collection Nationaal Museum van Wereldculturen.

Creolizing Fashions

The scant available literature on the development of the koto states that several aspects of the style were influenced by European ideas on decency, status and fashion.[50] Though the latest fashions from Europe were popular and influential in sartorial life in the colonies, it seems superficial and ignorant, and even a continuation of colonial violence, to simply attribute the koto and its different elements to European intervention. One long-held myth on the origins of the kotomisi is that a planter's wife had ordered her enslaved women to wear large and voluminous costumes, in order to deal with the wandering eye of her husband. This idea is supported by David Lowenthal, in his publication of 1960 on the Guianas, where he states that '*kotomissie* is local reinterpretation or invention rather than authentic survival . . . [it] was the costume of Moravian converts, not of tribal Africans'.[51] It may be the case that some of the colonial women wanted their servants to wear more clothes because of Christian values and the European idea of modesty. However, it is a denial of processes of cultural formation, creolization and hybridization – where all sorts of ideas and practices come together and form complete new shapes and beliefs – to think that Europeans alone could enforce such a change, even when considering the large differences in power. More logically, enslaved women were influenced by the fashions of women of higher rank and saw dress as a means to acquire status, hence taking agency themselves.

Another example of the dominant idea of European origin concerns assumptions about the aforementioned koi, a lengthy cushion-like textile object to make the koto stand out more widely. The koi is argued to be a variant of the 18th and 19th century cul de Paris, or in general of European fashions accentuating specific aspects of the female body, such as hips, waist and buttocks. If anything, however, the function of the cul de Paris may have inspired Afro-Surinamese women to design their own shapeshifting garment piece. Placing it on the small of the back (Figure 4.7), not the bottom, developed a new style element, as is often done in fashion design.

African aesthetics and hybrid solutions for aspects such as functionality were also influential in the development of dress styles that eventually led to the kotomisi, that is a complete, new and unique style, neither completely European nor African. As Christine Checinska writes, 'It is out of such collision, contradiction, and turmoil generated by movement and migration that creolized black aesthetics ... emerge; after all, creolization was and is a process of contention not blending'.[52] People transported to the Americas came from all over Africa, and took multiple dress styles (and their signifying qualities) with them. African elements such as bare breasts, wrapping the body with large volumes of decorated cloth (Figure 4.8), and folding head cloths, merged with European styles such as long voluminous skirts, covered bodies, and shaped silhouettes through additional wear, leading to the distinct shape of the kotomisi today.

A more nuanced understanding of processes of cultural hybridization dismisses and disrupts the still broadly supported perception of koto as an object of submission. Former enslaved and free Afro-Surinamese women and makers had agency in its creation and development. As Buckridge also notes:

> Slave women were able to 'make fashion' and be creative with their Creole dresses ...the women were very much aware of the various styles of dress worn in Europe. They observed what their mistresses wore and were able to adapt these clothes to their tastes and particular circumstances. Their dress styles reflected creativity and innovation on the part of slave and freed women.[53]

New developments from areas other than Europe gained attention and interest in the colonies, as trading expanded and Japanese prints, Chinese designs and Indonesian Javanese (called yampanesi) became trendy in early koto fashion. Ideas about fashion styles such as the koto can also be decolonized and decentred by paying attention to other fashion histories that developed beyond, but simultaneously to, those within the NMVW collections. When examining dress styles from the Frieze town of Hindeloopen c.1850–1874, we can speculate that it was not always the European fashion capitals that were influential in terms of spreading fashion ideals and ideas, but also local Dutch styles. For example, the women in Figure 4.9 wear voluminous skirts

Figure 4.7 Photograph of a young woman with a 'koi' on her back. TM-60005964. Collection Nationaal Museum van Wereldculturen.

Figure 4.8 Group portrait of women, Elmina. 1870–1890. Photographer: unknown. TM-60024048. Collection Nationaal Museum van Wereldculturen.

Figure 4.9 Detail of the print *27 figuren in Hindelooper klederdracht* (27 figures in folk dress from Hindeloopen). By Hendrik Lap (1824–1874). PTA 187-022. Collection Fries Museum, Leeuwarden.

and long-sleeve jackets and the headwear greatly resembles the angisa styles in Suriname. Friesian headscarves indicated the marital status of their wearer, and were thus not that different from African signifying ways of communicating identities. The textiles used by the Frieze women were similarly produced in European factories that reproduced textiles from all across the world (such as Indian madras). Furthermore, Hindelooper women gave their textiles names, as did West-African and Afro-Surinamese women.[54] Passed from mother to daughter, everyone remembered the name of the cloth that embellished grandmother and granddaughter alike. Sometimes the cloth was named after the ship's captain who had brought it, or the first woman who wore it. Sometimes the name developed from the pattern.[55] Since striped or checked cotton from Friesland was also popular in the West Indies, it is possible that Frieze women living in Suriname inspired creole fashions as much as the aforementioned wider European trends.

The Koto Today

Since the 1880s, the silhouette and essential elements of the koto have altered little, although its colour combinations, patterning, measurements, motifs and accessories have changed according to new developments in fashions from around the world. The koto was part of a globally influenced, 19th century local fashion system in which expressions of ethnicity were shaped through the fashions that people wore.[56] This stopped when kotomisi disappeared from the streets of Paramaribo in the early 20th century and European dress styles, became more accessible and functioned as the symbol of modernization.[57] As is the case with 'folk dress', kotomisi was relegated to the back of public memory and worn only by elderly women, or on special occasions.

However over the last five years, younger Afro-Surinamese generations in Suriname and the Netherlands have become interested in koto ensembles again, re-igniting them with contemporary meaning in processes of self-fashioning. Cultural awareness is growing among young people looking for new ways of connecting with their heritage and expressing their multiple identities. Kotomisi has increasingly become a popular key marker of identity of Afro-Surinamese women. In the Netherlands, the koto functions as a pars-pro-toto for Afro-Surinamese culture, and as a tool used in the symbolic construction of community, which makes it a political expression.[58] During special festivities, such as keti koti (when the abolition of slavery on 1 July 1863 is celebrated in the public domain of larger cities in the Netherlands), many Afro-Surinamese women wear the style elaborately and according to the latest fashions. While not considering it as fashion (when fashion is still associated with global Western styles), they do recognize it as fashionable, referring to the simultaneous functioning of several systems within the same geographical locality. As such, kotomisi is performance, of race, of gender and of class, but also of history and of fashion. Old and young are designing new koto styles, including angisas, while honouring its heritage qualities. Specific makers are well-known for their koto making skills, and people go to them to have dresses made. The NMVW

Figure 4.10 Waarderi (appreciation) koto (left) and Tu Kondre Uma (two countries woman) koto by Jürgen Joval, 2018. Collection Museum van Wereldculturen, inventory numbers 7194 and 7195. Photograph: Irene de Groot.

collected two kotos by Jürgen Joval (in 2018 and 2019), a young Surinamese fashion designer who uses new techniques such as photoprint and applique to fashion his kotos, reinstalling links between the koto and wider global fashion systems (Figure 4.10). In 2019, the Dutch Klederdrachtmuseum (Costume Museum) organized an exhibition on kotomisi, and called for designers to reinvent the koto in a competition. The winner of this competition was Dutch Surinamese Cheyenne Nelson, with her contemporary take on the koto (Figure 4.11).

Figure 4.11 Design Cheyenne Nelson, winner competition Klederdrachtmuseum, 2019. Photographer: Rob Bosscher. © Klederdrachtmuseum.

Conclusion

In the few written and oral histories available, the koto has been, and often still is, defined, including among Afro-Surinamese people, as a European invention. By looking at the history of the development of the koto style as it is today, a much broader and more hybrid history of change and innovation becomes visible. Europe's influence within slave societies was immense, but that does not mean it was the single factor in determining dress practices and 'doing' fashion. Other cultural influences, such as African, Indian, Indonesian and Japanese styles and motifs, shaped koto fashion. The koto is a clear example of hybridization and global intracultural design practices, giving evidence of multiple ingredients that fashioned these objects. The koto exemplifies how dominated peoples could and did have agency in creating culture, and were not passively subjugated to a colonial cultural supremacy. It embodies creolization or bricolage, of conscious but also organic combinations of cultural preferences, restrictions and tastes that made it the transcultural item that many Afro-Surinamese people today see and use as one of the key markers of their cultural identity.

The koto is a unique Afro-Surinamese cultural invention that has been through different phases of local and diasporic validation. It is located in specific geographies that include both local and global fashion systems functioning simultaneously, and proves that fashion is not a fixed characteristic of material culture, but a contextual social concept depending on diverse and overlapping factors. Not only is fashion by definition about change, but ideas about fashion also change over time. What fashion is, or when fashion is, is determined by defining fashion as a social phenomenon that is incomprehensible without context. What and when fashion is changes across time and space. Fashion is not a characteristic or quality of a piece of clothing, but a cultural possibility. As such, the koto has a socio-cultural biography that takes it from local fashion to everyday dress, to heritage costume, to national symbol, and back to fashion again, not only in linear developments since the end of the 19th century, but also overlapping through time. For museums, categorization is central to acquisition, documentation and educational efforts. In that respect, fashion as a concept can help ethnographic museums argue against the continued presence of colonial ideas about non-European material culture as being static, non-changing or pre-modern. The multiple identities of the koto are proof that such colonial ideas can be thrown out for good.

My research has brought me from reading and thinking about the important role of clothes and fashion in colonial times, to realizing how this relates to the current decolonial debate. In the time that this chapter has taken to write, a lot has changed in the Dutch museum world, both because of larger political events and movements worldwide, such as the death of George Floyd and Black Lives Matter, and the debate on the restitution of museum objects in Dutch society. Working with decolonial approaches involves looking critically at one's own role within the colonial institution, including whether or not I can legitimately write about cultural objects such as the koto. As a curator, I have a complex set of responsibilities towards these collections, within which I hope to support a growing understanding of the koto as an important form of cultural expression within Dutch society, as well as to contribute to broader discussions on ethnographic collections and possibilities for a decolonial approach.

Notes

1. See the dual language publication by the director of the Koto Museum in Paramaribo for an informative introduction to the angisa: Christine van Russel-Henar. *Angisa Tori: De geheimtaal van Suriname's hoofddoeken/Angisa Tori: The Secret Code of Surinamese Headkerchiefs* (Paramaribo: de Stichting / the Foundation Fu Memre Wi Afo, 2008).

2. Ann Laura Stoler, *Along the Archival Grain: Epistemic Anxieties and Colonial Common Sense* (Princeton, NJ: Princeton University Press, 2010).

3. Steeve Buckridge, *The Language of Dress: Resistance and Accommodation in Jamaica 1750–1890* (Lubbock, TX: Texas Tech University, 2004) 61, 77.

4. Eric Wolf, *Europe and the People Without History* (Berkeley, CA: University of California Press, 1982).

5. Buckridge, *The Language of Dress*. On the historically formed colonial assumptions on ethnicity and fashion, see also Sarah Cheang, 'Ethnicity'. In D. A. Baxter, Ed. *A Cultural History of Dress and Fashion in the Age of Empire, Vol. 5* (London: Bloomsbury, 2017).

6. A closed workshop on this topic was held on 14–15 November 2019 at the NMVW, co-organized with the Research Collective for Decolonizing Fashion (RCDF).

7. Mary Ellen Roach Higgins, Joanne Eicher and Kim Johnson, *Dress and Identity* (Albany, NY: Capital Cities Media Inc., 1995) 7.

8. Yuniya Kawamura, *Fashion-ology* (Oxford: Berg, 2004).

9. For more on style as agency, see Carol Tulloch, *The Birth of Cool: Style Narratives of the African Diaspora* (London: Bloomsbury, 2016) 4.

10. That fashion belongs to the West is argued by many, for example Mary Ellen Roach and K. E. Musa, *New Perspectives on the History of Western Dress: A Handbook* (New York: NutriGuides, 1980); Elizabeth Wilson, *Adorned in Dreams: Fashion and Modernity* (London: I.B. Taurus, 2007); Joanne Entwistle, *The Fashioned Body: Fashion, Dress & Modern, Social Theory* (Cambridge: Polity Press, 2015).

11. Frantz Fanon, *Zwarte Huid, Witte Maskers* [1952] (Amsterdam: Octavo, 2018); Edward Saïd. *Orientalism* (New York: Pantheon Books, 1978); Bill Ashcroft, Gareth Griffiths and Helen Tiffin, *Postcolonial Studies: The Key Concepts* (Abingdon and New York: Routledge, 1998).

12. Jennifer Craik, *The Face of Fashion: Cultural Studies in Fashion* (London: Routledge. 1993); Jennifer Craik, *Fashion: The Key Concepts* (Oxford: Berg, 2009); Angela Jansen and Jennifer Craik, *Modern Fashion Traditions: Negotiating Tradition and Modernity through Fashion* (London: Bloomsbury, 2016); Sandra Niessen, Ann Marie Leshkowich and Carla Jones, Eds. *Re-Orienting Fashion: The Globalization of Asian Dress* (Oxford: Berg, 2003).

13. Malcolm Barnard, Ed. *Fashion Theory: A Reader* (Abingdon and New York: Routledge, 2007) 2–4; Linda Welters and Abby Lillethun, *The Fashion Reader*, 2nd edn (London: Bloomsbury, 2014) xxv.

14. Ingrid Loschek, *When Clothes Become Fashion: Design and Innovation Systems* (Oxford: Berg, 2009).

15. See Cheang, 'Ethnicity', 143

16. 'Fashion' can be discussed as a cultural system of specific elements, as can other cultural concepts, such as religion, art or kinship.

17. Laddy van Putten and Janny Zantinge, *Let Them Talk* (Paramaribo: Mededelingen Surinaams Museum, 1988) 17–19.

18. van Putten and Zantinge, *Let Them Talk*; workshop discussions with local Afro-Surinamese communities, e.g. at OBA Bijlmerplein, for the opening of the *Saya en koto; lagen van stof en van tijd*, a collecting exhibition, 23 June 2019, organized by Imagine IC; koto workshop at Opleiding Meestercoupeur, 5 March 2020, organized by Modemuze and Imagine IC: www.modemuze.nl/blog/mapping-routes-gesprek-over-een-koto-verzameling (accessed 12 May 2020).

19. The foundation of a kotomuseum in Paramaribo in 2009 by Christine van Russel-Henar shows recognition of the importance of the *koto* as Surinamese cultural heritage.

20. Sometimes yaki is written as jaki or jakki.

21. Officially, slavery ended in Dutch colonies in 1863, though recently, communities of descendants of enslaved people have called for this date to be pushed to 1873, when the ten-year period of obliged labour ended and contract labourers from India and Asia replaced the workforce. Hans Buddingh, *De geschiedenis van Suriname* (Amsterdam: Nieuw Amsterdam, 2012) 183, 217.

22. See workshop discussions, footnote 18 above.

23. M. Balkenhol, 'De kotomisi en haar kinderen: Slavernij en erfgoed nieuwe stijl in Nederland', *Oso, tijdschrift voor Surinaamse Taalkunde, Letterkunde, en Geschiedenis*, 31 (2) (2012) 55–71. These sentiments were also expressed in several interviews and informal talks with Afro-Suriname women at the workshops detailed in footnote 18 above.

24. van Putten and Zantinge, *Let Them Talk*, 19; Bea Brommer, *Bontjes voor de Tropen: De export van imitatieweefsels naar de tropen* (Brussels: Gemeentekrediet, 1991) 10.

25. See Robert Duplessis, *The Material Atlantic: Clothing, Commerce and Colonization in the Atlantic World, 1650–1800* (Cambridge: Cambridge University Press, 2015).

26. Osnaburgs were linen materials from Europe, deriving their name from one of the centres of their production, Osnabruck. There were many other centres of production, though of differing levels of quality. Chris Schriks and Sylvia de Groot, *Reis door Suriname: Een bewerking van Voyage au Surinam van P. J. Benoit* (Zutphen: De Walburg Pers, 1980) 69, 71; Adriaan van Berkel, *Amerikaansche voyagien: Behelzende een res na rio de Berbice [...]* (Amsterdam: Johan ten Hoorn, 1695); J. D. Herlein, *Beschryvinge van de volk-plantinge Zuriname [...]* (Leeuwarden: Meindert Injema, 1718).

27. Karwan Fatah-Black, 'Suriname en de wereld 1650–1800: Een Atlantisch en mondiaal perspectief', *OSO: Tijdschrift voor Surinamistiek en het Caraïbisch Gebied*, 31 (2) (2012) 177–191.

28. Brommer, *Bontjes voor de Tropen*, 10.

29. In NA 2.20.01 NHM 5202 (1781, 1791). Nationaal Archief (National Archive) Den Haag.

30. Buckridge, *The Language of Dress*, 123–124.

31. Theo van Lelyveld, 'De kleeding der Surinaamsche bevolkingsgroepen in verband met aard en gewoonten'. In *De West-Indische Gids* (1919) 1e jrg., Dl. I: 259n; see also Tamara Walker, *Exquisite Slaves: Race, Clothing, and Status in Colonial Lima* (Cambridge: Cambridge University Press, 2017).

32. Herlein, *Beschryvinge van de volk-plantinge Zuriname*, 96; Wim Hoogbergen and Marjo de Theye, 'Surinaamse vrouwen in Slavernij'. In *Vrouwen in de Nederlandse Koloniën. Zevende jaarboek voor vrouwengeschiedenis* (Amsterdam: Stichting Jaarboek voor Vrouwengeschiedenis, 1986).

33. van Putten and Zantinge, *Let Them Talk*, 20.

34. Museum Rotterdam Inventory Number 20983.

35. Susan Legêne, *De bagage van Blomhoff en van Breugel: Japan, Java, Tripoli en Suriname in het negentiende eeuwse Nederlandse cultuur van het imperialisme* (Amsterdam: KIT Publishers, 1998) 238–239.

36. See Sterre Snijders, 'Rapport Onderzoek Kotomisipoppen' (unpublished) (Leiden: RCMC, 2018).

37. Melville J. Herskovits and Frances S. Herskovits, *Suriname Folk-Lore* (New York: Columbia University Press, 1936) 4; Ilse Henar-Hewitt, *Surinaamse Koto's en Angisa's* (Paramaribo: Offsetdrukkerij Westfort, 1990).

38. Surprisingly, the work of Arnold Borret (1848–1888) is not in the NMVW collection, but in the collection of the Royal Netherlands Institute of South East Asian and Caribbean Studies.

39. Herskovits and Herskovits, *Suriname Folk-Lore*; van Putten and Zantinge, *Let Them Talk*.

40. Benoit, 1839 cited in Schriks and de Groot, *Reis door Suriname*, 35.

41. ibid., 31

42. ibid., 35

43. Cynthia McLeod, *Elisabeth Samson: Een vrije, zwarte vrouw in het 18ᵉ eeuwse Suriname* (Groet: Uitgeverij Conserve, 2008) 101.

44. See also Karwan Fatah-Black, *Eigendomsstrijd: De geschiedenis van slavernij en emancipatie in Suriname* (Amsterdam: Ambo/Anthos, 2018) 39.

45. Benoit cited in Schriks and de Groot, *Reis door Suriname*, 35.

46. van Putten en Zantinge, *Let Them Talk*, 38; Alex van Stipriaan, 'Het slaafgemaakte lichaam: Paradox van het Surinaams apartheidssysteem in de negentiende eeuw', *De Negentiende Eeuw*, 39 (3/4) (2015) 307–328; van Lelyveld, 'De kleeding der Surinaamsche', 259.

47. Gerrit Schouten (1779–1839) was one of the first recognized Surinamese artists. He made watercolours but was most famous for his dioramas of Surinamese local life, which he made for colonials to take home as souvenirs. See Clazien Medendorp, *Kijkkasten uit Suriname: De diorama's van Gerrit Schouten* (Volendam: Stichting LM Publishers, 2010).

48. van Putten and Zantinge, *Let Them Talk*, 24.

49. See also Buckridge, *The Language of Dress* for similar customs in Jamaica.

50. Herlein, *Beschryvinge van de volk-plantinge Zuriname*; Benoit, 1839; van Lelyveld, 'De kleeding der Surinaamsche'; van Putten and Zantinge, *Let Them Talk*.

51. David Lowenthal, 'Population Contrasts of the Guianas'. In *Geographical Review*, 50 (1) (1960): 54.

52. Christine Checinska, 'Aesthetics of Blackness? Cloth, Culture, and the African Diasporas', *TEXTILE*, 16 (2) (2018) 124.

53. Buckridge, *The Language of Dress*, 63

54. van Putten and Zantinge, *Let Them Talk*, 17–19; Brommer, *Bontjes voor de Tropen*, 19; Herskovits and Herskovits, *Suriname Folk-Lore*, 4.

55. Brommer, *Bontjes voor de Tropen*, 19

56. Cheang, 'Ethnicity'.

57. Joanne B. Eicher, Sandra Lee Evenson and Hazel A. Lutz, *The Visible Self: Global Perspectives on Dress, Culture and Society*, 3rd edn (Fairchild Books, 2008) 52.

58. M. Balkenhol, 'De kotomisi en haar kinderen. Slavernij en erfgoed nieuwe stijl in Nederland', *Oso, tijdschrift voor Surinaamse Taalkunde, Letterkunde, en Geschiedenis*, 31 (2) (2012) 55–71.

CHAPTER 5
COATS AND TROUSERS: REDRAWING THE MAP TO RESCRIPT THE NARRATIVE
Abby LILLETHUN and Linda WELTERS

Introduction

Coats and trousers are globally ubiquitous in fashion today. They are worn by people of all ages and may be worn together as a suit of matching or coordinated fabric, or they may be treated as separate pieces within a wardrobe to be combined with additional garments. Coats are overgarments that cover the upper body, have sleeves, and open in the front. Trousers are bifurcated garments that cover the lower torso, crotch area, and legs.

Surveys of Western fashion generally assign early evidence of coats and trousers to images found in Persian art dating back 2,500 years.[1] One book stated simply that the 'Medes, the most esteemed of the Persians' subjects, and Scythians wear outfits comprising tunics, trousers, and ... coats with front openings and rolled collars ...'.[2] On trousers alone, the common story line suggests that the Romans adopted trousers called feminalia from the 'barbarians' in Gaul;[3] one source explained that 'During the imperial period, Roman soldiers adopted knee-length trousers that were placed under the tunic in cold weather. These garments were similar to those worn by the Gauls, a northern European tribe'.[4] In such narratives the story of coats and trousers focuses primarily on their relationship to Europe.

The development of coats and trousers is worthy of accurate portrayal in the history of fashion, not least because of their prominence in contemporary dress. This study responds to the question: what does the consideration of broader transcultural exchanges reveal about how histories of coats and trousers could be rewritten? The archaeological record (including extant garments), art works, and texts serve as the source material for this study, and the work of other scholars contextualizes the evidence drawn together here. This study redraws the coat and trousers map extending it beyond Persia and Gaul to include ancient evidence of these garments across the latitudinal span of Eurasia and into North Africa (see Figure 5.1). A redrawn map of the occurrence of coats and trousers projects a new narrative, one that replaces the reductive Western European trope with evidence from Central and Eastern Asia, and points to ancient trade routes as primary in the rewritten narrative. Further, it participates in the decolonizing of the history of fashion. In conventional fashion histories, European colonizers are credited with spreading their tailored dress styles across the globe – specifically the English, French, Dutch, and Spanish – and displacing indigenous dress. Drawing on the work of Aníbal Quijano, we seek to disrupt the power of coloniality that perpetuates Europe's cultural

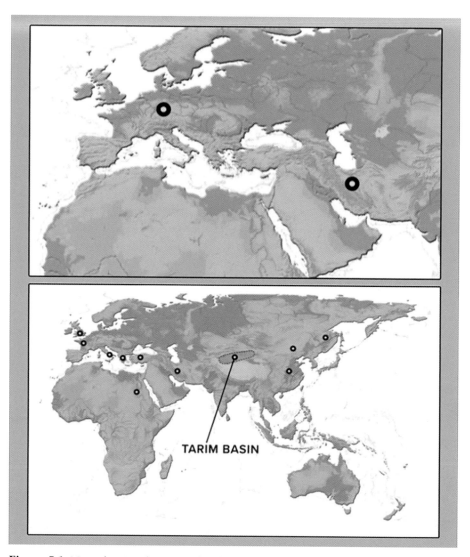

Figure 5.1 Maps showing the geographical scope of coats and trousers in the old and new narratives. Background map used by permission of Thomas Talessman, www.worldhistorymaps. info/index.html. Illustration: Fafar Bayat. *Top*: Map showing Gaul and Persia, the locales of evidence of trousers in the prior historical narrative. *Bottom*: A redrawn map indicating sites of early evidence of coats and trousers that spans Eurasia and includes North Africa.

dominance in the writing of dress history.[5] Instead of focusing only on the West, we present an interconnected narrative that demonstrates complexities and nuances in the history of coats and trousers.

Evidence from Persia and Europe

As previously mentioned, Western dress histories attribute the introduction of coats to Persia and trousers to both Persia and Gaul. The ancient site known as Persepolis, in present-day Iran, figures prominently in accounts of Western fashion histories as its sculptures depict various tribes both wearing and carrying coats and trousers. Persepolis was built between 520 and 486 BCE by the Achaemenid Empire. Sculptures on the Apadana staircase walls, carved in bas-relief, portray Iranian tribes bringing sleeved coats and footed trousers as their tribute to the emperor (Figure 5.2).[6] The Medes are the only tribe depicted wearing coats, albeit with pendent sleeves. The Greek author Xenophon (c. 431 BCE–354 BCE) claimed that the coat was adopted by the Persian nobility from the Medes who rode horseback as cavalry for the Persian Empire. He called it kandys.[7]

Roman feminalia are shown in the Colonne Trajane (Trajan's Column) erected in 113 CE in commemoration of Rome's victory over the Dacians, which added to Rome's

Figure 5.2 Bas-relief, eastern stairway walls of the terrace stairway, Persepolis Palace, Apadana. Dignitaries addressing the party of Nowruz celebration. 520–486 BCE, Achaemenid Empire. Islamic Republic of Iran. Photo by PHAS/Universal Images Group via Getty Images. Medes, an Iranian tribe, wearing sleeved coats.

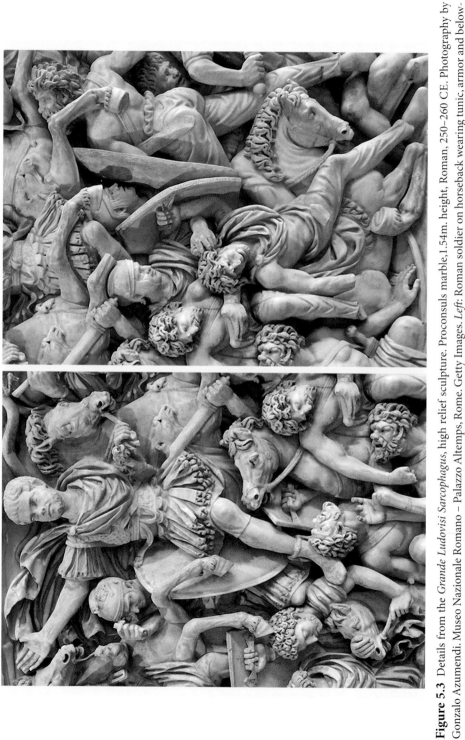

Figure 5.3 Details from the *Grande Ludovisi Sarcophagus*, high relief sculpture. Proconsuls marble, 1.54m. height, Roman, 250–260 CE. Photography by Gonzalo Azumendi. Museo Nazionale Romano – Palazzo Altemps, Rome. Getty Images. *Left*: Roman soldier on horseback wearing tunic, armor and below-the-knee feminalia under his tunic. *Right*: Two bare-chested Goths, one on a fallen horse and the other standing. They wear loosely fitted ankle-length trousers.

portion of the Black Sea coastline. The Roman feminalia, also in bas-relief, end below the knee. It is difficult to tell from the sculpture how this bifurcated garment was constructed. How a garment is made provides clues to its origin, development, and transfer to other cultures. What other sources might provide information about trousers?

Evidence includes additional Roman sculptures, illuminations (illustrations) in medieval prayer books, and surviving clothing. Another Roman artwork in bas-relief, the Grande Ludovisi sarcophagus created in 250–260 CE, depicts Romans and Goths in battle. The Goths were a Germanic people who eventually toppled Rome. In a scene from one side of the sarcophagus (Figure 5.3), the central figure on horseback wears feminalia, a form of trousers, while two bare-chested Goths wear ankle length trousers. The image shows no drawstring or other stabilizing method at the top of the trousers; however, their rolled-over tops suggest a cincture or leather belt holding the trousers in place at the waist. The sculptor did not render any seamlines.

Rare, small bronze sculptures of tribal Gaulish and Germanic males dating to the first and second centuries depict men in garb like that worn by the Goths in the Ludovisi sarcophagus.[8] They are also bare chested and wear long trousers. Vexing to the fashion historian, once again, is the lack of any indication of seamlines. The structure of their trousers cannot be ascertained, although they show fullness at the waist and a rolled top like the Goths' trousers; however, they appear to be more voluminous through the thigh because of deep wrinkles.

To further explore the question of how trousers were made, we turn to European bibles and prayer books from the Middle Ages. Often pages were 'illuminated,' or illustrated, with contemporary scenes. In the Luttrell Psalter (c. 1325–1335 CE), male field workers wear short tunics or shirts over nether garments termed braies, which appear to be draped. The Maciejowski Bible (1240–1260 CE) reveals the draping method: men working the ground with tools wear bifurcated garments consisting of a single piece of cloth wrapped between and around the legs, with the corners tied to a cord at the waist (Figure 5.4). It is worth noting that ancient Mediterranean cultures – the Egyptians, Greeks, and Romans – associated draped garments (such as those they wore) with civilized society. Conversely, cut-and-sewn garments, originally made from animal skins, were associated with 'barbarians' (e.g., peoples who did not speak Greek or Latin). The highest status clothing in these ancient cultures was draped from woven fabric. It is not surprising, then, that in the early European Middle Ages men retained the preference for draped garments. Except for Roman soldiers wearing feminalia, it was not until the Renaissance that high-ranking Europeans in the developing urban centers traded mantles, loose tunics, and draped trousers for more closely fitted garments.

Yet, European tribes of earlier centuries had cut-and-sewn trousers. A rare archaeological survival is a bifurcated garment, commonly called the Thorsberg trousers, found in a northern German peat bog that dates to no later than 300 CE (Figure 5.5).[9] The pH level of peat bogs is ideal for preservation of protein, in this case wool. The Thorsberg trousers include footlets sewn to the bottom of the trouser legs. It is important to note that the trousers were made from two shaped tubes rather than being draped.

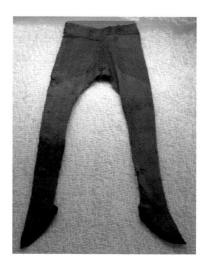

Figure 5.4 Redrawn detail from the Maciejowski Bible, French, 1240–1260 CE, Ms M. 638, fol. 12V. The Pierpont Morgan Library. Redrawing: Fafar Bayat. The man wears braies draped from a single piece of cloth wrapped between and around the legs, with the corners tied to a cord at the waist.

Figure 5.5 Thorsberg trousers. Wool. German, no later than 300 CE, Museum für Archäologie Schloss Gottorf Landesmuseum, Germany. Adapted from photography by Andreas Franzkowiak. Creative Commons Attribution – ShareAlike license (CC-BY-SA 3.0), while retaining dual licensing with the GNU Free Documentation License (GFDL). www.gnu.org/licenses/fdl-1.3.html. The Thorsberg trousers are made of wool fabric sewn from two shaped tubes for the legs, a crotch piece, and belt loops at the waist.

To summarize, the evidence shown in Roman sculptures is inconclusive as to how trousers were constructed. Medieval illuminated manuscripts reveal lower-body men's garments derived from the ancient Mediterranean preference for draped clothing. However, the Thorsberg trousers provide irrefutable evidence that Germanic tribes wore cut-and-sewn cloth trousers by about 300 CE, which possibly evolved from animal skin garments.

Many centuries later, as European men's upper-body garments became shorter and more fitted than the prior loose tunics, Europeans began wearing tight hose, one for each leg, that could only be achieved through cutting fabric and sewing it into a tube for each leg and attaching them with 'points' (i.e., ties) to an upper body garment (e.g., the pourpoint, or doublet). After some experimentation with the crotch area, a rudimentary type of trousers with a crotch covering came into fashion in Europe. By 1500, young men donned close-fitting bifurcated garments known in fashion history as 'hose' (e.g., trunk hose, nether hose); however these are not directly related to the leg-covering trousers discussed here. The relationships between the trouser variants of the 1st- and 2nd-century European tribal groups, Roman feminalia, 4th-century Thorsberg trousers, and the draped braies of the Middle Ages in Europe are unknown at this time.

We now turn to the evidence for coats. Sleeved coats of the type seen at Persepolis – the kandys – migrated west, first to Greece in the late 5th century BCE at which time the kandys became fashionable among Athenian women and boys.[10] A woman depicted on the marble gravestone of Myttion (c. 400 BCE) wears such a garment over her draped chiton (Figure 5.6). Later, Imperial Roman women also wore front-opening coats as illustrated in a Roman floor mosaic at Piazza Armerina at the Villa Romana del Casale in Sicily dating to around the 3rd to 4th century CE.[11]

Excavations of tombs near Antinoë in Graeco-Roman Egypt add Persian-style riding coats to the record. These coats, which were assumed to accommodate horseback riding, have collarless necklines, are fitted to the upper body, close on the left side, and feature a knee-length, side-flared skirt. One coat found with a male body wearing a shirt and a pair of wrapped leg coverings has been radiocarbon dated to 443–637 CE.[12] Such coats are depicted in contemporaneous Byzantine and in later Islamic art (Figure 5.7).[13] By the

Figure 5.6 Grave stele of Myttion, no. 78.AA.57, 71.1 × 24.1 × 8.9cm, marble with polychromy, c. 400 BCE, unknown maker. The J. Paul Getty Museum. Digital image courtesy of the Getty's Open Content Program. Myttion, a Greek woman, wears a kandys, a sleeved coat, over her chiton.

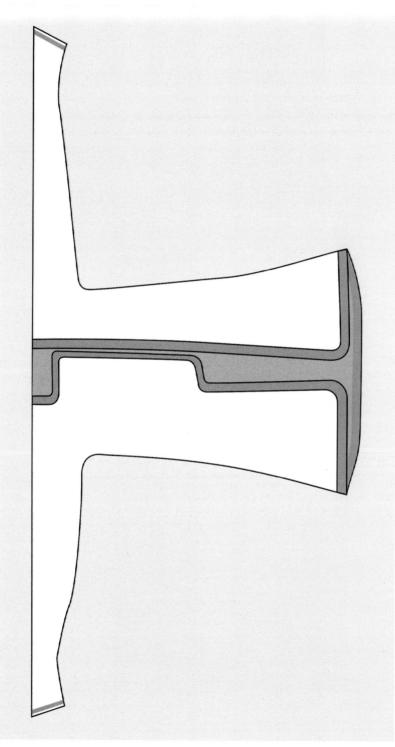

Figure 5.7 Redrawing of Horseman's Coat. Wool and cashmere with linen-backed borders. 443–637 CE., Antinoë (Egypt), 120 x 252cm, including sleeves. Stiftung Preußischer Kulturbesitz, Staatliche Museen zu Berlin – Skulpturensammlung und Museum für Byzantinische Kunst, Berlin (9695). Redrawing: Fafar Bayat. The type of Persian-style riding coat is present in contemporaneous Byzantine and in later Islamic art.

late Roman Empire, coats were well-known in the Mediterranean world as the garb of the peoples of eastern Byzantium.[14] The Byzantine Empire, which began as an extension of the Roman Empire with its sartorial inheritance of tunics and mantles, gradually adopted clothing styles of its eastern neighbours. By the 12th century, Byzantine empresses' appearance changed from layered long tunics to long tunics worn with kaftans, a form of coat with wide sleeves and front openings.[15]

In Europe proper, the kaftan-like coat evolved into the 15th-century robe known as a houppelande, which was worn by both men and women. This elite garment, with its voluminous shape and elaborate trailing sleeves, displayed the sumptuous patterned silks of Byzantium and the Italian city-states. Yet, the garment itself had its origins in lands east of Byzantium in Southwest Asia.

What were the antecedents of the coats and trousers that became popular in Persia, North Africa, and then in Europe? Multiple and overlapping stories exist in the current literature as discussed above. We now shift our attention eastward to Central Asia to redraw the map regarding the origins of coats and trousers.

Asian Contexts: Tarim Basin

Over the last fifty years, archaeological excavations in the Tarim Basin and its surroundings have uncovered cemeteries dating from the Bronze Age through the Iron Age to the Silk Road era (2000 BCE – 500 CE).[16] The Tarim Basin is located in Eastern Central Asia in China's northwestern Xinjiang Uyghur Autonomous Region. It is bordered on three sides by mountains, and to the east by the Gobi Desert. It encompasses the Taklamakan Desert, which provides starkly arid conditions ideal for artifact preservation. The remains of some individuals even have eyelashes.[17] Mair's description of the basin as 'the nexus of Eurasia' implies contact and exchange between numerous cultures across human history.[18]

Among the clothing excavated from burials are coats and trousers. Based on multidimensional analysis of horse remains that reveal evidence of human interaction with horses, many scholars assert that horse domestication occurred about 6,000 years ago in the Eurasian steppes and that horseback riding followed about 2,500 years later.[19] Many scholars also associate the development of trousers with horseback riding.[20]

The oldest known extant trousers, two pairs dating to between the 13th and 10th centuries BCE, were found at Turfan, an ancient site at the northeastern edge of the Tarim Basin (see map in Figure 5.1).[21] The location was an oasis on prehistoric trade routes and later on the Silk Road. It is worth noting that the Asian steppe region, where many believe that horses were domesticated in the Neolithic era, lies north over the Tian Shan mountains, and access between the steppe and the Tarim Basin is on the basin's northeastern rim where the trousers were discovered.

The trousers consist of three pieces woven to shape (Figure 5.8). Using woolen yarns, the weaver made two identical leg pieces which widened from the hipline to the waist. Geometric designs are woven into the fabric. A third piece, the crotch piece, consists of a striped fabric with stepped selvages. To assemble the trousers, the two leg pieces were

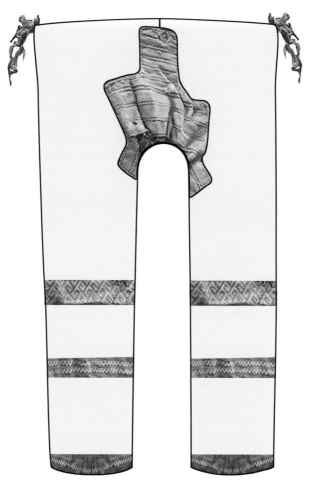

Figure 5.8 Redrawing of the 'oldest known trousers'. Woven of wool (find # 2003 SYIM 21:19, after Xinjiang, 2011) from the Yanghai site, tomb M2. Redrawing by Fafar Bayat. The 'oldest known trousers', radio-carbon dated to between the 13th to 10th centuries BCE, are made of two tubes of woven cloth, embellished with stitching, and joined with short center front and back seams and a stepped diamond-shaped crotch gusset.

folded at the sides and stitched at the inseams, which formed two tubes. These tubes were joined with short seams at the waist center front and center back. Then the two leg sections were spread apart and the stepped crotch piece was placed to span the space between the two legs, overlapping the leg edges, and sewn in place. Cords tied the trousers on the body at the waist. This construction created an ideal garment for individuals who spent most of their lives on horseback. In fact, the trousers were found in context with horse bones, suggesting that they were worn by horse riders.[22]

Also found in the Tarim Basin, at Sanpul Lop on the southwestern rim of the basin, was a pair of wool knee-length trousers dated to between the 2nd century BCE and the

2nd century CE. The legs are two tubes of 36cm-wide fabric joined by a square crotch piece described as 'rich and thick'.[23] Rather than being overlapped like the Turfan trousers, the crotch piece was inserted like a gusset, allowing free leg movement.

Excavated burials also produced coats. One of the oldest was found on a 'mummy' known as Cherchen Man, dated to 1000 BCE at Zaghunluq cemetery, proximate to Cherchen in the southeastern part of the basin, where desiccation from burial in the dry and salty soil preserved the bodies and clothing. Cherchen Man, preserved in a flexed position with knees bent, was buried in a shirt cut like a coat and held closed by a cord belt; the hem extended to his hips, covering the waist of his trousers. It is impossible to know the precise construction of his trousers without destroying the mummy. The cut of his long shirt is simple, which replicates the construction of a coat: two lengths of cloth form the front and back without seams at the shoulder. The two fabric lengths are sewn together at the center back and are open in front. Tubes of fabric attached at the arm openings, one on each side of the shirt, function as sleeves.[24] Cherchen Man's burial also had a coat that was found folded and placed under a horse saddle. The coat of brown wool with red cuffs and hem edge is constructed similarly to the shirt, except the sleeve circumference tapers from shoulder to wrist. Trousers found nearby suggest a model for those of Cherchen Man; they are formed of two tubes with a square crotch gusset applied with a yellow yarn on top of the pant tubes in a manner similar to the construction of the oldest known trousers.[25]

A spectacularly preserved coat dating between the 5th and the 3rd centuries BCE came from Subeshi cemetery on the north central edge of the basin (Figure 5.9). The pale, yellow coarse wool has 'a thin warp but a more dense weft'.[26] The coat is enhanced by a narrow stand-up collar and sleeves that taper from shoulder to wrist. At the sides of the two cloth panels that comprise the coat body, triangular inserts that start at the underarm add volume and create a flared hem.

Yingpan Man, excavated from his undisturbed Tomb 15 in the Yingpan cemetery located in the northeastern Tarim Basin, dates to between the late 4th and early 5th centuries.[28] The deceased was a Caucasian and measured six feet six inches in height; he was unusually tall. His ethnicity is thought to be Sogdian and he may have been a merchant in this important location along the Silk Road. His extremely sumptuous attire is the most complete set of clothes yet found in the region. His silk and wool coat, belted with a yellow silk sash, closed to the right in the style of Asia's western regions. A miniature coat had been placed on top of his sash. The predominantly red coat's woven pattern portrays confronting bulls and Greco-Roman putti indicative of transcultural exchange with Mediterranean and/or Persian design aesthetics and motifs.[29] Unhemmed dark red silk trousers embroidered with multiple colours of wool threads in a lozenge and floral design cover his lower body.

Persian textile patterns entered the Chinese fashion system east of the Tarim Basin by 455 CE, which is when a Sassanian (Persian) embassy was established in the Northern Wei dynasty (386–534 CE).[30] According to Kuhn, there was 'a great deal of informal exchange between China and Central Asia of textiles and the techniques for making them', and Sogdians who were Iranians residing in Central Asia, east of the Tarim Basin, were important in that exchange.[31]

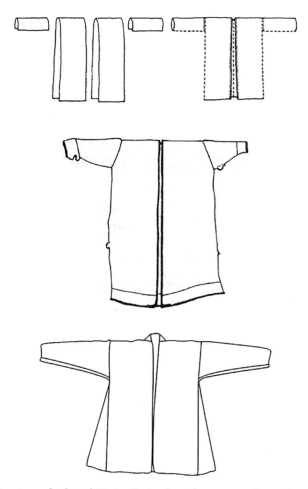

Figure 5.9 Drawings of selected Tarim Basin sleeved garments. Top and middle drawings: garments found with Cherchen Man, ca. 1600 BCE. By permission of Elizabeth Wayland Barber. Bottom drawing: Woolen Robe, 5th–3rd centuries BCE, drawing by Fafar Bayat[27]. *Top*: Cherchen Man's shirt shows that the fabric length runs from hem to hem. *Middle*: A woolen coat found with Cherchen Man. *Bottom*: Robe with triangle inserts in the side seams.

That the Chinese innovated numerous weaves and the looms to make them is well recognized among textile scholars. Of importance in this examination of coats and trousers is a textile named jin, a term that broadly denotes Chinese polychrome silk fabrics. Jin textiles were already present in the Bronze Age and continued development into the Song Dynasty (980–1279 CE), known for its enjoyment of fashion. Jin was restricted to the elites, and colourful 'luxurious silks, produced with gilded threads, became highly fashionable'.[32] Partial remains of a pair of jin fabric trousers in a weft-faced compound tabby weave were excavated from Tomb 170 at Astana, in the Tarim Basin's northeastern region. They date to 386–581 CE.[33] An overcoat of gilded jin in a compound weft-faced twill weave (samit) dated to the 12th century was found in the eastern sector of the Tarim Basin, in northwest China. The textile design is patterned with interlocking roundels, each enclosing two birds. It shows influences from cultures to the west that were fashionable in the Song dynasty; the pattern was called 'circular road' or 'heavenly corona'.[34] Sogdians were welcomed into the Chinese dynastic culture and served in official roles; they may have aided in the transfer of such motifs/textiles. This sumptuous coat, made with a front closure overlapping to the right, may have been a gift from the current dynasty to a diplomat.

The presence of numerous coats and trousers in the vast Tarim Basin indicates a long history of their use along trade routes connecting cultures across Eurasia. This history includes the appearance of textile motifs outside of their place of origin. We now turn attention further east in Asia to investigate the distribution of coats and trousers beyond the Tarim Basin.

Asian Contexts: East of the Tarim Basin

Archaeologists who excavated the Tarim Basin are unanimous in their description of the population of the region as multi-ethnic.[35] Some mummies display characteristics that are more European than Asian. Trade took place along ancient routes, bridging east and west.[36] Barber posits that the presence of coats and trousers around the Tarim Basin reflects the locals' adoption of dress forms from those people with whom they had contact.[37] The Tarim Basin is the location of a fascinating set of archaeological finds that show cross-cultural influences on the styles of the region, and the kinds of coats and trousers that were worn as a result.

That coats were worn elsewhere in Asia is evidenced by a figural lamp stand of a Mongol youth wearing a coat (Figure 5.10). Dated between the fourth and the third centuries BCE, it was created in northeastern China during the Warring States period (340–287 BCE) of the Zhou dynasty (1046–256 BCE). The figure wears a sleeved coat tied closed with a belt, and with a collar and decorative border. Slightly later, the famous Terracotta Warriors of Chinese Emperor Qin Shi Huang, dating to 210–209 BCE and unearthed in Xian in eastern China, wear coats and trousers.

In Chinese dynastic cultures, a fabric width for each distinct weave was specified in the dress code system, and textiles were restricted according to social rank. Coat structure was based on a top section spanning from sleeve end to sleeve end, including the shoulder area, which attached to a skirt or bottom section. Both the upper section and the lower section were made from multiple lengthwise strips of fabric.[38]

Because textiles were so valuable, they were sometimes woven to the shape of garment pieces, thus avoiding waste of precious yarns.[39] An example of such a garment is a coat from northeastern China's Liao dynasty (907–1125 CE). The coat is of jin in a weft-faced compound twill, a samit, patterned with medallions containing four lions each, placed in a background of dragon fish, and floral motifs on a red ground.[40] The sleeves taper from the shoulder to a narrower wrist. The coat has a standing collar, closes to the left side, and the hem flares due to gores at the sides.

Figure 5.10 Figural lamp stand, bronze, eastern Zhou, Warring States, 4th–3rd centuries BCE, height 30cm, no. 31.976. Maria Antoinette Evans Fund, Boston Museum of Fine Art, www.mfa.org/collections/object/figural-lamp-stand-17842. This Mongol youth from eastern China wears a coat that closes with an overlap, and has straight sleeves.

The Jin Dynasty (1115–1234 CE), situated on the eastern coast of China and north of the Song region, also enjoyed gold-enhanced jin fabrics, even exporting them to the Song dynasty. A song titled *The Records of Hearsay on the Pine Forests North of the Plains* portrays the story of Hong Hao (1088–1155 CE) who was a Song envoy to the Jin dynasty. It provides a clue as to who the weavers of such textiles may have been.[41] The lyrics document Uyghur weavers living near modern day Hebei province in Yanshan, stating that they were 'skilled at working with twisted gold thread'.[42] A dark red-brown coat of tabby weave found in the tomb of Wanyan Yong (1123–1189 CE) at Achang in Harbin in northeastern China and dated to 1162 CE displays gold decorative bands on the top of the sleeve lengths and near the coat hem.[43] The ground textile is a tabby weave and the bands are a weft-faced twill in a pattern of pseudo-Kufic or Turkish-style writing. The stylized writing in the decorative bands suggests contact between Arab and eastern China dynastic cultures, whether via transplanted Uyghur weavers from the Tarim Basin region, or via exchange through trade routes across the continent, or via sea routes combined with land routes. The Liao dynasty coat's construction is in the style of sleeved coats found around the Tarim Basin, rather than the dynastic model of a top-and-sleeve section joined to a bottom skirt section. The cut of the coat also suggests adoption or exploration of stylistic influences from Central Asia.

The Silk Road land routes consisted of varied paths traversing the Eurasian continent and sea routes stretching from the eastern China coast to the Persian Gulf and Red Sea. Long distance trade was accomplished both by linked short-haul trips and long trips with multiple stops. Traders exchanged materials, technologies, ideas and concepts, and included were textile technologies, weave structures, motifs, dyes, and fibers. Also, part of the long transcultural exchange were garment types and garment construction methods, such as gussets, sleeve types, and closures. Examples used in this analysis point to motifs and garment styles that traversed across cultures. Greco-Roman and Byzantine motifs spread eastward, appearing in Chinese and Central Asian textiles. Coat and trouser garments moved westward from Central Asia into Europe. The Persian riding coat style, which most likely had roots in the coats of the nomadic tribes of the Asian steppes, was worn in northern Africa during the Greco-Roman period. Complex textile patterns in multiple colours, first made possible by Chinese weaving innovations, were worn in Bronze Age Central Asia, brought there through trade.[44]

Conclusion

Although gaps remain in tracing the adoption of coats and trousers, it is argued that coats and trousers originated in Asia and arrived in Europe via prehistoric and ancient trade networks. The important roles of coats and trousers in diverse fashion systems across history, and their continuity in contemporary fashion systems, demands that their narratives be rescripted to reflect this transfer.

The earliest clothes were made from plant materials and animal skins. Later, the development of yarns from plant and animal fibers led to clothing made from textiles once weaving was developed sometime between 25,000 and 7,000 years ago. However, due to the fragile nature of organic materials, evidence of both skin and woven clothing in prehistory is scant. Therefore, scholars may only guess at how garments developed. Skin garments probably served as the models for woven garments, and innovations for fit, function, and decorative qualities occurred along the way. The earliest known trousers are a leap forward from wrapped leather or felted fiber leggings; they would be more stable on the body and protect the sensitive crotch. For this study a key point concerning trousers is that they were in use in Central Asia by the 13th century BCE, and presumably in the Asian steppes before then. Regarding coats, the one buried with Cherchen Man, also in Central Asia, is approximately four centuries earlier than those depicted on the walls at Persepolis.

With this rewriting of the narrative of coats and trousers, the spatial aspects of their occurrence demand a redrawn map inclusive of Asia (Figure 5.1). The existing narrative connecting ancient Persian dress and that of Iron Age Gaul to the development of Western style clothing and its eventual spread across the globe through colonization is replaced with the narrative of coats and trousers developing in the East and spreading to Eurasia and North Africa. In this way, the Eurocentric storyline is dislodged by a more complex and longer historical narrative.

Notes

1. Blanche Payne, Geitel Winakor and Jane Farrell-Beck, *The History of Costume: From Ancient Mesopotamia Through the Twentieth Century*, 2nd edn (New York: Harper Collins, 1992); Phyllis Tortora and Sara B. Marcketti, *Survey of Historic Costume,* 6th edn (London and New York: Bloomsbury, 2015).

2. Payne et al., *The History of Costume,* 23. The Scythians were a group of nomadic tribes from Southern Siberia who extended their influence over Central Asia from 900 BCE to 200 CE ('Introducing the Scythians,' Blog British Museum, 30 May 2017, https://blog.britishmuseum.org/introducing-the-scythians/ (accessed 12 July 2019)). Ancient Greek historians considered both Goths and Scythians to be barbarians.

3. Payne et al., *The History of Costume,* 107–08.

4. Tortora and Marcketti, *Survey of Historic Costume,* 95.

5. Aníbal Quijano, 'Coloniality and Modernity/Rationality,' *Cultural Studies* 21 (2–3) (2007) 168–78.

6. 'Persepolis', www.livius.org/articles/place/persepolis/persepolis-photos/persepolis-apadana-east-stairs/ (accessed 12 July 2019)

7. Mireille Lee, *Body, Dress, and Identity in Ancient Greece* (New York: Cambridge University Press, 2015) 123.

8. For example, see accession no. 1859, 1126.1, The British Museum, a small statue of a Gallo-Roman man.

9. Graham Sumner, *Roman Military Clothing, Vol. 2: AD 200–400* (Botley: Osprey, 2003), 35.

10. Elfriede Knauer, 'Toward a History of the Sleeved Coat: A Study of the Impact of an Ancient Eastern Garment on the West,' *Expedition,* 21 (1) (1978) 23.

11. ibid, 27.

12. Helen Evans and Brandie Ratliff, Eds. *Byzantium and Islam: Age of Transition, 7th–9th Century* (New York: Metropolitan Museum of Art, 2012) 171.

13. Evans and Ratliff, *Byzantium and Islam,* 167–168). The Eastern Roman Empire was established by Constantine in 324 CE in a town called Byzantium; it became the Byzantine Empire, which was overtaken by the Ottoman Turks in 1453 CE.

14. Cäcilia Fluck, 'Dress Styles from Syria to Libya'. In Helen C. Evans and Brandie Ratliff, Eds. *Byzantium and Islam: Age of Transition, 7th–9th Century* (New York: Metropolitan Museum of Art, 2012) 160.

15. Linda Welters and Abby Lillethun, *Fashion History: A Global View* (London and New York: Bloomsbury, 2018) 109.

16. Victor Mair, Ed. *Secrets of the Silk Road* (Santa Ana, CA: Bowers Museum, 2010).

17. Victor Mair, 'The Mummies of East Central Asia', *Expedition*, 53 (3) (2010) 26.

18. ibid, 32.

19. David Anthony, *The Horse, the Wheel, and Language: How Bronze Age Riders from the Eurasian Steppes Shaped the Modern World* (Princeton, NJ: Princeton University Press, 2007).

20. Elizabeth Wayland Barber, *The Mummies of Ürümchi* (London: Pan, 1999) 37.

21. Ulrike Beck, Mayke Wagner, Xiao Li, Desmond Durkin-Meisterernst, and Pavel E. Tarasov, 'The Invention of Trousers and Its Likely Affiliation with Horseback Riding and Mobility: A Case Study of Late 2nd Millennium BC Finds from Turfan in Eastern Central Asia', *Quaternary International*, 348 (2014) 224–35.

22. Beck et al., 'The Invention of Trousers'.

23. Mair, *Secrets of the Silk Road*, 153.

24. Barber, *The Mummies of Ürümchi*, 25.

25. ibid., 37–49.

26. Mair, *Secrets of the Silk Road*, 147.

27. Barber, *The Mummies of Ürümchi*, Figures 2.3 and 2.12; Mair, Ed. *Secrets of the Silk Road*, Figure 36-2.

28. Mair, *The Mummies of East Central Asia*, 30.

29. Ulf Jager and Victor Mair, 'The Yingpan Man'. In Victor Mair, Ed. *Secrets of the Silk Road* (Santa Ana, CA: Bowers Museum, 2010) 56.

30. Dieter Kuhn, 'Reading the Magnificence of Ancient and Medieval Chinese Silks'. In Dieter Kuhn, Ed. *Chinese Silks* (New Haven, CT: Yale University Press, 2012) 30.

31. Kuhn, *Reading the Magnificence,* 30, 494 n.117. See above.

32. ibid., 51.

33. Dieter Kuhn, Ed. *Chinese Silks* (New Haven, CT: Yale University Press, 2012) 176.

34. Zhao Feng, 'Silks in the Song, Liao, Western Xia, and Jin Dynasties'. In Dieter Kuhn, Ed. *Chinese Silks* (New Haven, CT: Yale University Press, 2012), 202, 268, 270–271.

35. Spencer Wells, 'Genetic Affinities of the Tarim Basin People'. In Victor Mair, Ed. *Secrets of the Silk Road* (Santa Ana, CA: Bowers Museum, 2010) 81–87.

36. Mair, *Secrets of the Silk Road*.

37. Barber, *The Mummies of Ürümchi*.

38. Kuhn, *Reading the Magnificence*, 22–4.

39. ibid., 24.

40. ibid., 52

41. Etienne Balazs and Yves Hervouet, Eds. *Song dai shu lu [A Sung Bibliography]* (Hong Kong: Chinese University Press, 1978) 109–110.

42. Feng, *Silks in the Song*, 283.

43. ibid., 283, 285. Wanyan Yong was Prince of Qi (also known as Emperor Shizong of Jin).

44. Angela Sheng, 'Textiles from the Silk Road: Intercultural Exchanges Among Nomads, Traders, and Agriculturalists', *Expedition*, 53 (3) (2010) 33–43, www.penn.museum/documents/publications/expedition/PDFs/52-3/sheng.pdf (accessed 12 July 2019).

SECTION II
NATIONALISM, TRANSNATIONALISM AND FASHION

INTRODUCTION TO SECTION II
Erica DE GREEF

Fashion has long created cultural, social and political distinctions. Simultaneously, it has blurred differences, weaving together disparate narratives and aesthetics to form hybrid, borderless identities. In this sense fashion proclaims identities, as much as it expands upon the entanglements of identity and place. In this section, we take a closer look at the production of national and transnational fashions as a result of global politics. The authors' perspectives explore the reclamation of local fashion stories and practices, increasingly fulfilling historic and contemporary aesthetic needs, for both indigenous communities and global societies. Additionally, they assert the complexity of entangled relations between regional fashion systems that are often overlooked in favour of the singular Westernization of fashion globalization.

The chapters reflect on fashion as embodied ways of being in the world, or as strategies of resistance and invention for negotiating cultural memory or crafting communities of practice. In the process of bringing these narratives together, it is necessary to embrace divergent definitions of dress and fashion, so as to trouble and broaden the definitions of fashion and globalization. The authors invite us to consider local fashion adoptions and evolutions, and ask us to welcome diverse voices and histories to form a more truly global fashion discourse.

Fashion entrepreneur Chepkemboi J. Mang'ira explores the powerful convergence of a digital platform, traditional Kenyan accessories and historical research in a highly collaborative project aimed at decolonizing contemporary African fashion. Mang'ira shares the various stages of the project, its reception and its potential for crafting new aesthetic narratives that are deeply rooted in the past, yet answer to the current call for cultural diversity and sustainability in the face of a branded, Western fashion homogeneity.

The intersection of media platforms, youth culture and contemporary fashion also informs Koma Kyoko's chapter. Her in-depth investigation of the evolution of the Japanese sub-culture kawaii involves a range of actors and multi-directional flows between France and Japan. The chapter allows for a nuanced reading of the transboundary relations that contributed to the construction of kawaii, a transnational style that disrupts simple binary definitions, and articulates the circularity of meaning-making inherent to global fashion phenomena.

Exploring questions of place, history and absence, as well as national aesthetics and cultural identity, through the work of contemporary fashion designers in Aotearoa New Zealand, Harriette Richards invites us to examine the impact of colonization on local fashion. Despite indigenous cultures having long, rich histories of corporeal fashioning, these have been all but excluded from global fashion histories dominated by Western sartorial ideals. Richards argues for a decolonizing of fashion history to develop more diverse representation with designers telling their own stories.

Through a case-study of the early 20th century fashion of the creole Chinese/ indigenous community of the Malay Archipelago in Singapore, Courtney Fu explores the development of a unique hybrid fashion identity. In her chapter, Fu confronts the limits of fashioning a national stereotype by presenting the hybrid fashionabilities of these women who refuse the stereotype. By doing so, the notion of agency is reclaimed within a broader revisioning of tradition as praxis and traditional aesthetics as continually evolving.

We hope that these chapters offer potential strategies for decolonizing the discourse around fashion globalization by inviting a closer listening to current debates around localization, nationalism, decoloniality, and multi-directional global histories, fashions and politics.

CHAPTER 6
#OWNYOURCULTURE: DECOLONIZING FASHION THROUGH TRADITIONAL JEWELLERY
Chepkemboi J. MANG'IRA

Introduction

There is a popular saying in Swahili, 'mwacha mila ni mtumwa', loosely translating to 'one who throws away their culture is a slave'. The irony is, while this is such a popular proverb, it is rarely applied in reality with regards to Kenyan fashion. When compared to our ancestors of the 19th century and before, the majority of Kenyans have abandoned their original way of dressing – of wearing intricately woven beads, feathers, and leather dress. This is largely attributed to forceful miseducation of the association of all Kenyan traditional attire with evil according to the Christian missionaries.[1] The worst part of this miseducation was that this was taught to young children, thus leaving future generations of Kenyans looking down upon and disowning all aspects of their heritage, from language to attire. It is only a handful out of 42 tribes that still appreciate their beadwork and have stylized it over time (as of the 2019 census). In the fashion space, designers may dabble in using some form of beadwork in their collections but as a whole the beadwork styles are classified by the public, and even some fashion insiders, as 'traditional', often with negative connotations attached.

My name is Chepkemboi J. Mang'ira, and I am the founder of #OwnYourCulture, an online platform that encourages young Kenyans to embrace their heritage through styling and with traditional accessories.[2] My aims for developing the online platform were to promote, preserve and educate youth in Kenya and beyond on traditional jewellery and its relevance in the fashion of today. This work began as a social media hashtag and page showcasing different ways that traditional accessories can be fashionable. I left it open for users to share stories of their culture or stories passed down in their communities alongside the styled photos. I am a journalist by training,[3] and a fashion entrepreneur and decolonization activist.[4]

A myriad of situations and self-introspections, as well as my volunteer work in fashion forums, led to the start of #OwnYourCulture. Looking back, the culmination point of this was as I was preparing for the Festival for African Fashion and Arts (FAFA), a major Kenyan fashion event. As a fashion blogger, I had to ensure I dressed the part, as well as representing Kenyan designers. With a minimal budget, I spent a lot of time researching what outfit I would wear. At the time, I followed South African fashion as I felt their street style section of magazines featured people that looked like me – afro hair and clothes from stores similar to what we had in Nairobi. I would browse their work to see the latest style trends and search for inspiration for my own designs. I came across a man dressed in a white vest and white jeans and Maasai necklace and I absolutely loved the look! That's when an idea began taking root near the second anniversary of my blog, just as I was creating a new strategy for it. I created a synonymous Instagram page (see Figure 6.1), and arranged photoshoots with any willing photographer (from my brother, to my neighbours and friends) to capture my outfits styled with traditional beads.

I have also immersed myself as the purveyor of this movement. Every day since the start of this #OwnYourCulture campaign, I have dressed in traditional accessories, at all gatherings, on public transportation, to work, and all the way to fashion events. I used and still use myself as a walking installation. The purpose of this, in my own small way, is to get more individuals offline accustomed to the idea of wearing 'traditional' accessories as part of normal or everyday fashion and to spark converzations on the beauty of our past cultures. The feedback was positive, with more and more people commenting on how beautiful and wearable traditional accessories are.

I chose traditional jewellery as my tool to decolonize fashion in Kenya, and I am using both real-world and digital platforms to share that. This chapter is about my own work, and my online community's contributions to decolonizing fashion through the use of traditional jewellery.[5] Throughout this chapter I use different terminologies to describe the jewellery – there is the local Kenyan contextual English where the term 'traditional' is used to describe the fashion of the mid-20th century and before. I will also use terms such as everyday clothes/normal fashion to denote the accepted standards of dress in Kenya, which is suits and ties for men, and for women, skirt suits, below-the-knee dresses and coats, with minimal accessories and a preference for European style straight hair wigs and weaves.[6] The reason I chose jewellery to start decolonizing fashion in Kenya is because of the symbolism, beadwork patterns and colour choices that carry a lot of Kenyan histories, such as community identification, age group identification, status identification, and design creativity.

Implementation and Adaptation

In the section that follows, I explore how the #OwnYourCulture movement began in June 2014 and how it developed. It was an idea whose beginning and aim was to change attitudes towards traditional fashion. In the discussion that follows, I share some of the strategies I employed in developing the campaign. I share this process to show the intricate interconnection between digital storytelling and perception, and how this trickles down into the offline world.

The process of inviting citizen participation was simple – style yourself with traditional jewellery, take a photo, upload it to social media (specifically Instagram) and add the #OwnYourCulture tag alongside a story passed down from your community. My deciding factor for selecting participants was the 'traditional-ness' of the accessory. I devised a selection criterion to enable the message to be better understood – the accessory had to be from or inspired by (and with clear relation to) traditional Kenyan dress. If the criteria were met, the post would be shared on all our platforms, appealing to our human need for being appreciated. As the project's followers grew, there were

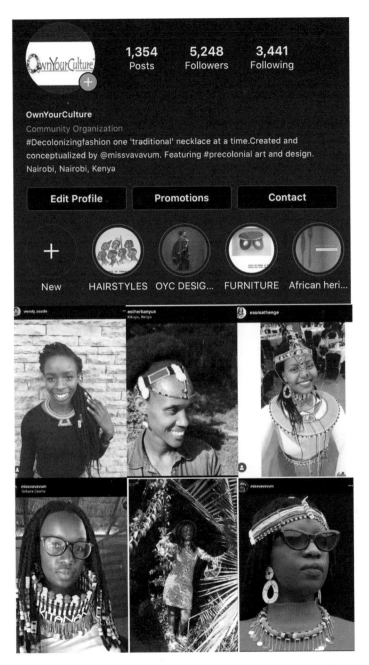

Figure 6.1 Snapshot of the #OwnYourCulture page. Top row – Wendy Osodo, 27, insurance professional; Esther Kanyua, 37, in a Turkana head piece; Esther Mathenge, Human Resource professional, 26, in assorted Maasai jewellery. Bottom row – myself in Turkana ceremonial neck piece; Maureen Shelmith in leso (Swahili fabric) dress and assorted beadwork (photograph by Perpetua Adoyo); and myself in Samburu head piece and Maasai necklace (photograph by Perpetua Adoyo).

many different interpretations of what taking pride in traditional fashion meant to the participants. There are bead accessories available at local shops designed with little or no traditional history significance, or those that were created specifically for the European market during the colonial period. Due to their ready availability and cheap price, participants wore them and used the #OwnYourCulture tag. At this point, according to the images submitted, the understanding of traditional fashion was any locally beaded item. This served as a unique and insightful reflection of the public understanding of traditional Kenyan fashion.

There exists a daily caravan market in Nairobi known as Maasai Market where beaded jewellery, crafts and art from Eastern, Western, Central and Southern Africa are sold. On interviewing the artisans, they each noted that the majority of their customers were tourists, or Kenyans from the diaspora, or Kenyans travelling abroad, buying jewellery to gift them as souvenirs. I felt it was imperative to maintain a standard style of accessorizing that related to traditional fashion, as opposed to just posting any kind of beadwork. On the social media page, it was and still is important to showcase traditional Kenyan fashion as accurately as possible. This meant thorough research using photography from the national museums and libraries was necessary, to learn and educate the participants on traditional and precolonial fashion. I shared this research through precise and short posts on the online platforms, and I would make sure to answer all the participants' questions (such as in Figure 6.4) while referencing museum texts and other sources.

Through the #OwnYourCulture social media pages, participants had learnt and were able to differentiate traditional beads from contemporary designer ones, and this was made evident in their posts. They would send images of family heirlooms or tag pages involving traditional fashion in the comments sections. They had even reached a point they were able to differentiate between beadwork styles from various communities and would often tag the #OwnYourCulture pages on such posts. Around eight months into the project, I noticed a new demand for knowledge about other communities. Due to the dominance of data on Maasai culture, most participants were dressed in these accessories, which prompted me to research and showcase styles from different tribes. This then led me to create a team of bead-workers and designers that began recreating traditional jewellery from other tribes, whose designs would then become available for sale. Looking back, I believe this team helped in the growth of #OwnYourCulture because through them we were able to create design replicas of a range of traditional Kenyan tribes. To solidify the project, I would make sure to participate in fashion events to display these items, as well as interact offline with the participants. Our booths at various fashion events were always popular as many people were interested in discovering new information about traditional Kenyan jewellery. In fact, many visitors could not believe that the designs were actually inspired by photographs of our ancestors. I often included mini-educative sessions around these accessories, even educating my own team members. Many followers of #OwnYourCulture expressed their fascination in learning that every Kenyan tribe designed fascinating jewellery and attire, dispelling the misconception that only a handful of Kenyan tribes created or wore beautiful beadwork. Posts highlighting information on lesser known tribes performed well, with many followers commenting

Figure 6.2 Chepkemboi J. Mang'ira, posted in November 2019. Photograph: Perpetua Adoyo.

and sharing the posts with their friends. There has been positive response and fascination from followers on the various East African beadwork styles from each community. This goes to show the missing links and misunderstanding of our fashion history.

I undertook research in books and museum documentation from the National Museums of Kenya, and anthropological institutes such as the British Institute of Eastern Africa and Kenya Archives. I found evidence of design styles that seemed to have travelled around East African communities. The current accessory style of the Datoga tribe in Tanzania is very similar to that of the Kikuyu, Luo, Maasai and Kalenjin communities of the early 1900s. I also noticed that what was worn at a certain time period by one tribe was often soon adopted by another tribe some years later. These are just a fraction of the interesting aspects of traditional fashion that I uncovered through my own research. I realized that there is so much more context that designers can make use of today. One example is a neck piece that I am wearing in Figure 6.2 that was once worn by young

Maasai brides in the 1970s, which now is worn by Samburu men,[7] and to the trained eye could even resemble traditional Turkana neck pieces, albeit different in size. I would often make use of these facts, and compare them on the #OwnYourCulture platforms to prompt discussions. The online interactions were often limited to comments, as well as short digital style emoticons and private messages asking for more references so they could research the images themselves. It was my prerogative to ensure that this was just not a passing fad, but a long-lasting critique of what we accept as fashion and why.

South African street-style from fashion sites such as Elle South Africa, According to Jerri and For Fashion Freaks often featured individuals styled in traditional beaded accessories (even some wearing Kenyan beadwork), which I would then repost as motivation for showcasing the tremendous ways our accessories are relevant fashion items, including for Kenyans themselves rather than just for tourists. The initial re-posts on the #OwnYourCulture social media accounts featured the South African street-style posts, as well as posts by Africans living in the diaspora, traditional jewellery merchants, and editorial photographs that had been featured in magazines (see Figure 6.3). All this reposting was done in a bid to showcase the diversity of and place for traditional accessories in fashion.

In running and directing this campaign, I have noted that women are at the forefront of digital influence in imagery submissions and even interaction. In retrospect this could be attributed to the fact that today traditional jewellery is considered womenswear, even though in the past this was very different, where both men and women adorned themselves excessively in jewellery. This echoes the necessity of making space for other forms of fashion expression to include more diverse gender narratives. The next steps for the growth and future of the #OwnYourCulture campaign included clearer information and images of traditional style identities. I was to embark on yet more research on what was worn in the past, from museums and books, as well as speaking to anthropologists from the National Museums of Kenya and the Kenya Archives, and tribal elders in towns such as Kajiado, Baringo, Turkana, Kuria, Arusha and Kampala.

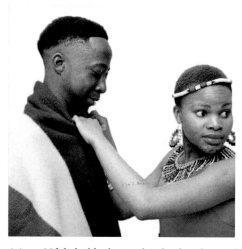

Figure 6.3 Alex Nkosi in a Ndebele blanket and Yolanda Khanyisile Sibanyoni in a Zulu headband and Xhosa necklace.

Nine months into the online #OwnYourCulture campaign, the various social media accounts (Instagram, Facebook, WhatsApp and Twitter) began gaining traction and we received orders from new and old followers for newly made accessories, representative of their cultures. The ethical thing to do at this point was to work with rural women who were most familiar with the design styles in demand. I reproduced the design images from my image research processes and from old colonial photographs. We would customize these pieces to fit the more contemporary lifestyles of today's customers, for example using more monochrome colours that would be work-friendly, or match the work or school dress codes. Another method that we used was repurposing some traditional neckwear designs as earrings or hair accessories. This proved useful in that #OwnYourCulture participants could now wear pieces of their own traditional cultures. Some participants would immediately post images of our designs, and this would then lead to inquiries on traditional fashion as well as requests for the customized jewellery.

To encourage various forms of participation, one year into running the campaign, I implemented a best dressed tag every week whereby the best, most uniquely dressed participant would be posted across all social media accounts and highlighted. In a bid to spread the message further, I also searched for and joined Facebook groups with similar aims of promoting African style and beauty. Many active groups focused on embracing natural hair. With the improved interaction from the curated content, I began to appreciate and understand the importance of great quality images of real people. I collaborated with photographers such as Jossy Ndiho in 2015, where I styled myself in different outfits and traditional jewellery. It was important to consistently put out new images in order to encourage continuous participation and engagement. In 2016, I decided to invite a broader involvement from fashion media (from bloggers to magazines) to help spread the message. I went on to work with some of the country's top style bloggers, including Wamboi Karebe, a self-described artist of life with vast experience as a stylist in Kenya.

In 2018, the campaign co-hosted the Hairitage Festival, celebrating natural hair, African beauty, African fashion and locally made products. The festival was founded by the Nurtured Knotts Group administrators, Nakhulo Khaimia and Nyasuba Lando

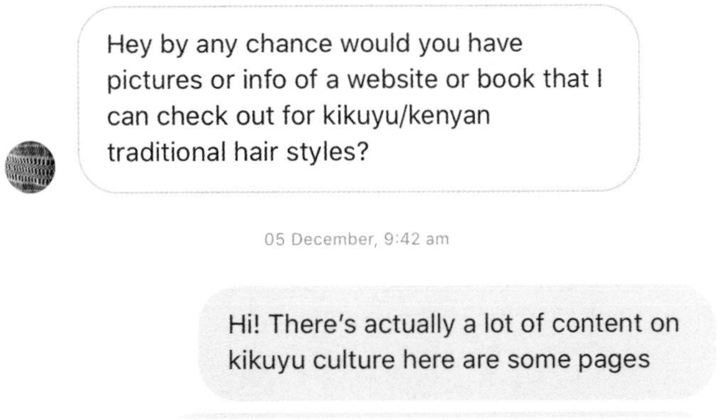

Hey by any chance would you have pictures or info of a website or book that I can check out for kikuyu/kenyan traditional hair styles?

05 December, 9:42 am

Hi! There's actually a lot of content on kikuyu culture here are some pages

Figure 6.4 An enquiry on information about traditional hairstyles from Wambui, 24, a piloting student.

Lando. The theme in 2018 was #OwnYourCulture, from which I was able to observe how the theme was being interpreted offline. Many attendees arrived dressed up and on theme (see Figures 6.5 and 6.6), with different interpretations of traditional dress. For the festival editions outside of the city, such as the one held in Nakuru (a town 200km from Nairobi), I noted a similar resistance towards traditional jewellery as had been evident in Nairobi when I started my campaign. Many people still did not understand how one can be educated and still value, even cherish, traditional accessories.

In the daily running of the #OwnYourCulture campaign, and without prior planning or expectations, I did notice that some themes appeared. Firstly, there were participants who still deemed traditional accessories 'too much' and resisted the idea of wearing them. Another group of participants, while supportive of the project, still felt uncomfortable wearing traditional accessories, and would instead hang accessories on their walls at home. It has even become popular to have Pokot,[8] Marakwet[9] and Samburu circular necklaces serve as home décor items.

Like any fashion subculture there are trends and styles that have developed within the #OwnYourCulture community. Narrower or smaller pieces are often preferred as they work well in office settings. Some participants are also slowly adjusting to the idea of wearing precolonial or traditional fashion. This is still rooted in the after-effects of colonialism more than half a century later, whereby elaborate traditional dress is seen as

Figure 6.5 Hairitage Festival attendee, Tindi Kamwetu, 33-year old teacher.

Figure 6.6 Wachu Suzanne Wanjaria, Museum Professional, wearing a Himba-inspired hairstyle. Photograph: Perpetua Adoyo.

unsuitable. Recently, a directive from the president to allow workers in some of the Kenyan corporate offices to wear kitenge outfits on Fridays has been greatly supportive to and appreciated by the local fashion industry. In addition, the growth of the #OwnYourCulture community, and online boutiques around it, has shown the country's thirst for original and decolonized fashion that pays homage to diverse ancestral heritages. The self-sustaining #OwnYourCulture community continues to influence and inspire others to embrace the values, creativity and diversity of African heritage, accessories and fashion.

#OwnYourCulture and Decolonizing Kenyan Fashion Efforts

In this section, I will look at the roots of the disapproval towards traditional fashion to briefly contextualize the #OwnYourCulture project. As I have mentioned before, the negative perception of traditional fashion began during the colonial period, reinforced through stringent measures that were taken to ensure that Kenyans reject every bit of their culture. Ngugi wa Thiong'o[10] writes on the reinforcement of colonial practices, where in colonial Kenya children were taught to dismiss their own culture. To date it is still illegal in some schools to speak in one's tribal language. Even wearing natural hair in some schools is still prohibited.

In the 1960s, as Kenya worked towards gaining independence, the government sought to decolonize Kenya by renaming places, removing statues, and adapting Kiswahili as the national language. However, it seems that traditional fashion took a back seat amidst all this. Song and dance were preserved and encouraged,[11] and still remain popular today. Some political leaders at the time would always wear traditional items during important ceremonies. The first President of Kenya, Jomo Kenyatta, alongside prominent politicians of the time such as Jaramogi Odinga and Tom Mboya, often sported a beaded hat from the Luo[12] community called ogut tigo. However, this style seems to have since disappeared from the public save for a few extant pieces in museum collections and those worn by a handful of political leaders.

There have been efforts made, by both private individuals and the government, to create design competitions whose aim was to establish a national Kenyan dress that represented the various peoples of Kenya. One of the earliest attempts was that of Mary Kadenge in the 1960s but, according to past newspaper articles, this quest failed due to extreme cultural differences among Kenyans. The next attempt was by Margaret Akumu Gould in the 1980s in which she collaborated with the Kenya Tourism Board and a group of designers. The winners were Christine Ndambuki for her Nigerian-inspired men's kaftan and Wacu of Wacu Designs for a dress for women made from kikoi – a hand-loomed, cotton cloth popular throughout Eastern Africa. However, these competitions came to an end, and the outfits disappeared. The intention had been to instil a Kenyan dress that would be symbolic of Kenya, and which would receive the same respect as the wearing of a formal suit. In 2004, the government yet again organized a competition to find a national dress. The resulting garments were not well received by the public, as they were seen to be too expensive.[13] Some variations of these attires however survived, and these are still made by tailors. The most common national dress practice, however, is to embroider the colours of the Kenyan flag onto clothes.

Regional beauty pageants are perhaps one of the few places where traditional aesthetics are still appreciated. Traditional dress also remains a key component of national celebrations. Close inspection of the designs of the entertainers at these events shows that the current designs are not as bold and lively as those from earlier eras. Traditional attire also still appears in annual school music festivals, which sees students from primary school to college participate in diverse events. Plays and dances encourage and promote Kenyan culture, however the dress and accessories are still classified in categories that make them seem inferior to contemporary fashion. There are still ongoing efforts to find the ultimate Kenyan attire that features our diversity and history, although these are on a smaller scale, usually targeting a few designers or fashion students. It is for these reasons that the work of #OwnYourCulture towards decolonizing fashion is so important, especially in terms of perceptions, attitudes and appreciation of Kenyan identities.

Conclusion

I would like to emphasize the importance of this work in decolonizing fashion, specifically the power of digital influence in achieving this goal. With conscious use, digital influence can be used to facilitate positive change within a society. From the #OwnYourCulture campaign, it is evident that online activities trickle down to the offline world. What may start out as just an image that one takes to participate in the campaign, may go on to inspire similar-minded people to be more curious and conscious of their culture, and eventually even lead to a demand for better representation in other media as well as in retail spaces. The digital is so influential that it can influence other formats such as shops, thereby creating new work for bead-workers – and a whole new supply chain is born. Activism has changed immensely with the digital revolution. Today, change is one click away.

With regards to decolonization, it has been clear to me that in order to sustain the effects of the campaign, there must be collaborative efforts made between the makers, wearers and consumers, that consistency and clarity in messaging is key, and that an ongoing call-to-action is required in order to see the results of its implementation and various interpretations. There must be a practicality attached to the decolonization methods whereby the actual people that can help facilitate the change are enlisted in these activities. This has been made easier by the digital world, whereby activism and calls-to-action can be mobilized together, so as to demand better representation and visibility. Within the digital environment, this work can be documented and its evidence can then be used to ask the relevant authorities for change.

Even as the work continues, there are still some people that would not like to be associated with traditional jewellery, as a matter of aesthetics, claiming that it is not up to standard in comparison with Western jewellery. They do not want to be 'othered' in association with traditional jewellery, as it is seen as something that is only acceptable when worn by artists or creatives. This goes to show how much work there is still to do in decolonizing mental attitudes towards traditional Kenyan fashion. To echo Walter Mignolo and Rolando Vasquez,[14] there is a need to create a place for plurality in fashion. In working on this campaign, there have been many challenges to the rules of fashion (and specifically jewellery). East African beadwork has very different design aesthetics to that of the West. In the #OwnYourCulture community, we are all constantly experimenting with fashion trends and styles; the key lies in its aesthetic pleasure.

In terms of fashion globalization, this virtual community has made clear that they are aware of the issues, and they want to actively participate in showcasing their diversity to show that traditional jewellery is still relevant today. This virtual community shows that fashion is no longer in the hands of a few people. Consumers of fashion are now more aware of the processes involved, and fashion systems can no longer work to exclude or narrow down other people's fashion histories.

I share all the above because #OwnYourCulture is important in the fashion sphere in that it shows there is a thirst for including and seeing traditional fashion. There is a thirst for making space for ourselves 'to see ourselves'. This #OwnYourCulture work and its adjunct processes are important to be shared so that we can see other ways of being, and even implement a more cohesive and inclusive fashion ecosystem, based on similar relationships with and respect for the diversity of African fashion. The #OwnYourCulture campaign goes to show that traditional fashion is valid and can be very much part of today's world, not just a snippet of other fashion perspectives.

This chapter is important in the academic sphere as it captures the practicality and actualities of practicing decolonization. It encapsulates the process of drawing from the academic sphere to the realities of asking ordinary people to participate in their own unique ways. Theories and terminologies are great but the real effect on real people is through such an enactment that asks people to contribute and participate. I believe in starting wherever one is at. There are free tools that can be made use of today that can contribute towards positive change. There is importance in cultivating a culture and a heritage not only for its economic and aesthetic impacts, but also to instil a sense of pride in people.

I want you, the reader, to understand that traditional fashion is still very much relevant today, not just as a tourism product! There is method, history, originality and meaning to the adornments. I want you, the reader, to understand that we cannot just put whole 'other' fashion systems on the back burner in the name of modernity. Fashion is a sense of self-expression, and in Kenya, has been an expression of its people. Each ornament has had meaning and significance for families and tribes throughout history. And each ornament has to be given its rights and respected as part of fashion both as critical and creative acknowledgement. Every day, I wear the accessories that I have researched, and reproduce them (when I can), because I want more people to appreciate their fashion relevance. This work is important to me because I want more accurate stories to be shared that are inclusive and truthful. I would also love to see the same reflected within Kenyan society in terms of a sense of pride and appreciation for our traditional fashions. In my context, it resulted in creating a demand and supply based upon heritage, not just what outsiders deem fashionable, but rather from looking inward and determination by the people themselves based on their own criteria. Some examples may depend solely on our weather or cultural patterns.

In conclusion, fashion needs to be reported on, written about, and created from a people's context, and not just from Western perspectives. It needs to be all-encompassing, while at the same time it must enable, as well as create, ways amongst ourselves to discern creativity, authenticity, quality and even surprise, so that we can develop systems that will help us strengthen our communities and our appreciation of these communities. To reinforce what Achille Mbembe terms the notion of 'pluriversity',[15] this campaign is about including others and acknowledging, understanding and respecting their ways of being. Through these decolonization efforts, other styles of expression can be allowed to thrive on their own, for the benefit of many people, and to honour ancestral efforts. Let us not be 'mwacha mila ni mtumwa' – the ones who throw away their cultures. Let us instead #OwnOurCulture.

Notes

1. This is common knowledge in Kenyan society. Students are taught in history class that traditional jewellery is believed to have been tied to heathenism and thus the missionaries saw it fit to discard all aspects of it. It is also common knowledge among the older generations of Kenyan society, so much so that there is even a name and classification of traditional jewellery.

2. I would like to express gratitude to the various authors whose books have influenced my work, including Joy Adamson's *The Peoples of Kenya*; Mohammed Amin, Duncan Willets and Brian Tetley's *The Beautiful People of Kenya*; Hassan Arero and Zachary Kingdon's *East African Contours Reviewing Creativity and Visual Culture*; Arthur Danto, R. M Gramly, Mary Lou Hutgren, Enid Schildkrout, and Jeanne Zedler's *Art/Artifact: African Art in Anthropology Collections*; Alan Donovan's *My Journey through African Heritage*; Angela Fisher and Carol Beckwith's *Painted Bodies: African Body Painting, Tattoos & Scarification*; and *Faces of Africa*; Holy Ladislav's *The Art of Africa: Masks and Figurines from East and Southern Africa*; Ewel Mafred and Anne Outwater's *From Ritual to Modern Art, Tradition and Modernity in African Sculpture*; Nakamura, Kyoko's *Adornments of the Samburu in Northern Kenya*; Nigel Pavitt's *Kenya: A Country in the Making 1880–1940*; Ngugi wa Thiong'o's *Decolonizing the Mind*; and Kenji Yoshida and John Mack's *Preserving the Cultural Heritage of Africa*.

3. I studied at the University of Nairobi, Bachelor of Arts, Media Studies, graduating in the class of 2013.

4. I primarily work with artisans who specialize in traditional jewellery; I do this by training them on techniques as well as discussing with them the best design methods for the jewellery. I also run the #OwnYourCulture online platform, promoting traditional jewellery as a decolonizing fashion activist. The subject of identity has been close to me given the different names of tribes I have as well as my lack of understanding of my English name, coupled with studying and living alongside Ethiopian, Somali and Indian children who seemed so rooted in their identity and their culture. They always had names representative of their respective towns of origin, while my names seemed to cause confusion in school. So, this got me curious from an early age as to where people and names come from, and especially why I could never comprehend my own English name.

5. I would like to express deep gratitude to the following photographers, whose work was instrumental: Jeri Muchura, Abdalla Hassan Agil, John Ogweno and Perpetua Adoyo. I would also like to thank the Kurlly Diaries Facebook members for their consistent support and contributions from the early days. I would also like to thank Yvette Mumanyi, Winnie Awuor Awino, Nicole Muchai and Phonsina Archane for their time, participation, audience and blogger contribution. I would also like to thank stylist Lucy Robi for her constant support and encouragement, I would also like to thank Leanne Tlhagoane for highlighting and sharing the importance of the work, I want to thank Justine Mbugua and Muthoni Ndonga for giving #OwnYourCulture a platform offline, I would also like to thank my team of bead-workers headed by Salome Seremon Mure and most importantly I would like to thank the #OwnYourCulture community for their passionate participation and contribution.

6. Kenyan men and women do also sport casual wear such as jeans and t-shirts. This everyday clothing also shows a preference for European fashion.

7. A semi-nomadic pastoralist Nilotic group, from North Central Kenya. They still keep their traditional culture and can always be found styled in their colourful jewellery and red body paint.

8. The Pokot are a subtribe of the Kalenjin-highland Nilotes, living in the West Pokot and Baringo counties in Kenya. They still carry out their traditional way of living as pastoralists and adorn themselves with traditional hairstyles and jewellery.

9. Marakwet are another subtribe of the Kalenjin, living in Elgeyo-Marakwet county. They are still using traditional jewellery for ceremonies.

10. Ngugi wa Thiong'o, *Decolonizing the Mind* (London: James Currey, 1986) 18.

11. Robert M. Maxon, 'Social & Cultural Changes'. In B. A Ogot and W. R Ochieng, Eds. *Decolonization & Independence in Kenya* (London: James Currey; Athens: Ohio University Press, 1995), 142.

12. A Nilotic ethnic group from Western Kenya.

13. ArtMattersInfo, 'Kenya's Quest for Elusive National Dress Continues' (2008), https://artmatters.info/2008/09/futility-of-kenyas-quest-for-national-dress/ (accessed 12 July 2019).

14. Walter Mignolo and Rolando Vasquez, 'Decolonial AestheSis: Colonial Wounds/Decolonial Healings'. *Decolonial Aesthesis*, July 15, 2013, https://socialtextjournal.org/periscope_article/decolonial-aesthesis-colonial-woundsdecolonial-healings/ (accessed 9 May 2020).

15. Achille Mbembe, 'Decolonizing Knowledge and the Question of the Archive' (unpublished public lecture) (Wits Institute for Social and Economic Research, 2018), https://wiser.wits.ac.za/system/files/Achille%20Mbembe%20-%20Decolonizing%20Knowledge%20and%20the%20Question%20of%20the%20Archive.pdf (accessed 12 July 2019).

CHAPTER 7
KAWAII FASHION DISCOURSE IN THE 21ST CENTURY: TRANSNATIONALIZING ACTORS
KOMA Kyoko

Introduction

Kawaii or 'kawai' is a French loanword that means an aesthetic of Japanese origin evoking the world of childhood, of which an example is kawaii fashion, according to the French dictionary *Le Petit Robert* (2018). The key characteristics of kawaii fashion, such as pastel colours and imaginary characters, could be considered marginal Japanese fashion in French contexts. This chapter interrogates the direct or indirect tactics of *transnationalizing* – rather than globalizing – Japanese kawaii (cute or immature) style as a non-Western fashion that is considered to be 'different' from modern Eurocentric social norms.

Kōichi Iwabuchi explained, 'the intricacy and disjunctiveness of emerging intra-Asian popular cultural flows under globalizing forces are better expressed by the term *transnational* as opposed to *international* or *global*.'[1] His concept follows the idea put forward by Ulf Hannerz, an anthropologist who defined 'transnational' in his book, titled *Transnational Connections: Culture People Places*.[2]

In this chapter, I explore the different ways of diffusion through which this fashion phenomenon was constructed and disseminated by the discourses of several actors as an example of transnationalization in France. These diffusion processes include the direct discourses of wearers themselves in social networking services to construct niche fashions outside of the mass media; the direct discourses of the Japanese government in hope of exploiting the popularity of kawaii fashion already spontaneously circulating especially among French youths; the indirect discourses of mass media and publications; and the indirect discourses of some fashion brands that constructed and distributed, or 'appropriated', 'localized', and (re)globalized the kawaii style, as reported in the mass media.

According to the 7th edition of *Kojien* (2018), the dictionary of Japanese language, かわいい (pronounced kawaii in Japanese) means 'pitiful, poor; must love, feel deep affection; small and beautiful'. According to the *Nihon Kokugo Dai Jiten* (Japanese Language Grand Dictionary), already in use since the second half of the Middle Ages, the term means feelings of compassion towards women, children, or any weaklings, in comparison to 'think tenderly of . . .', かわいい, which is the feeling an elder/superior holds for his/her junior/inferior (Nihon Kokugo Dai Jiten in Japan Knowledge Lib.com[3]).

Nada Inada, a Japanese psychoanalyst, explained in his paper, published in 『思想』 (*Thought*, in English), that kawaii is 'a point of view on children, from kawaii existence to [a] beautiful one' as follows:

When one describes another as *kawaii*, they do not have an equal human
relationship; they have a strict pecking order.[4]

In the 1970s, the term kawaii started to be popularized by Japanese young women,
designating a type of behaviour, style of life, and feeling. Kawaii contents and products
seemed directly related to shōjō culture: since the middle of the 1970s in Japan, shōjō
started to be used as 'a variant form of a girl's character' – that is, a rounded handwriting
exclusively considered to be used by teenagers, because it is kawaii, according to Kazuma
Yamane in *Study on A Variant Form of a Girl's Character*.[5] The term kawaii started to be
used as a 'second order' cultural notion (whereas the 'first order' is for something to be
beautiful) under the initiative of Japanese women and girls, who use it to describe a
feeling, behaviour, lifestyle, or anything in Japan.[6] The shōjō culture started to become a
popular market in Japan in the 1970s,[7] which is considered as one of kawaii, comprising
shōjō, manga, fashion, idols, and fancy goods, such as Hello Kitty and dress-up dolls.[8] At
the same time, Otsuka discusses that the term kawaii tends to be 'something to be
graduated from, not only for shōjō, but also for the Japanese in general who do not
become mature in the modern age.[9]

Sharon Kinsella, a Japanologist studying this Japanese subculture from the United
Kingdom, presented in her paper, 'Cuties in Japan', that 'cute clothes were and are delicately
designed to make the wearer appear childlike and demure ...'.[10] In Japan, kawaii is
considered as an important keyword constructing an embedded Japanese normative
femininity since 1970 with changing significations designated by the term over time.[11]
Kawaii continues to be used in designating fashion or models in Japanese women's
fashion magazines, such as *an an*, the Japanese women's prototypical fashion journal,
launched in 1971, as the first foreign sister magazine of *Elle France*. The images of kawaii
as presented by the magazine *an an* can be seen as an example of how kawaii has been
used to represent an ideal image of Japanese women within Japan. The meanings of
kawaii used in *an an*'s feature pages have continued to be adapted to adhere to new
meanings of cool, natural, and even mature styles over time .[12]

Kawaii Fashion Transnationalizing in France

How did kawaii fashion 'arrive and thrive' in France? What can a close investigation of the
relationship between a Japanese aesthetic and a French fashion system tell us about the
ways in which fashion forms develop and 'change over' to social networking platforms
after their full-scale escalation since the middle of the 2010s? Fashion styles considered to
be kawaii outside of Japan – which have not corresponded to kawaii fashion developed in
the Japanese context, such as Harajuku street fashion or some Lolita fashions – have been
spontaneously accepted outside of Japan since around 2006. This is when a number of
new actors, such as fashion designers and the Japanese government, brought this Japanese
fashion into contemporary popular culture worldwide. It is important to note that this
marginal kawaii fashion style, which was firstly diffused amongst French wearers (who
used the internet to collect information on kawaii fashion and to create their own style

communities), does not correspond to a singular construction of a Japanese normative femininity, but rather to specific Japanese street fashions that started in the 1990s.

French television network Nolife disseminated Japanese pop culture in France from 2007 to 2018. Nolife's Japanese business manager Suzuka Asaoka explained that, from 2006 to 2007 when the Japanese girls' cartoon *Nana* was distributed, and the Harajuku Girls Collection was held at the Japan Expo (organized by Japanese Anime fans starting in the 1980s), the concept and aesthetics of Japanese Anime had begun to be diffused on French television, and Japanese popular and kawaii culture started to gain recognition.[13] In 2006, *Imidas* (a Japanese magazine which treats neologisms as indispensable to modern society for expressing several social conditions or manners and customs) defined kawaii as a 'state of popular culture exclusive to Japan, which is imported and firmly established abroad, focusing in particular on anime and manga'.[14] In 2006 the Japan Expo – organized as a French Japanese pop culture festival – was restarted after a one-year break. This coincided with a number of visitor shows, whilst Japanese pop culture, including the kawaii fashion craze, boomed.

I focus on the four main 'actors' that I consider to have played a major part in the transnationalizing of kawaii fashion since 2006. These are firstly the wearers who used the internet or who participated in the Japan Expo; secondly the Japanese government; thirdly the French fashion media; and lastly, fashion designers who presented their collections in France and London. I examine what each act of 'wearing' signifies, and whether these acts can be considered as 'appropriation', 'imitation', 'inspiration', 'theft', or 'articulation'.[15] To approach the globalization or transnationalization of kawaii fashion in this chapter, the significant representation constructed through fashion discourses and its transnationalization needs to be explored carefully.

Discourse on Constructing and Transmitting Fashion as Representation in Transnational Ages

This study investigates why we should analyse the discourse on fashion instead of real fashion, and is focused on how kawaii clothes became kawaii fashion, as constructed by fashion discourses in the media. Roland Barthes argued in his famous work *Système de la mode* that 'with parole, clothes becomes fashion', and that 'words and images are central to the production, circulation and dissemination of fashion'.[16] In addition, Barthes argued that 'the image freezes an endless number of possibilities, [while] words determine a single certainty ... What language adds to the image is knowledge'.[17]

Dominique Maingueneau, a French analyst of discourse, defines discourse as a trace of an act of communication that is socio-historically determined, based on the ideas of Michel Foucault.[18] Maingueneau adds that discourses legitimise the frame in terms of 'what is the knowledge, [and what is] the literature'.[19] In this study, kawaii fashion is understood, therefore, as a representation constructed through the discourses of three key actors (the wearers, the French fashion media, and the Japanese government) that were conditioned (by various forms of power) within a given moment (the early 21st century) across different societies (France and Japan).

Barthes analysed fashion discourse in the mid-1950s and 1960s, when Parisian haute couture dominated, and when fashion discourses were constructed within fashion journals that transmitted them globally. Nowadays, with the development of information technologies such as the internet and social networking services, non-Western fashion, including subcultures such as kawaii fashion, can be transmitted to other countries, even if the Western mass media do not treat them as important. In other words, the power of gatekeepers, noted by Barthes in the 1950s and 1960s, has been interrupted by new forms of distributed technologies. Non-Western kawaii fashion can therefore be examined through the theoretical premises of, among others, global versus transnational, dominant actors versus several actors, and strategies versus tactics.

The development of communication tools, such as the internet and social networking services, permit people to share information transnationally between individuals and small groups who can freely modify or develop them. It is useful to examine the acculturation and representation of kawaii fashion as formed transnationally in the discourses of several actors in order to understand how it has, on a transborder basis, been created and spread among individuals and groups in other countries. These actors include practitioners of kawaii fashion, the media, wearers, fashion designers, and national institutions. Knowledge of kawaii fashion wearers' practices was attained through the internet, as well as the exposition of Japanese culture and street fashion magazines, and was later appropriated by fashion designers in Paris and London as a 'design source'. Kawaii fashion was then 'auto-appropriated' by the Cool Japan Policy[20] as a 'pure' Japanese cultural artefact, which was re-offered to the world. Kawaii fashion therefore expanded transnationally, not only from the top down,[21] but also from the bottom up through several actors.

It is important to consider how all these actors relate to the development of kawaii fashion. Following Hannerz's discussion, Iwabuchi has argued that when non-European, especially Asian, cultural information and artefacts go beyond borders, in this 'transnational arena, the actors may now be individuals, groups, movements, business enterprises, and in no small part, it is this diversity of organization that we need to consider'.[22] This notion of several actors is related to Bruno Latour's Actor Network Theory that Joanne Entwistle uses to support her discussion of fashion as a set of overlapping markets that brings many different actors – human and non-human – into play in order to sell particular sorts of goods, labelled 'fashion' or 'fashionable'.[23]

1. First Actor: Kawaii Fashion Wearers

In response to the kawaii fashion trend, two groups wearing kawaii fashion in France were the Rainbow Team and L'Association Rouge Dentelle & Rose Ruban, who organized online forums to promote interaction between wearers starting in 2008 and 2009, respectively. Rainbow Team was organized by French wearers of kawaii fashion, inspired by Harajuku street fashion and FRUiTS style magazine led by Shoichi Aoki.[24] Aoki was the publisher and photographer of street fashion in Japan, who since 1997 has presented the freshness of Japanese street fashion in his magazine FRUiTS.[25] In his book, FRUiTS, Aoki describes his subjects as fresh and colourful, and often refers to the wild and quirky street style of Tokyo.[26] These fashion styles presented in *FRUiTS* have been hailed as kawaii[27], and became the main source of inspiration for Rainbow Team.[28] L'Association Rouge Dentelle & Rose Ruban, on the other hand, was organized by French Lolita fashion wearers. These wearers were mainly inspired by Lolita fashion aesthetics, which are characterized by frilly dresses, knee socks, and bonnets.[29]

The online forums of these two French groups were organized to show the organizations' fashion and information, as well as to communicate among wearer-members of each online forum. At the same time, Japanese popular cultural festivals in France, such as the Japan Expo, served as these groups' 'community place' where wearers could wear the clothes they want. Wearers published their kawaii fashion and activities on the internet (see Figure 7.1).

Participants in the Japan Expo 2013 in France were asked by e-mail 'what is kawaii style for you?' Their answers were varied, and included: kawaii is, among other things,

Figure 7.1 Hika, wearer of kawaii since 2006 in the Rainbow Team, and later in the Street Japan Style team, Paris.

Figure 7.2 Street Japan Style, a community of French wearers of kawaii established by Lutin Harajuku, createur of kawaii fashion style 'Mad & Kawaii' that organized Harajuku Fashion Walk in Paris. Photograph courtesy of Street Japan Style, Liliana Costa.

pastel colour design for children. According to some French Lolita fashion wearers it would be 'strange' or 'non-daily' to wear childish clothes in France. Some Lolita-style wearers do not consider their own style as kawaii[30], as some sub-genres of Lolita are not fundamentally built around a kawaii image, but a more classical and elegant image. On the other hand, 11 of the 19 French Lolita wearers I interviewed answered that Lolita is a mix of European and Japanese styles, seven said it is European, and one thought wearing kawaii style allowed them to be closer to Japanese culture.[31] Could their activities – such as wearing kawaii fashion, particularly Lolita fashion, considered by its wearers as fashion of European origin, that is, as fashion created through the result of appropriation of fashion of European origin by Japanese wearers – be considered as a kind of re-appropriation of this Lolita fashion, through which Western dress was appropriated by Japanese wearers? Kawaii fashion was inspired by the occidental fashion style, diffused among a segment of the youth, and re-acculturated by several French actors such as fans/wearers, and the designer's creative act of kawaii-inspired style could be considered admiration or cultural appropriation of kawaii fashion (see Figure 7.2).

2. Kawaii/Kawai: Definition of Kawaii Fashion by Wearers Redefined in the French Mass Media and Books

French mass media and publications started to define what *kawaii* fashion was in the noughties. In the *Dictionnaire du look* published in France in 2009, the kawaii style was defined as Harajuku street fashion: 'the kawaii world [designated by] the fans of Japanese culture. Rocked by manga, [it] is the world of the child, [it is] terribly cute [and] full of stars, pandas, babies and fireflies'.[32]

An article concerning the kawaii style was published in *Glamour France* in April 2010; it had a caption reading 'KAWAII! From the first ray of sunlight, we adopt the preppy look of Japanese women'. Three years later, an *Elle* online article titled 'Manga Girl', which was released in April 2014, described Western luxury and the first fashion brands, such as Marc by Marc Jacobs, Balenciaga par Nicolas Ghesquière, Fendi, Prada, Chanel, Mango, H&M, and Esprit, as 'colourful and humoristic street fashion, that is kawaii'.[33]

Could it be said that the kawaii fashion character in question was not presented as the French standard, but rather French fashion magazines and books considered it as an 'ethnically fashionable' style[34] that is immature, childish, and has a touch of manga style? It started to be considered in Japan in 2006 that the boom of kawaii in the 2000s reflected an admiration for kawaii across the globe, particularly in France.[35] The kawaii that has been acculturated in France tends to be defined as Japanese proper and seen as the traditional aesthetics of Japanese society in the Japanese context: this is promoted by the Japanese government's 'Cool Japan' strategy, through their support for promotional events such as Japan Expo, Tokyo Crazy Kawaii, and financial support for Japanese companies aiming to expand overseas.

3. Auto-Appropriation or Re-Acculturation? Kawaii Fashion Reconstituted and Re-Distributed Abroad by the Japanese Government

The kawaii style that was acculturated in France led to a re-acculturation or redefinition as 'Japanese proper' and as traditional aesthetics in Japanese society through the governmental 'Cool Japan' strategy. After the spontaneous boom of kawaii style by French wearers and organizers of the Japan Expo, how did Japanese public diplomats or public institutions promote their own kawaii fashion, not as kawaii fashion acculturated by French wearers, but as Japanese proper fashion created by Japanese?

First, in 2009, the Japanese Ministry of Foreign Affairs (MOFA)[36] appointed three kawaii ambassadors who would wear Japanese fashion that is considered kawaii abroad for one year. As an example, Misako Aoki, then kawaii ambassador for Lolita fashion, visited more than 45 cities in 25 countries.[37] Following this initiative, in 2013, the first Japanese pop cultural festival, titled 'Tokyo Crazy Kawaii Paris' was organized by Japanese industries and held in Paris[38] (see Figure 7.3). This festival was supported by the Subsidy of Japan Contents Localization and Promotion Support (J-LOP), under the 'Cool Japan' strategy, and focused on presenting kawaii fashion as both Harajuku street fashion and Lolita fashion. The mission of 'Tokyo Crazy Kawaii', was to promote the beauty of the Japanese language and Japan's creativity to the world and to help local French people accept 'kawaii culture' as a part of their lifestyle and not as a one-time trend. Within this mission, stress was put on the fact that kawaii was something that originated in Japan, and therefore Tokyo Crazy Kawaii could offer a unique Japanese experience to the French people participating in the event.[39]

Figure 7.3 Report of Ministry of Economy, Trade and Industry of Japan showing support for the event Tokyo Crazy Kawaii Paris, www.kantei.go.jp/jp/singi/titeki2/tyousakai/kensho_hyoka_kikaku/dai5/siryou6.pdf (accessed on 21 June 2020).

Regarding the location of the first event, the Tokyo Crazy Kawaii Committee chose Paris. According to its official webpage:

France is a country that receives the highest number of visitors in the world, and people in France have the highest standard of fashion and beauty. They like Tatami and Bonsai, which have been considered as one of Japanese traditional culture, even though they may not be familiar with Japan's anime and manga, which could be considered as a second notion of beauty. The Tokyo Crazy Kawaii is an event to experience 'authentic' Japan, enabling the world to see Japan.[40]

This 'authentic' Japan could be said to have been constructed through auto-appropriation of kawaii appropriated/constructed in France by the Japanese government. Moreover, the Ministry of Foreign Affairs of Japan published a magazine named *Nipponica* from September 2013 onwards to further promote Japanese (i.e. kawaii) culture overseas. Through these national efforts, kawaii fashion, which had been treated as a marginal fashion style, started to gradually be constructed and disseminated by Japanese media as 'kawaii Japan'.[41] From 2011, when the Cool Japan office of the Ministry of Economy, Trade and Industry (METI) was established, kawaii was even used on public diplomatic occasions such as the above-mentioned Tokyo Crazy Kawaii. The intention of Crazy

Kawaii in Paris was to allow the Japanese to demonstrate that kawaii culture, as recognized in France at the Japan Expo (which was organized by French people) should be redefined for French fans/visitors as Japanese proper culture by the Japanese. It is however, not clear to what degree the Crazy Kawaii campaign succeeded, as after one year the event was suspended.

However, from 2014 onward, the attitude of the METI towards kawaii changed suddenly. The ministry started to declare kawaii as a short-lived culture, and ceased its active promotion in favour of the promotion of other aspects of more 'traditional' Japanese culture such as performing arts and craftwork.[42] The promotion of kawaii culture using explicit kawaii discourse by the Japanese Government overseas can therefore be called short-lived. After 2014, the promotion of kawaii became more indirect and discreet, through the above-mentioned promotion of other aspects of Japanese culture.

4. Appropriation vs Inspiration, or Strategy vs Tactics? Representation of Kawaii by the French, Japanese and London's Fashion Designers

The act of appropriation is often conditioned by some form of power, such as 'industrial', 'ideological', 'economic', 'political', or 'institutional'[43], which could be criteria for judging whether an activity is deemed appropriation or inspiration. Ziff and Rao show that 'cultural transmission can be seen as an appropriative practice – a process whereby dominant groups may be criticized and challenged when they borrow [with diverse powers] the cultural forms associated with subordinate groups'.[44]

However, in this research the act of appropriation is considered as a positive action, expressed through the following three situations. In each case, appropriation is not considered as a one way domination of one group over the other, but as a collaborative act between groups.

Firstly, Michel De Certeau's definition of strategy, which he used in his work *L'invention du quotidien, Tome 1: Arts de faire*[45], in which appropriated culture can in turn use its appropriation as a strategy to support a more profound global spread of said culture. Secondly in the case where a certain type of culture is divided as mainstream culture and subculture, mainstream culture can appropriate subculture and through this appropriation legitimise the subculture. Thirdly, an appropriation of other cultures not through ideas of control or power, but as homage to that culture.

This kawaii fashion distributed among wearers through the internet was re-appropriated by fashion designers belonging to the Paris and London fashion worlds, such as these collections: Louis Vuittons Spring/Summer 2016 ready to wear (see Figure 7.4), Comme des Garçons Spring/Summer 2018 ready to wear (see Figure 7.5), Ryan Lo Fall 2017 ready to wear London (see Figure 7.6). The representations of kawaii fashion as created by these three designers have varying interpretations in the captions of their photos on the mobile app Vogue Runway Application. First, the caption for Louis Vuitton was written as 'Nicolas Ghèsquière . . . His reference points were many: Wong Kar Wai's 2046 and the anime series Evangelion came up backstage'.[46]

Figure 7.4 Louis Vuitton: Runway – Paris Fashion Week Womenswear Spring/Summer 2016. Photograph: Pascal Le Segretain/Getty Images.

The style, evoked by manga and anime (specifically, the anime series Evangelion) is considered as a kind of kawaii fashion in France. This type of fashion was constructed by the *Le Monde* journalist Carine Bizet in her article titled 'Paris supports stylists', dated 8 October 2015.[47] 'As the first model . . . [is] a beautiful Asian with red hair . . ., this gang of punk and 'kawaii' dolls have a saintly look'. What is remarkable, however, is that the same journalist called Harajuku Fashion Japoniaiserie (niaiserie means stupidity in French) instead of Japonaiserie in the article of *Le Monde* dated 17 January 2014, about half a year earlier.[48] Therefore, kawaii style could be considered as a kind of appropriation of Japanese street fashion by the Fashion luxury company Louis Vuitton for French luxury clients.

By contrast, the caption on the Vogue Runway Application for Comme des Garçons was: 'Hello Kitty and plastic kiddy novelties were piled up as neck-pieces and embedded in space princess wigs. The face and blonde tresses of a blue-eyed manga princess adorned a floor length coat'. 'The Kawakubo angel – a timelessly chic fashion goddess in her imposing white tweed suit – stood out as the singular persona manifested at the centre of a colourful, surreal, cartoonish, kawaii toy and computer game-referencing parade'.[49] Even ten years after the kawaii boom among French wearers and seven years after the Cool Japan strategy, the referencing of kawaii by fashion brand Comme des Garçons, a Japanese brand itself, can be considered as auto-appropriation. As a result of this auto-appropriation of kawaii, works by designers and brands such as Comme des Garcons, kawaii's popularity was expanded beyond the appeal of streetwear and subcultural fashioning.

Figure 7.5 Comme des Garçons, during the women's 2018 Spring/Summer ready to wear collection fashion show in Paris. BERTRAND GUAY/AFP via Getty Images.

Figure 7.6 Ryan LO, Backstage at London Fashion Week, February 2017. Photograph: Tristan Fewings/Getty Images.

Moreover, the caption on the Vogue Runway Application for Ryan Lo,[50] a designer from Hong Kong presenting his ready to wear collection in London, was: 'the designer's key reference this season was recently defunct Japanese style magazine *FRUiTS*, a publication that can claim a good deal of the credit for the international fame of the cute as pie, uber consuming Harajuku girl'.[51] This designer could be motivated not by the (un)conscious domination included in the act of appropriation but by the inspiration evoked through the homage of/respect for the magazine *FRUiTS*, which ceased publication in Japan.

Although these three designers adapt kawaii fashion as a design source, the discourse of *Elle* on Chanel,[52] takes the kawaii fashion source as 'big eyes for a manga doll effect', 'ultra-coloured evoked the kawaii icon', which *Elle* tended to connect with K-Pop. This could be an appropriation. Therefore, each fashion designer adopted their kawaii design source but in a different way.

As mentioned above and noted in this research, we reconfirm that the act of appropriation is considered as an act of collaboration between different groups. Considering the abovementioned cases of Louis Vuitton and Chanel, big luxury brands from France have created a new fashion style inspired by kawaii fashion as appropriative action. By doing so, this appropriation gave way to a further global spread of kawaii fashion that surpassed the limited circle of fans. This appropriation can therefore be considered a *strategy*, following Michel De Certeau's definition.[53] 'Legitimised' kawaii fashion could indirectly and tactically be distributed globally using the strategic power and the media of the Western fashion world.

In the case of Comme des Garçons and Ryan Lo, these brands appropriated kawaii to create each of their fashion styles. They are not European brands, but the designers were able to present their collections in Europe in cities such as Paris or London. Comme des Garçons auto-appropriated the kawaii marginal style, and Ryan Lo developed his collection as an homage to *FRUiTS* magazine, not as an intention to steal kawaii fashion culture.

Conclusion

Kawaii fashion can be constructed and transmitted through several actors, such as wearers, the mass media, the Japanese government, and fashion designers in a transnational communication space. Nowadays, as digital media has developed and multiple actors can spread information by themselves, Japanese fashion culture can be 'found' in digital transnational communication spaces by others who do not share the language and culture of Japan.

As I mentioned above, each act of constructing kawaii by the four actors examined, namely wearers/internet users, the media, the Japanese government, and fashion designers, can be considered as admiration, appropriation, auto-appropriation, or inspiration. Different from globalized Western fashion transmitted mainly through mass media, non-Western trends, such as kawaii fashion, can be considered transnationalized fashion in digital society. These trends are constructed by different actors from different backgrounds with different types of power, and can therefore change and develop in various directions through different forms of appropriation.

Thanks to the development of digital media, former 'unknown' non-Western fashion styles can spread more easily through different actors, each taking on a new interpretation and stimulating others to take part in the appropriation process. Through this research project, I propose that the current rather negative interpretation of appropriation can perhaps develop into new, different and more positive definitions, focusing on ideas of strategic distribution, support and collaboration in the future.

Notes

1. Iwabuchi Koichi, 'Taking 'Japanization' Seriously: Cultural Globalization Reconsidered'. In *Recentering Globalization: Popular Culture and Japanese Transnationalism* (Duke University Press Books, 2002) 16.

2. Ulf Hannerz, *Transnational Connections: Culture People Places* (Routledge, 1996).

3. https://japanknowledge.com/lib/display/?lid=200200f2c1f00Pp7nf8d (accessed 17 May 2020).

4. Nada Inada (なだいなだ), 'Aru kodomokan – Kawaii sonzai kara utsukushii sonzai he', 「あるこども観-カワイイ存在から美しい存在へ」 *Shisō* 『思想』 (1969) 1073, 1080.

5. Yamane Kazuma (山根一眞), *Shōjo hentai moji no kenkyū* 『少女変体文字の研究』 (Kōdansha, 1986).

6. Shuichi Masubuchi, *Kawaii Syndrome* (NHK publishing, 1994) 18–19.

7. Eiji Otsuka argued that kawaii culture could be Shōjo Bunka, which began to thrive in the 1970s Japan, and this is when shōjo played a central role in the society of consumption. Eiji Otsuka (大塚英志), *Shōjo Minzokugaku* 『少女民族学』 (Kobunsha 1989) 47–68.

8. Ibid., 48–49.

9. Ibid., 249.

10. Sharon Kinsella, 'Cuties in Japan'. In Brian Moeran and Lise Skov, Eds. *Women, Media and Consumption in Japan* (Abingdon: Routledge, 1998) 220–254.

11. For more information concerning the change in meaning of the term kawaii over time see Tanaka Hiromi and Koma Kyoko (田中洋美と高馬京子), 'Gendai Nihon no media ni okeru gendā hyōshō – Joseishi "an・an" ni okeru joseizō no hensen', 「現代日本のメディアにおけるジェンダー表象 ― 女性誌『an・an』における女性像の変遷」 *Meiji Daigaku jinbunkagaku kenkyūjo kiyō* 『明治大学人文科学研究所紀要』87 (2020) 1–46.

12. Ibid.

13. Interview by author on January 21, 2011.

14. *Imidas,* Shueisha, 2006.

15. Denise Nicole Green and Susan B. Kaiser, 'Fashion and Appropriation', *Fashion, Style & Popular Culture*, 4(4) (March 2017) 148.

16. Roland Barthes, *The Fashion System* (Berkeley: University of California Press, 1990).

17. Ibid., 13, 14, 17.

18. Dominique Maingueneau, *Analyser des textes de communication* (Armand Colin, 2016).

19. Ibid.

20. According to the Cabinet Office of Japan, 'Cool Japan' includes contemporary Japanese culture and products such as animations, manga, characters, and games. Japanese traditional cuisines and commodities in which people discover new values are also 'Cool Japan', as are Japanese high-tech robots and cutting-edge green technologies. www.cao.go.jp/cool_japan/english/pdf/cooljapan_%20initiative.pdf (accessed 14 May 2020).

21. Peter McNeil explains Simmel's trickle-down theory as follows: 'everyone was breeding increasingly more sophisticated and different strains of roses, the people sensed that breeding roses was only of secondary relevance to their lives and no longer a sign of success. This is a classic example of what has come to be called, for the topic of fashion, the trickle-down theory'. Agnès Rocamora and Anneke Smelik, Eds. *Thinking through Fashion* (London, New York: I.B.Tauris, 2016) 69.

22. Iwabuchi Koichi, 'Taking 'Japanization' Seriously: Cultural Globalization Reconsidered'. In *Recentering Globalization: Popular Culture and Japanese Transnationalism* (Duke University Press Books, 2002) 16.

23. Joanne Entwistle, *The Fashioned Body: Fashion, Dress and Social Theory* (Cambridge: Polity Press 2016: Kindle version) 5635.

24. www.instagram.com/fruitsmag/?hl=ja (accessed 21 June 2020).

25. Aoki Shoichi, *Fruits* (Phaidon, 2001).

26. www.bbc.com/culture/article/20170920-the-outrageous-street-style-tribes-of-harajuku?referr=https%3A%2F%2Fwww.google.com%2F (accessed 14 May 2020).

27. Koma Kyoko, 'Kawaii as Represented by Wearers in France Using the Example of Lolita Fashion'. In Koma Kyoko, Ed. *Representation of Japanese Popular Culture in Europe* (Vytautas Magnus University, 2013) 67–82.

28. Among these eclectic street styles presented in *FRUiTS*, we can also find decora (lolita) style, and other lolita related styles. *FRUiTS*' style was therefore broader than only classical Lolita style.

29. https://ejje.weblio.jp/content/Lolita+fashion (accessed on 14 May 2020).

30. Koma Kyoko, 'Kawaii as Represented by Wearers in France Using the Example of Lolita Fashion'. In Koma Kyoko, Ed. *Representation of Japanese Popular Culture in Europe* (Vytautas Magnus University, 2013) 67–82.

31. Ibid.

32. Original text: 'Fan de culture japonaise, le monde kawaii. Bercé par les mangas, est celui de l'enfance: Rempli d'étoile, de bébés pandas et lucioles trop mignonnes'. De Géraldine de Margerie, *Dictionnaire du look* (Poche, 2011) 131.

33. www.elle.fr/Mode/Dossiers-mode/Manga-Girl (accessed 21 June 2020).

34. Margaret Maynard, *Dress and Communication* (Manchester University Press, 2004).

35. "Kawaii' sekai ni kaze Nihon ga utahime no kokoro wo toraeta', 「「カワイイ」世界に風 日本が歌姫の心をとらえた」 *Asahi Shimbun*, January 1, 2006.

36. www.mofa.go.jp/announce/event/2009/2/1188515_1152.html (accessed 16 September 2019).

37. https://lineblog.me/aokimisako/ (accessed 20 February 2020).

38. www.crazykawaii.com/en/ (accessed 10 September 2013); https://prtimes.jp/main/html/ rd/p/000000001.000007447.html (accessed 16 September 2019).

39. www.crazykawaii.com/en/ (accessed 10 September 2013); https://prtimes.jp/main/html/ rd/p/000000001.000007447.html (accessed 16 September 2019).

40. www.crazykawaii.com/en/ (accessed 10 September 2013); https://prtimes.jp/main/html/ rd/p/000000001.000007447.html (accessed 16 September 2019).

41. 'Sekai ga gyōten Kawaii Japan', 「世界が仰天 [KAWAII★JAPAN], May 9, 2012, 16–56.

42. www.kantei.go.jp/jp/singi/titeki2/cool_japan/pdf/mission_sengen.pdf (accessed 1 May 2016).

43. Bruce Ziff and Pratima V. Rao, Eds. *Borrowed Power: Essays on Cultural Appropriation* (New Brunswick, N.J.: Rutgers University Press, 1997) 7.

44. ibid.

45. Michel De Certeau, *L'invention du quotidien, Tome 1: Arts de faire* (Paris: Union générale d'éditions, 1980).

46. This collection also was treated in *Vogue.com* online. www.vogue.com/fashion-shows/ spring-2016-ready-to-wear/louis-vuitton (accessed 21 June 2020).

47. www.lemonde.fr/fashion-week/article/2015/10/08/paris-soutient-les- stylistes_4785444_1824875.html (accessed 21 June 2020).

48. www.lemonde.fr/mode/article/2014/01/17/les-japoniaiseries_4348998_1383317.html (accessed 21 June 2020).

49. This collection also was treated in *Vogue.com* online. www.vogue.com/fashion-shows/ spring-2018-ready-to-wear/comme-des-garcons/slideshow/collection#15 (accessed 21 June 2020).

50. This collection also was treated in *Vogue.com* online. www.vogue.com/fashion-shows/ fall-2017-ready-to-wear/ryan-lo (accessed 21 June 21 2020).

51. Uber was used during this period in countries such as France and Belgium among young people to state a superlative. The meaning is equivalent to "ultra".

52. Elle, 'On adore le look K-Pop du défilé croisière Chanel de Séoul', https://www.elle.fr/Beaute/ News-beaute/Make-up/On-adore-le-look-K-Pop-du-defile-croisiere-Chanel-de- Seoul-2948226 (accessed 5 January 2020).

53. Michel De Certeau, *L'invention du quotidien, Tome 1: Arts de faire* (Paris: Union générale d'éditions, 1980).

CHAPTER 8
ERASURE, FORGETTING AND THE PRACTICE OF MEMORY: DECOLONIZING FASHION IN AOTEAROA NEW ZEALAND
Harriette RICHARDS

Introduction

... he was tataowed all over the face, with a streak of red paint over his nose and across his cheek ... He had a flaxen garment ornamented with a beautiful wrought border and under it a petticoat made of the sort of cloth which they call Aooree Warow, on his ears hung a bunch of teeth, and an ear ring of Poonamoo, or greenstone ... By his dress, carriage, and the respect paid to him, we supposed him to be a person of distinction among them.

Sydney Parkinson, 1773[1]

In his seminal 1969 book *Traditional Māori Clothing*, anthropologist, historian, and kaumātua (elder) Sidney Hirini Moko Mead uses notes made by European colonialists such as Scottish botanical illustrator and natural history artist Sydney Parkinson, as well as detailed drawings and historical photographs, to recount the technological and functional changes of Māori clothing prior to and following colonization. Thinking through the ways in which the forms and techniques of Māori dress changed over time, the text provides a comprehensive account of this dynamic aspect of Māori culture and illustrates the fact that, despite assumptions to the contrary, Māori had a sense of fashion long before the arrival of colonists such as Parkinson.[2] What is interesting about Mead's text, beyond the many examples it cites, is the way it situates dress and clothing culture as something other than mere costume. While Mead may not use the word 'fashion' in his account, Patricia Te Arapo Wallace's later analysis of his work and the history of Māori garments mobilises the term as an important concept through which to theorise Māori dress cultures in Aotearoa.[3]

Unlike the way Western fashion is often theorized – as that which is preoccupied with the new,[4] that which constantly changes,[5] that which constitutes a commercial industry and a networked global system[6] – Wallace conceives of early Māori fashion as 'an inherent part of human social interaction and a means by which individuals of status and power have displayed their importance'.[7] Fashion, in Wallace's estimation, is not limited to prevailing Western conceptualizations. Rather, it is a universal practice of symbolic representation. She suggests that, in order to recognize the deep significance of Māori clothing cultures, we must move beyond 'an exclusively Western concept of "fashion"'.[8]

However, even thinking beyond limited conceptions of fashion, Wallace's argument becomes entangled with other Western understandings of fashion, for example as a contradictory practice that simultaneously innovates and remains that same[9] and as a definitive system of gendered and classed distinction.[10] The ways fashion has been theorized are many, yet these various understandings have wielded enormous influence over global fashion cultures, especially in the political practice of differentiating between Western 'fashion' and non-Western 'costume'. Identifying the many and complex ways fashion can be understood is not only a key factor in the project of (re)thinking and decolonizing fashion (see Introduction, this volume); it is also fundamental to the process of acknowledging the practices of repudiation that frame fashion, and to analyzing the neglect of Māori dress in accounts of New Zealand fashion history.

In this chapter, I argue that the history of fashion in Aotearoa New Zealand has experienced two distinct moments of erasure and forgetting. First, the colonial project enacted widespread re-imagining of indigenous cultures. The establishment of new social and cultural hierarchies in the colonies meant the sidelining of much indigenous heritage and practice. In Aotearoa New Zealand, this included the colonial disavowal of Māori fashion cultures, whereby 18th and 19th century colonial categorization positioned Māori garments as 'ceremonial dress' or 'costume' rather than fashion. Ongoing practices of colonization in the settler state throughout the 20th and into the 21st centuries have ensured the persistence of this perception, as well as the long-standing omission of Māori garments from narratives of New Zealand fashion history, which has only recently begun to be redressed (thanks to the work of scholars such as Wallace). Second, the triumph of Pākehā (white New Zealander) fashion designers – including Zambesi, WORLD, Karen Walker, Nicholas Blanchet, Kate Sylvester and Nom*d – at Sydney and London Fashion Weeks at the end of the 1990s took the country, and the international fashion community, by surprise. The seemingly unlikely nature of New Zealand's incursion into the global fashion sphere caused media commentators and critics alike to claim that New Zealand fashion had emerged 'from nowhere'[11] out of what had previously been a 'sartorial wasteland'.[12] The dismissal of fashion in New Zealand prior to the late 1990s was demonstrative of the 'ruthless forgetting'[13] with which the concept of Western fashion is bound. In order to unpack how this history of conscious erasure and ruthless forgetting has contributed to New Zealand fashion, I reflect on the relationship between time and memory in fashion, the ways in which these dismissals occurred, and the work of contemporary Māori designers and advocates who are changing understandings of fashion in Aotearoa New Zealand.

Isolated within the South Pacific Ocean and at the periphery of the global economy – a global economy predicated on a problematic dichotomy between the centre and its margins – Aotearoa New Zealand is a marginal place, 'an unsettled state in a sea of islands'.[14] In this settler colonial place, bound by unsettling anxieties,[15] there are multiple liminal spaces between different conceptualizations and understandings of the past. Acknowledging this multiplicity of history is a fundamental aspect of the project to unsettle the colonial present. If we are to counter colonial practices of disavowal and the system of forgetting by which modern – by extension, Western – fashion functions, the dominant narratives of fashion as having arrived on New Zealand shores simultaneously with the arrival of Pākehā, and the stories of an independent New Zealand fashion industry as having emerged either in the 1940s, post WWII,[16] or 'from nowhere' in the late 1990s,[17] then we must tell more complex fashion stories. By drawing attention to the practices of erasure and forgetting that continue to haunt fashion in Aotearoa New Zealand, this chapter positions fashion as a practice of memory, contends with stories that have gone untold, and contributes to the project of decolonizing fashion in the settler colonial context.

Fashion Memory

The relationship of fashion (however theorized) to time and temporality is intricate and complex. Barbara Vinken suggests that fashion's 'most intimate relationship is its relation to time'.[18] Western understandings of fashion argue that it is firmly situated within the present, characterized by the perennial preoccupation with the pursuit of newness and 'nowness'. This pursuit is so complete, Roland Barthes wrote in *The Fashion System*, that fashion 'disavows the past with violence'.[19] Fashion abolishes long-term memory to such a degree that it perpetuates 'an amnesic substitution of the present for the past'.[20] Following Barthes, Karen de Perthuis observes: 'In fashion's metaphysical universe there is no time to grow old. Individual fashions burst on the scene, appearing for all the world as if they expect to live forever, only to be trampled underfoot by fashion's mania for novelty'.[21] The ambivalence of fashion towards the past is evidence of the spirit of modernity with which Western fashion is intricately woven. This system of forgetting, through which the system of fashion functions, corresponds with the capitalist mode of production. For Friedrich Nietzsche, 'ruthless forgetting' encapsulates the essence of modernity.[22] The very act of forgetting is an act of modernity. It is not an unconscious forgetting but, rather, a conscious act, in which memory is deliberately obliterated.

Despite the strength of this avowed pursuit, this line of argument continues, fashion signifies more than just the present. It also frequently references a lost past through the aesthetic modes of a time that has long since been and gone. That Western fashion encapsulates both the present and the past simultaneously was recognized by Walter Benjamin, who famously wrote that fashion is ultimately determined by the *tigersprung*, the tiger's leap into 'the thickets of long ago'.[23] Fashion is inherently haunted by the very same past that it so vociferously denies. As de Perthuis argues, the recurrent nature of fashion, the fact that fashion continues despite its erasure of its own past, has the capacity to 'bestow the value of longevity on fashion that its notorious capriciousness otherwise denies'.[24] Western fashion thus has an ambivalent relationship to time: time past is lost, but not mourned; time now is haunted, but blithely. Regardless of the constant recurrence of fashion and the lasting quality of material garments themselves, the concept of ruthless forgetting in contemporary Western fashion prevails. The capitalist system within which fashion functions ensures that a cycle of erasure and refashioning continues to dominate.

What is so interesting about this capitalist forgetting is that it mirrors – somewhat distortedly, and far less violently – the processes of erasure and re-writing that accompany the settler colonial project. Practices of repudiation and denial are central to the colonial past, and remain so within the settler colonial present. From stories of place in Hawai'i[25] and Southeast Kansas,[26] to understandings of indigenous Australian agriculture[27] and the history of civil conflict in Aotearoa New Zealand, settler colonialism has been shaped by the 'art of forgetting'.[28] Erasing indigenous histories, cultures and practices through dispossession and dismissal, colonial hierarchies have reigned over political narratives and nation-building. It was this 'reorganizing of memory'[29] that built the distinction between fashion and costume as part of the political project of denigrating the legitimacy of indigenous material cultures.

While such practices of forgetting have long prevailed, important scholarship (including this volume and the work of the Research Collective for Decolonizing Fashion more broadly) is now redressing this historical erasure. Fashion has a particularly potent role to play in the decolonization of historical narratives, precisely because of the complex relationship between fashion and time, and the role fashion plays as a practice of memory that is 'material, embodied and enacted'.[30] Indeed, Ulrich Lehmann, in line with Benjamin, suggests that fashion is the cultural object 'that alters our perception of history'.[31] Rather than providing evidence of conventional linear historical narrative, fashion provides an alternative, far more nuanced imagining of historical progression. 'Fashion works erratically through its method of quotation. It wilfully cites any style from the past in a novel incarnation or present rendition ... Fashion thus constitutes an aesthetic rewriting of history'.[32] If we take fashion to be a practice of cultural memory, it can act as a material conduit through which to reconstitute its own past. In Aotearoa New Zealand, fashion has played an important role in disguising history. However, it has also played, and is playing, an increasingly significant role in reclaiming history, restoring memory. Despite the fact that, as de Perthuis notes, memory is frequently positioned as the 'enemy of fashion', that the entire existence of fashion is 'tailored on a perpetual act of wilful forgetting', and that this 'wilful amnesia allows it to occupy an eternal present',[33] fashion also has the potential to reflect the past and remind us of those elements of history that had otherwise been forgotten, ignored or denied. Indeed, fashion is one of the most evocative forms through which we encounter the afterlife of the past; it 'holds the sometimes unbearable gift of memory'.[34]

In the settler colonial context of Aotearoa New Zealand, the gift of memory is certainly unsettling, at times unbearable. However, this process of recalling uneasy memory, contending with the anxieties of an uncomfortable past, is crucial to the project of the settler colonial present.[35] Acknowledging the ways in which aspects of history have been wilfully denied in the production of New Zealand fashion discourse is also fundamental to the practice of decolonizing fashion. The ways in which fashion's 'amnesia' has played out in Aotearoa New Zealand, first through the colonial practices of disavowal and second through the capitalist processes of forgetting, have shaped a recurrent narrative of fashion history. However, recent publications[36] and exhibitions (especially through the New Zealand Fashion Museum, founded by Doris de Pont in

2010) have sought to re-configure linear, limited accounts of fashion history in Aotearoa New Zealand. By presenting vital research examining the forgotten, overlooked and dismissed dimensions of fashion history, this scholarship is changing perceptions about what New Zealand fashion has been and can be. Continuing to illuminate the practices of denial and forgetting that have shaped, and continue to haunt, New Zealand fashion, is necessary in order to better understand the complexity of local/global dynamics in this context as well as the ambivalence of New Zealand fashion to its sense of place and history.

Colonial Disavowal

Since colonization in the 18th and 19th century, Māori garments, including kahu kurī (dog skin cloaks), korowai and kākahu (feathered cloaks), and pounamu (greenstone) jewellery and taonga (treasure), have been categorized as costume rather than fashion. This categorization of dress cultures as *not* fashion is not unique to Aotearoa New Zealand.[37] The project of colonization was intent on relegating indigenous clothing practices to the past, representative of 'uncivilized' ethnic dress in contrast to the 'civilized' clothing habits of European colonialists. Familiar moral arguments for colonization as a civilizing mission prevailed in New Zealand, as in neighbouring Australia and other colonial outposts. Margaret Maynard remarks on the central role of dress within colonial race relations and the importance of European clothing habits, not only in 'civilizing' indigenous Australians but also in reproducing social hierarchies in the colony.[38] Similarly, dress practices were crucial to the colonial process in Aotearoa New Zealand. Early settlers brought new materials, styles and techniques, which Māori used to modify existing garments, as well as European-manufactured clothing, which Māori 'readily adopted'.[39] By the early part of the 19th century, Chanel Clarke notes, 'there was little distinguishing Māori dress from that of their European counterparts'.[40] However, the ways in which Māori adopted European garments reflected earlier Māori fashion cultures, with garments used to symbolize political power and social status. It was, as in Australia, missionary influence that had a more profound effect on Māori dress and fashion. As Clarke continues, the 'key mission was to civilise Māori so that they could be converted more readily to Christ'[41] – and this process began with clothing. Missionary women 'domesticated' indigenous women by conforming them to the ideals of European morality and encouraging them to cover their bodies with dark full-length gowns. As the European population grew, and with it the moral influence of Christianity, 'the function of Māori garments gradually changed from clothing to ceremonial costume'.[42]

Colonial perceptions of Māori garments assumed that they were static and unchanging, used only for protection and symbolic of an 'uncivilized' people. However, as has been made evident by the work of scholars such as Mead[43] and Wallace,[44] Māori garments prior to and following colonization were far from fixed. As Wallace writes, Māori dress was in fact 'the product of an ongoing process of discovery, experimentation and creativity ... it evolved continuously from the practices associated with the Eastern

Polynesian origins of the first settlers'.[45] Furthermore, far from simply being practical items providing shelter and protection, Māori fashion also functioned as symbolic clothing through which cultural meaning and value was, and can still be, understood, as Mead makes clear through his analysis of colonial texts such as that by Parkinson cited above. Given the primacy assigned to the concept of change within modern, Western conceptions of fashion,[46] and the presumption that the dress habits of cultures such as Māori were unchanging, it is little wonder that the clothing cultures of non-Western peoples have been relegated to the domain of costume rather than fashion. Yet, even when it has been acknowledged that Māori dress evolved over time and served as a symbolic system of great social and cultural significance – as Western fashion is categorized – this has not been enough to change perceptions of Māori garments as no more than costume.

The very fact that Māori garment styles and their symbolism changed over time is what leads Wallace to argue for their significance as a distinctive fashion culture. The most defining feature in theoretical conceptualizations of Western fashion is change. However, as Victoria Rovine points out, while 'change is crucial to the distinction between fashion and other dress practices … recognizing change requires an appreciation of the historical and cultural context within which dress innovations occur'.[47] As such, Rovine suggests that 'fashion is the manifestation of an impulse to innovate, rather than simply change that may be motivated by other factors such as the availability of materials, or adaptation to climatic changes'.[48] Early Māori garments were certainly reliant on experimentation due to available materials and climatic conditions. As Wallace notes, 'the cooler, temperate climate of Aotearoa presented the newcomers with considerable clothing challenges'.[49] While Māori settlers could make barkcloth after establishing paper mulberry trees, the material was likely 'impractical for local purposes', in which case, Māori had to use 'trial and error' to develop warmer, rain resistant garments from the native flora and fauna, as well as the Polynesian dog they brought with them.[50] While these early experimentations were made out of necessity, as time progressed, Māori began to innovate based on impulse, producing new styles to symbolize political power or social status. Specific designs varied between iwi (tribes) and from region to region and, 'in regions remote from European influence, the designs of diverse dogskin cloaks continued to evolve in the early nineteenth century'.[51] Given the changing nature of Māori fashions over time, due to both necessity and innovative impulse, 'what is currently recognized as "traditional Māori dress" can be identified as a European construct'.[52]

While change is a key defining feature in how Western fashion is understood, it is important to note that change alone does not constitute fashion. Rather, Eurocentric conceptions of fashion are also reliant upon the capitalist system of globally networked exchange. Thus, while Māori, both prior to and following colonization, evidently had a robust form of identifiable fashion culture, it was a thoroughly different fashion system to that which Māori designers work within today.[53] It is also important to recognize that this dismissal of Māori adornment as nothing more than 'ceremonial costume' was a calculated, politically motivated project, through which European morals, ideals and social processes could be enforced and codified in the colonial settlement. Far from an instance of forgetting, this process was one of erasure and displacement, relegating dynamic Māori fashion cultures to a static perception of tradition.[54] Remembering this original disavowal is not only necessary in decolonizing fashion and its historical narrative in Aotearoa New Zealand, it is also vital to unsettling the settler colonial present.

Cultural Cringe

The colonial disavowal of Māori adornment as a legitimate form of fashion, and significant dimension of New Zealand fashion history, was accompanied in the late 1990s by a second instance of erasure, this time in the form of ruthless forgetting. This second repudiation was very different to that which was enacted as part of the colonial project. However, it is useful to consider the two instances in conjunction as together they provide evidence of the long-standing sense of cultural cringe in Aotearoa New Zealand – both in relation to Māori aesthetics as 'other' and in terms of a national sense of being an 'outsider' on the global margins – and the ambivalence towards place and history that informs this drive to silence and forget.

In 1997, four Pākehā fashion designers – Wallace Rose, Zambesi, WORLD, and swimwear label Moontide – showed collections at the second Australian Fashion Week in Sydney. The collections were praised vociferously, lauded for their inventiveness, their creativity and originality. In 1998, a larger contingent – now including Karen Walker, Nicholas Blanchet, Kate Sylvester and Workshop – were invited to show. That year, the impact was even greater. Zambesi received a standing ovation, both Karen Walker and Nicholas Blanchet secured major overseas accounts in New York and London,[55] and articles quickly appeared declaring New Zealand 'the new Belgium'[56] and Zambesi 'New Zealand's answer to Dries Van Noten'.[57] Following the participation of 'The New Zealand Four' – Zambesi, WORLD, Karen Walker and Nom*d – in a combined show at London Fashion Week in 1999, New Zealand fashion was propelled onto the international stage. Words such as 'dark', 'edgy' and 'intellectual' were used with abandon by the fashion press in their descriptions of the Zambesi, Nom*d and Karen Walker collections and were picked up back home as actuality. Despite the disjunct between those descriptors and the reality of, for example, the WORLD collection – which was, by contrast, brightly coloured and playful – they were judged by the New Zealand government and media commentators to be complementary to rewriting the 'national brand' image of New Zealand. Perpetuating the idea that 'New Zealand's edge lies in an independent spirit that celebrates fresh, creative and unconventional thinking' suited perfectly the millennial political agenda that wished to promote a vision of New Zealand as a place of creativity, independence and originality, rather than bucolic paradise.[58]

Imagining a new fashion story that suited the political needs of the millennial moment meant that 'all notions of the past were removed. In the place of a unique local fashion history, we had New Zealand fashion as a *tabula rasa* – start date February 1999'.[59] Of course, this notion of Aotearoa New Zealand prior to the late 1990s being a 'sartorial wasteland'[60] was far from the truth. The designers who showed at these international fashion weeks did not come 'from nowhere', and their influence and aesthetics did not emerge out of a vacuum. In denying the work of any previous designers, the millennial narrative overlooked their influential impact on the New Zealand fashion industry and aesthetic identity. This lack of recognition for previous designers thus 'severely limited the ability of contemporary New Zealand fashion design to explain the origins of its own uniqueness'.[61]

One of the most common questions asked following the showcase of these Pākehā designers at London Fashion Week in 1999 was 'how "being from New Zealand" influenced their designs'.[62] This question was interesting, not only because it reflected the idea that antipodean fashion was something of an oxymoron, but also because it suggested that national fashion should reflect a sense of cultural identity. The idea of 'New Zealand fashion' was curious because it appeared 'international', rather than what was expected as 'national' or 'cultural'. Maureen Molloy notes:

> The most successful New Zealand collections of 1997–2001 were inspired not by traditional motifs such as the bush, the sea, and the sky, nor by the traditional design motifs of indigenous people of the region. Instead they exhibited a cosmopolitan pastiche that was deeply marked by both irony and nostalgia for a European past. The description of New Zealand design as distinctive owed more to these ironic 'takes' on British, French, and East Coast United States fashion and subcultures of seventy years ago than to the so-called colonial ingenuity and local landscape influences with which it was credited.[63]

The fact that that many Pākehā designers have been, and continue to be, more willing to reflect on their settler colonial cultural history and sense of place through association with the symbols of borrowed, international cultural capital is illustrative of the multiple dimensions of New Zealand's cultural cringe. While some commentators who attended New Zealand Fashion Week (NZFW) in its early years, such Colin McDowell, who attended the second NZFW in 2002, suggested that New Zealand designers should 'use more of Māori culture' in their work,[64] such calls were largely for the use of Māori textiles and patterns in Pākehā design, rather than for greater inclusion of Māori designers in the NZFW program or support for emerging Māori designers. There are examples of Pākehā designers adopting the iconography of Māori culture. However, these are more frequently examples of what has become known as 'Kiwiana', rather than genuine collaborative design. Just as the colonial disavowal of Māori fashion cultures represented a sense of cultural cringe towards the indigenous 'other', so too the millennial forgetting demonstrated a repudiation of New Zealand fashion history perceived as provincial, peripheral and inconsequential.

Pākehā designers have often been ambivalent about representing their work as indicative of an externally perceived 'New Zealand', instead choosing to tread 'a precariously poised path that negotiates a fine line between their national affiliation as New Zealanders (with the implications of rurality and marginality that this national affiliation stereotypically brings) and expressing themselves through a modernist trope mobilised via metropolitan, sophisticated and/or ironic tropes'.[65] In the global fashion system, where questions of cultural appropriation are rife, the production of culturally, historically, or geographically specific fashion in a settler colonial context is not simply a matter of applying 'indigenous designs to commercial entities'.[66] While Pākehā designers remain committed to a certain sense of 'New Zealand-ness', they also continue to draw upon metropolitan aesthetics for their collections, privileging European motifs over indigenous ones, legitimizing Pākehā cultural history over Māori. Overcoming the culture of colonial disavowal and cultural forgetting in New Zealand fashion means questioning the cultural cringe that has ensured the sidelining of much of New Zealand fashion history and contending deeply with the 'unsettling anxieties'[67] that this history has embedded within the settler colonial present.

Contemporary Fashion in Aotearoa New Zealand

The project of decolonizing fashion in Aotearoa New Zealand has gained in strength since the mid-2000s, with the spectre of fashion memory becoming increasingly resonant. No longer relegated to the realm of 'costume', Māori fashion has carved out a distinctive space in the industry and publications such as those by Labrum, McKergow and Gibson (2007), Hammonds, Jenkins and Regnault (2010) and de Pont (2012), and exhibitions at the New Zealand Fashion Museum, have begun to re-think New Zealand fashion history. The recognition of past disavowal through engagement with the material and oral histories of Māori fashion cultures has seen the emergence of Māori designers in an industry that had previously denied Māori design as 'fashion'. These practices of memory, both in and through the fashion of Aotearoa New Zealand, have affected 'our understanding of who we are' and have provided us with new 'feelings of belonging'.[68]

One of the most significant initiatives to support the decolonization of New Zealand fashion has been Miromoda, the Indigenous Māori Fashion Apparel Board (IMFAB). Established in 2008 by Ata Te Kanawa and Rex Turnbull, Miromoda has played, and continues to play, a vital role in supporting Māori designers navigating the requirements of the domestic fashion industry as well as the global fashion system. In 2009, the year after its establishment, Miromoda became a permanent feature of the NZFW program and, in 2015, the showcase was moved to a new schedule time, when the designers would have a larger number of buyers in the audience – increasing their commercial potential. The Miromoda showcase, featuring winners of the Miromoda Fashion Design Awards, has become one of the most highly anticipated shows of the NZFW program. Since the establishment of Miromoda, Te Kanawa notes 'there have been very noticeable changes. If we were considered the 'Māori' novelty show in the beginning, this is no longer the case … There are increased Māori designers and the model agencies have increased the Māori people on their books tenfold. We cast the only four Māori models available across several agencies in 2008. The only other brown faces were in security. Now there's a

Figure 8.1 Designer Kiri Nathan (Ngāpuhi, Tainui) on stage following the first Kiri Nathan solo show at NZFW, 29 August 2018.

Māori-owned model agency [Ataahua Models] disrupting the mostly established agencies'.[69] This change can be seen across the industry, including on the cover of New Zealand's premier fashion magazine *Fashion Quarterly*, which featured transgender Māori model Manahou Mackay on the cover of their final issue in April 2020.[70]

Miromoda alumni include designers such as Kiri Nathan (Ngāpuhi, Tainui), whose designs (including korowai, kākahu and pounamu taonga) have been worn by Jacinda Arden, Barack Obama, Meghan Markle, the Duchess of Sussex, and Chelsea Winstanley, co-producer of the film *JoJo Rabbit* and the first Māori woman to be nominated for an Academy Award. In 2018, Nathan was the first Māori designer to have a solo show at NZFW (Figure 8.1), and in 2019, she was awarded the prestigious BLAKE Leader Award, recognizing her significant contributions to leadership in Aotearoa New Zealand, especially her role in founding the Kāhui Māori Fashion Collective, an initiative that aims to further the activities of the IMFAB by sharing Māori fashion with the world and developing a culture of manaakitanga (caring for others) and tautoko (support) within the New Zealand fashion industry. Nathan, along with her husband, pounamu carver Jason Nathan, is committed to celebrating Māori culture and heritage through the Kiri Nathan brand, as well as supporting other Māori designers navigating the fashion industry, both in Aotearoa and abroad.

In 2019, Nathan led the second Kāhui Māori Fashion Collective hīkoi (journey/ march) to China, where eight Māori fashion designers had the opportunity to visit fabric markets and manufacturers and meet with influential industry stakeholders. One of the designers to participate was fellow Miromoda alumni Bobby Campbell Luke (Ngāti Ruanui). Having been awarded runner-up emerging designer in the 2015 Miromoda awards, Luke showed as part of the NZFW Miromoda showcase that same year. In 2019, he showed as part of a group show alongside four other Māori and Pasifika designers at Hong Kong Fashion Week and held his first solo show at NZFW. Luke's solo show, featuring his collection Whiri Papa ('the twinning of three threads'), was a standout in the 2019 NZFW program (Figure 8.2). Held at Auckland's Town Hall, the show included an evocative video projection, a moving performance of Māori songs by the Kapa Haka Roopu choir from Te Kura Kaupapa Māori o Hoani Waititi Marae, and a collection of pale garments paired with delicate woven kete (bags/baskets) (by Keita Tuhi, Ngāti Kahungunu) and pounamu jewellery. Journalists wrote admiringly of the impromptu haka tautoko (haka of support) that proud, weeping members of the audience performed at the close of the show.[71] Luke makes clear via his website and social media that he 'strives to decolonize fashion aesthetics' in Aotearoa New Zealand.[72] Through his work, Luke is pursuing a path that repudiates colonial erasure and ruthless forgetting, reclaiming fashion memory in design infused with a distinctive sense of place, history, and culture.

The work of organizations such as Miromoda and designers such as Kiri Nathan and Bobby Campbell Luke has been instrumental in changing perceptions about what constitutes 'New Zealand fashion'. In September 2019, the New Zealand Fashion Museum launched *Moana Currents: Dressing Aotearoa Now* at Te Uru Waitakere Contemporary

Figure 8.2 Designer Bobby Campbell Luke (Ngāti Ruanui) on stage following the first Campbell Luke solo show at NZFW, 28 August 2019.

Gallery in Auckland. The exhibition documented 'how our history of migration and cultural exchange is visible in what we wear and how we adorn ourselves', and sought to better understand the ways in which the cultures of the Pacific have informed a contemporary fashion identity in Aotearoa New Zealand.[73] Further, New Zealand Trade and Enterprise, once quick to capitalize on the international successes of a New Zealand fashion industry that emerged 'from nowhere' in the late 1990s, are now working with Māori designers to establish the Māori Fashion Coalition, which aims to provide Māori designers the authority to monitor copyright on disrespectful or appropriated Māori designs. Design, exhibitions and initiatives such as these demonstrate the many influential moves being made to decolonize fashion in Aotearoa New Zealand. However, it remains crucial that historical disavowals be remembered. Māori designers such as Nathan and Luke continue to tread a similarly 'precariously poised path' as Pākehā designers, yet rather than between the poles of global marginality and metropolitan sophistication, it is between an affiliation to a deeply rooted cultural affiliation and a global capitalist system, coded in the terms of settler coloniality. The potential for loss (of culture or identity) within this negotiation remains a shadowy, at times melancholic, presence in Māori design that weaves history into the present.

Conclusion

Fashion did not emerge – 'from nowhere' or otherwise – on the shores of this 'unsettled state'[74] with the arrival of European colonialists in the 1800s. Nor did it emerge in the 1940s, or suddenly in the 1990s. Rather, there has been a long, rich, and dynamic history of sartorial fashioning on these islands since well before the arrival of Pākehā. The colonial practices of disavowal which sidelined Māori fashion cultures as costume have long prevailed in the settler state. It has only been in recent years that sustained efforts by scholars, designers and advocates have begun to re-write the narratives of fashion history in Aotearoa New Zealand.

The two instances of erasure and forgetting that this chapter has outlined, coupled with complex cultural cringe – which has contributed to understandings of Māori aesthetics as 'other' to Western fashion, and to New Zealand itself as 'outsider' on the margins of the global fashion system – have long haunted the New Zealand fashion industry. The tensions and disconnections between recognition and dismissal have left liminal, in-between spaces in our imaginings of the past. Reclaiming these spaces and unpacking the practices of erasure and forgetting that have shaped fashion discourse in Aotearoa New Zealand is crucial to the project of decolonizing fashion. While the act of giving memory to history is an uneasy, 'sometimes unbearable', process, this example demonstrates that doing so provides space for far richer and inclusive fashion cultures to emerge.

Reflecting on the significance of clothing cultures for Māori tupuna (ancestors) and the role of contemporary Māori designers navigating the tensions between distinctive cultural fashion history and the global fashion system allows us to widen our understandings of what constitutes fashion, moving beyond simplistic binary distinctions between fashion and costume and attending more closely to the role of memory, history and place in contemporary design. As Rovine makes clear, fashion is 'a medium particularly well suited to storytelling'.[75] The fashion production of Māori, both prior to colonization and in the hands of contemporary designers such as Kiri Nathan and Bobby Campbell Luke, tells poignant, evocative stories about local cultural history as well as a long heritage of global connectivity and influence. Similarly, the fashion production of Pākehā tells lucid, striking stories about cultural cringe and a complex sense of inferiority, as well as the processes of carving out a distinctive aesthetic identity on the margins of a global fashion system. As such, Aotearoa New Zealand has much to offer in the process of decolonizing fashion discourse, rethinking fashion globalization, and understanding fashion as a practice of memory.

Notes

1. Cited in Hirini (Sidney) Moko Mead, *Traditional Māori Clothing: A Study of Technological and Functional Change* (Wellington, Auckland, Sydney: A. H. & A. W. Reed, 1969).

2. I conceive of fashion as a creative, material practice of cultural representation. I use the words 'dress', 'clothing' and 'fashion' to refer to worn objects of social and cultural consequence. I contend that inserting this understanding of fashion into theorizing of Māori dress not only acknowledges the deep social and cultural significance of Māori clothing cultures but also contributes to the project of dismantling narrow, Western conceptualizations of fashion and the colonial binary that defines Western fashion in contrast to non-Western, costume or non-fashion.

3. Patricia Te Arapo Wallace, 'Traditional Māori Dress: Recovery of a Seventeenth-Century Style?' *Pacific Arts*, 1, (2006) 54–64; Patricia Te Arapo Wallace, 'He Whatu Ariki, He Kura, He Waero: Chiefly Thread, Red and White', In Bronwyn Labrum, Fiona McKergow and Stephanie Gibson, Eds. *Looking Flash: Clothing in Aotearoa New Zealand* (Auckland: Auckland University Press, 2007) 12–27.

4. Roland Barthes, *The Fashion System* [1967] (Berkley and Los Angeles, CA: University of California Press, 1990).

5. Elizabeth Wilson, *Adorned in Dreams: Fashion and Modernity* (London: Virago Press, 1985).

6. Yuniya Kawamura, *Fashion-ology: An Introduction to Fashion Studies* (Oxford: Berg, 2004).

7. Wallace, 'He Whatu Ariki, He Kura, He Waero', 13.

8. ibid, 13.

9. Jean Baudrillard, *For a Critique of the Political Economy of the Sign* (St Louis, MI: Telos Press, 1981).

10. Thorstein Veblen, *The Theory of the Leisure Class* [1899] (Oxford: Oxford University Press, 2007).

11. Maureen Molloy, 'Cutting-Edge Nostalgia: New Zealand Fashion Design at the New Millennium', *Fashion Theory*, 8 (4) (2004) 477–490.

12. Molloy, 'Cutting-Edge Nostalgia'; Claire Regnault, 'A Culture of Ease: Black in New Zealand Fashion in the New Millennium'. In Doris de Pont, Ed. *Black: The History of Black in Fashion, Society and Culture in New Zealand* (New Zealand: Penguin Books, 2012) 200–219.

13. Frederic Nietzsche, 'On the Uses and Disadvantages of History for Life', In Daniel Breazeale, Ed. *Untimely Meditations* (Cambridge: Cambridge University Press, 1997) 57–123.

14. Jo Smith, 'Aotearoa/New Zealand: An Unsettled State in a Sea of Islands', *Settler Colonial Studies*, 1 (1) (2011) 111.

15. Lorenzo Veracini, 'Introducing', *Settler Colonial Studies*, 1 (1) (2011) 1–12; Lisa Slater, *Anxieties of Belonging in Settler Colonialism* (New York and London: Routledge, 2019).

16. Douglas Lloyd Jenkins, 'The Nineteen Forties: Stepping Out'. In Lucy Hammonds, Douglas Llyod Jenkins and Claire Regnault, Eds. *The Dress Circle: New Zealand Fashion Design since 1940* (Auckland: Random House New Zealand, 2010) 16–57.

17. Molloy, 'Cutting-Edge Nostalgia'.

18. Barbara Vinken, 'Eternity: A Frill on the Dress', *Fashion Theory*, 1 (1) (1997) 59.

19. Barthes, *The Fashion System*, 289.

20. ibid., 289.

21. Karen De Perthuis, '"I've Got T-Shirts Older than You!": Fashion, Clothes and Memory'. Paper presented at the Annual Conference of the Popular Culture Association of Australia and New Zealand, Sydney (30 June – 2 July, 2010) 1.

22. Nietzsche, 'On the Uses and Disadvantages of History'.

23. Walter Benjamin, *Illuminations* (New York: Schocken Books, 2007) 261.

24. De Perthuis, 'I've Got T-Shirts', 2.

25. Gaye Chan and Andrea Feeser, *Waikiki: A History of Forgetting and Remembering* (Honolulu: University of Hawai'I Press, 2006).

26. Levi Gahman, 'White Settler Society as Monster: Rural Southeast Kansas, Ancestral Osage (*Wah-Zha-Zhi*) Territories, and the Violence of Forgetting', *Antipode*, 48 (2) (2016) 314–335.

27. Bruce Pascoe, *Dark Emu: Aboriginal Australia and the Birth of Agriculture* (Broome, WA: Magabala Books, 2014).

28. Kynan Gentry, *History, Heritage and Colonialism: Historical Consciousness, Britishness, and Cultural Identity in New Zealand, 1870–1940* (Manchester: Manchester University Press, 2015).

29. Abdelmajid Hannoum, 'Memory at the Surface: Colonial Forgetting in Postcolonial France', *Interventions*, 21 (3) (2019) 369.

30. Heike Jenss, *Fashioning Memory: Vintage Style and Youth Culture* [2015] (London and New York: Bloomsbury, 2017), 8.

31. Ulrich Lehmann, 'Tigersprung: Fashioning History', *Fashion Theory*, 3 (3) (1999) 297.

32. Lehmann, Tigersprung, 301.

33. De Perthuis, 'I've Got T-Shirts', 2.

34. Jenni Sorkin, 'Satin: On Cloth, Stigma, and Shame'. In Jessica Hemmings, Eds. *The Textile Reader* [2012] (London and New York: Bloomsbury Academic, 2015), 59.

35. Slater, *Anxieties of Belonging*.

36. Bronwyn Labrum, Fiona McKergow and Stephanie Gibson, Eds. *Looking Flash: Clothing in Aotearoa New Zealand* (Auckland: Auckland University Press, 2007); Lucy Hammonds, Douglas Lloyd Jenkins and Claire Regnault, *The Dress Circle: New Zealand Fashion Design Since 1940* (Auckland: Random House New Zealand, 2010); Doris de Pont, Ed. *Black: The History of Black in Fashion, Society and Culture in New Zealand* (Auckland: Penguin Books, 2012).

37. Sandra Niessen, Ann Marie Leshkowich and Carla Jones, *Re-Orienting Fashion: The Globalization of Asian Dress* (New York: Berg, 2003): Victoria Rovine, *African Fashion, Global Style: Histories, Innovations, and Ideas You Can Wear* (Bloomington and Indianapolis, IN: Indiana University Press, 2015).

38. Margaret Maynard, *Fashioned from Penury: Dress as Cultural Practice in Colonial Australia* (Cambridge: Cambridge University Press, 1994).

39. Chanel Clarke, 'A Māori Perspective on the Wearing of Black', In Doris de Pont, Ed. *Black: The History of Black in Fashion, Society and Culture in New Zealand* (Auckland: Penguin Books, 2012) 45–47.

40. ibid., 47.

41. ibid., 47.

42. ibid., 49.

43. Mead, *Traditional Māori Clothing*.

44. Wallace, 'Traditional Māori Dress: Wallace, 'He Whatu Ariki, He Kura, He Waero'.

45. Wallace, 'He Whatu Ariki, He Kura, He Waero', 13.

46. Wilson, *Adorned in Dreams*.

47. Rovine, *African Fashion*, 15.

48. ibid., 15.

49. Wallace, 'He Whatu Ariki, He Kura, He Waero', 14.

50. ibid., 14.

51. ibid., 20.

52. Wallace, 'Traditional Māori Dress', 55.

53. Māori fashion culture prior to colonization therefore falls under what Rovine labels 'indigenous fashion': 'clothing innovations produced outside the global fashion system' (Victoria Rovine, *African Fashion, Global Style: Histories, Innovations and Ideas You Can Wear* (Bloomington and Indianapolis, IN: Indiana University Press, 2015) 9).

54. The concept of 'tradition', carrying with it problematic connotations of stasis and fixity, has been reclaimed by Rovine as a way to attend to the use of tradition in dress innovation (2015) 19.

55. Molloy, 'Cutting-Edge Nostalgia'.

56. Karen Floyd, 'Designers Prepare for Fashion Week', *The Independent* (Auckland), 28 April 1999, 2.

57. Regnault, 'A Culture of Ease', 204.

58. ibid., 207.

59. Hammonds, Jenkins and Regnault, *The Dress Circle*, 6.

60. Molloy, 'Cutting-Edge Nostalgia'; Regnault, 'A Culture of Ease'.

61. Hammonds, Jenkins and Regnault, *The Dress Circle*, 6.

62. Maureen Molloy and Wendy Larner, *Fashioning Globalization: New Zealand Design, Working Women and the Cultural Economy* (London: Wiley-Blackwell, 2013) 129.

63. Molloy, 'Cutting-Edge Nostalgia', 478.

64. Colin McDowell, cited in Peter Shand, 'Pieces, Voids & Seams: An Introduction to Contemporary New Zealand Fashion Design'. In Angela Lassig, *New Zealand Fashion Design* (Wellington: Te Papa Press, 2010), xiv.

65. Molloy and Larner, *Fashioning Globalization*, 93.

66. Shand, 'Pieces, Voids and Seams', xv.

67. Veracini, 'Introducing', 3.

68. Jenss, *Fashioning Memory*, 5.

69. Te Kanawa, personal communication, 11 August 2019.

70. On 2 April 2020, *Fashion Quarterly* announced it would be ceasing production after the shuttering of Bauer Media NZ in response to the Covid-19 crisis. Following the acquisition of the title by Auckland-based independent publisher Parkside Media, the magazine announced on 22 November 2020 that it would be making a comeback. The first issue of the renewed publication was launched on 14 December 2020.

71. Emma Gleason, 'Why designer Campbell Luke should be on your radar', *Fashion Quarterly*, 3 September 2019, www.fq.co.nz/nzfw/campbell-luke-nzfw (accessed 3 September 2019); Bek Wadworth, '5 emerging brands to watch from New Zealand Fashion Week', *Vogue*, 30 August 2019. www.vogue.com.au/blogs/spy-style/5-emerging-brands-to-watch-from-new-zealand-fashion-week/image-gallery/6ddd150eab2ddd2b6bc713e023a015e2 (accessed 30 August 2019).

72. Campbell Luke, https://campbellluke.co.nz/pages/our-story (accessed 30 August 2019).

73. New Zealand Fashion Museum, 'Moana Currents: Dressing Aotearoa Now' (7 September – 1 December 2019), http://nzfashionmuseum.org.nz/moana-currents-dressing-aotearoa-now/ (accessed 20 July 2020).

74. Smith, 'Aotearoa/New Zealand'.

75. Rovine, *African Fashion*, 6.

CHAPTER 9
WEARING ETHNICITY: NYONYA FASHION IN EARLY 20TH CENTURY SINGAPORE[1]
Courtney FU

Introduction

The 21st century has seen a resurgence of interest in Peranakan culture, especially in Singapore and Malaysia. A creole community descended from mixed marriages between indigenous Southeast Asia women and Chinese immigrant men, who could allegedly trace their origin to a mythical legend dating to the 15th century,[2] the Peranakan heritage is celebrated in Singapore as a national treasure testifying to a multicultural cosmopolitan past. It is also re-embraced by the Peranakan community as something salient and exceptional, that serves the purpose of distinction to counter the homogenizing effect of 21st century globalization. In 2008, a Peranakan museum was established in Singapore, and a former residential house of a Peranakan family was also turned into a museum, the Baba House,[3] showing Peranakan architecture style and interior decoration. In Malacca and Penang, the two other former Straits Settlements in the British colonial administrated Malaysia, a similar trend has been spotted, though with less government sponsorship.[4] Also in 2008, a Singapore Mandarin-language TV drama, *The Little Nyonya*, became a media sensation. It attracted phenomenal local viewership and received favorable ratings in other Mandarin-speaking markets, including China. In terms of publication, there has been a boom on books related to Peranakan material culture. Most are richly illustrated coffee table books that are targeted at a popular readership. Displayed in museum shops along with Peranakan-themed merchandise, a highly essentialized and romanticized cultural heritage is presented for public consumption. Visiting Peranakan museums and tasting their cuisines have become part and parcel of the booming heritage tourism, and Peranakan culture has been molded into a powerful marketing tool for national branding.

The Peranakan Association in Singapore, and those in Malaysia and Indonesia, see their mission as the preservation and promotion of their culture. Their public functions are occasions for colourful displays of sarong kebayas and batik shirts,[5] often accompanied by home-cooked Peranakan cuisine. Their members proudly announce their identity with the added prefixes of Baba and Nyonya to their names. However, in these efforts to promote and preserve Peranakan culture, certain elements have been given disproportionate emphasis, with others deliberately sidelined. Domestic and feminine aspects feature heavily in museum representations and Peranakan-themed merchandise, while political controversies and ethnic ambiguities are elided in order to present a harmless and palatable cultural heritage. As a result, the process reduces a highly complex and constantly evolving culture to something that is static, traditional, exotic, and locked in a timeless past. It engenders an impression of an authentic culture, uncontaminated by forces of capitalism, and one that deserves protection and preservation lest it be swallowed by the homogenizing process of globalization.

Understandable from a marketing point of view, publications on Peranakan fashion are invariably centered on the Nyonyas, with special attention given to one particular outfit – the sarong kebaya – an ensemble of open blouse of diaphanous materials and pastel colours matched with wrap-around skirt.[6] The singular focus on the sarong kebaya, to the neglect of other outfits, gives rise to the erroneous impression that it is *the* costume for Peranakan women, and exclusively for Peranakan women (known as Nyonyas). Menswear effectively escapes scholarly attention, though this is mainly due to the lack of surviving male garments. The craft of beadwork that decorates the surface of Nyonyas' mule slippers (kasut menak) and purses, and embroidery adorning their kebayas, are emphasized in these books as the feminine skills in measuring the marriageability of Nyonyas.[7] The fact that the sarong kebaya is not specific to Nyonyas alone has been highlighted by Peranakan scholar and private collector Peter Lee, who posits that the pan-archipelago outfit cannot be constrained by national or cultural borders.[8] It is a style donned by multiple Southeast Asian communities, native and foreign, residential and sojourn, all of whom played a role in its evolution. It is therefore *not* specific to the Nyonyas alone, whose wardrobe had been more diverse and multivariate than just the sarong kebaya.

Focusing on the Nyonyas in Singapore, this chapter attempts to redress the current imbalance in the discourse on Nyonya fashion by discussing their fashion experimentations with Chinese fashion undertaken during the first half of the 20th century. It counters the 'ethnocultural' representation of Nyonya dress as traditional, static, and in essence anti-fashion, a perception that inherits the colonial and Eurocentric fashion discourses and expressions of self-orientalism/exoticism on the part of Peranakan culture.[9] As Lee has demonstrated, there was no 'true' or 'pure' Peranakan costume to begin with. Through examining the rapid fluctuations in sartorial choices by Nyonyas in early 20th century Singapore, this chapter shows that the Nyonyas were quick to adapt to changes of the time, and that they had no fixed rules to abide by when it came to dressing. Rather, Nyonya fashion, as it had been in earlier times, evolved and responded with the prevailing trends of the times. What was salient, however, was their fluid identity which conditioned their sartorial choices whenever a combination of new socio-economic and political circumstances called for a new formulation of identity. Just as the current re-appreciation of sarong kebaya is a counter reaction to the accelerated globalization and Westernization of our times, similarly, the adoption of Chinese fashion a century ago was a response to the need for a new social space for the Peranakans in the volatile geopolitics that marked the early 20th century.

Changing Wardrobe: Switching Ethnicity

Dress and fashion pointed to a steady decline in the use of the *sarong* and *kebaya* among Straits-born Chinese women. Chinese women were beginning to realize how lacking in grace and beauty was the native wear compared to the jacket and trousers or the Shanghai gown, and today only a few women, most of them elderly, could be seen in the attire of the Malays.

While many still used the *sarongs* in place of pajamas, it was becoming unsuited to modern living conditions, and the general preference for the jacket and trousers, both as indoor and outdoor wear, was proof that the Malayan mode had long been regarded as out of date. [10]

This is an excerpt taken from an article titled 'Hands or Forks – Sarongs or Jacket or Gown, What Chinese Think' published in 1938 in the English-language newspaper *Singapore Free Press and Mercantile Advertiser*. The term 'Straits-born Chinese' began to gain currency around the turn of the 20th century and here referred to the Babas (male Peranakans) and Nyonyas (female Peranakans) residing in the Straits Settlements of Penang, Malacca, and Singapore.[11] Interviewing a few Babas, the article investigated attitudes to practices of eating and dressing, positioned along ethnic lines, though the content discussed represents several cultural ambiguities integral to the hybrid Peranakan culture. Concentrated in the port cities of maritime Southeast Asia where culture and people from all directions converged, the Peranakans had liberally blended cultural ingredients from all sources into their lives. There was no fixed recipe for the multidirectional borrowing, which varied from household to household. As such, the Peranakans could not be fitted squarely into any pre-existing racial categories. In the cosmopolitan and multicultural context of the port cities where people were free to mingle and dress to their own liking, there had been no need for official racial categorizations until the 19th century when the first census was conducted in 1824 in Singapore. For administrative purposes, race was a column to be filled in. At the same time, new intellectual currents of Social Darwinism and scientific taxonomy propelled a classification impulse that privileged Western cultures.[12] The first half of the 20th century was therefore not an era that celebrated hybridity or racial diversity. Amid the burgeoning sense of nationalism and anti-imperialism, there was a pressing need for clear articulation of ethnic identity and declaration of political allegiance, and creole communities like the Peranakans were left with diminishing spaces for ethnic ambiguity or in-between-ness.[13] Consequently, their hybrid culture was subject to attempts at classification.

Sarong kebaya was a pan-archipelago outfit whose origin and evolution reflected the multicultural and multi-ethnic influences of the cosmopolitan urban centers. Yet, as the quoted newspaper article reveals, sarong kebaya was being attributed as 'attire of the Malays' or the 'Malayan mode', a misperception that still continues today. Privileged Babas, inducted into Western culture through education and religion,[14] subscribed to colonial sensibilities and Western scientific taxonomy by imposing a hierarchy over their multivariate cultural traits, in which the Southeast Asian indigeneity was placed below the Chinese and European elements. Scholars today, driven by impulses for clarity and clear-cut demarcation, are also at fault in filtering a hybrid culture into various false categories.[15] The sarong and kebaya, an outfit that reflected asymmetrical citation in history from multiple ethnic and cultural sources, was given a Malay identity for convenience's sake,[16] so that the Nyonyas were seen as adopting a Malay style in an appropriation model that ignored how dress, like food, art, and even language in the region, evolved simultaneously and was interconnected amongst the many ethnic groups who converged in the port cities of maritime Southeast Asia.[17] All communities – local and foreign, native and migrant – had a role in the development and dissemination of the sarong kebaya. The ensemble therefore belonged to everyone in the archipelago as everybody had been a stakeholder in the development of, as well as a purveyor of the new style.

The 'Hands or Forks' article also highlights another phenomenon elided in the contemporary portrayal of Peranakan culture as invariably affluent and privileged. Eating with hands, commonly practiced by both Malays and Indians, was rarely associated with the Chinese Peranakans. Yet, as the article implied, it was a practice common enough to warrant a debate in the 1930s. The opulent displays of material culture in museums, ranging from utensils to furniture and jewelries, inadvertently generate an image of wealth across the Chinese Peranakan community. Indeed, there were Baba industrial magnates and business tycoons whose material legacy became the mainstay of the museums. However not all Babas and Nyonyas lived such a privileged life. Wealthy Peranakan families were a small fraction of the population, but their presence has been magnified in the museumization process to become representative of the entire community, while the lives of the less well-to-do Peranakans remain an under-studied area.[18]

Ascendency of Chinese Fashion

The newspaper article pointed to a clear ascendency of Chinese fashion by the late 1930s with a corresponding decline in popularity of the 'native attire' (the sarong kebaya). Images of prominent Nyonyas in the early 20th century provide visual evidence of this sartorial shift. Mrs Lee Choon Guan (née Tan Teck Neo, 1877–1978), daughter of a steamship tycoon in Malacca, was one of the first few Nyonyas to have received a private English education.[19] After her marriage in 1900 to Lee Choon Guan, a Baba businessman and philanthropist, she assumed an active public life mingling with the highest echelons in the British colony. Presiding over several mansions, she entertained frequently, earning her the title 'diamond queen' due to her dress style and her penchant for diamonds. However, throughout her high fame, she was rarely photographed in sarong kebaya despite her Nyonya origin.[20] Rather, the Chinese jacket and skirt ensemble was her choice of outfit throughout the 1910s and 1920s. In Figure 9.1, Mrs Lee Choon Guan adorned her Chinese jacket with two oversized brooches which looked like a modification of the kerosangs that traditionally used to pin baju panjang and sarong kebaya.[21] When cheongsam became fashionable in Shanghai in the 1930s, Mrs Lee switched to the new Chinese style which remained her sole choice of outfit for the rest of her life.[22]

Figure 9.1 Mrs Lee Choon Guan in a Chinese blouse and skirt ensemble against a European landscape setting. Her Nyonya stylistic preference was clearly shown by her hairstyle (sanggol) and oversized brooches resembling kerosangs that were used to pin baju panjang and kebaya. The feather fan and pointy heels were ostensibly European. Collection of National Museum of Singapore, c.1920s. Courtesy of the National Museum of Singapore, National Heritage Board.

Helen Yeo Hee Neo (1886–1951) was the wife of Song Ong Siang, a prominent member of the Straits Chinese community and leader advocating for its social reform. Song was the ultimate example of anglicized Baba. He received the Queen's Scholarship to study law in England, and was a devout Presbyterian, succeeding his father as the chairman of the Chinese Christian Association in Singapore. In all his extant pictures, he always dressed in impeccable Western suits as was the case with many Anglo-Chinese in British Malaya. His wife, Helen, on the other hand, followed Chinese fashions (Figure 9.2). Similarly to Mrs Lee Choon Guan, she dressed in the Chinese jacket/skirt outfit in 1910s and 20s, and switched to cheongsam when its popularity peaked in urban

Figure 9.2 Helen Yeo Hee Neo in Chinese jacket-skirt outfit, with her husband, Song Ong Siang in single-breasted suit. Lee Brothers Studio Collection, courtesy of National Archives of Singapore, c.1920.

Figure 9.3 Dr Lee Choo Neo, second from right, dressed in the latest fashion of lace kebaya with her friends in a garden, 1914. Collection of Mrs Vera Teo, Singapore.

centers in China in the 1930s. Her Nyonya identity, however, stood out when she did her hair in the sanggol style,[23] and accessorized her look with Nyonya jewelry. In some instance, she was seen wearing gelang kaki – gold anklets commonly worn by rich Nyonya girls – with Chinese outfits.[24] If we take the sartorial choices of these two prominent Nyonyas to be of socio-cultural significance, the fact that they chose to dress in Chinese styles despite their Nyonya origin signaled something more complex underneath the ascendency of Chinese fashion. In view of the political climate of the 20th century, what was the message that these Nyonyas wanted to convey with their dress sense?

It may appear that not all Nyonyas were in tune with the ascendency of Chinese fashion. Older women continued to dress in baju panjang, and younger women also demonstrated flexibility, switching between sarong kebaya and Chinese outfits. Dr Lee Choo Neo (1895–1947),[25] a Singapore-born Nyonya whose family had strong links with Java, was the first female doctor to practice in Singapore. Several photographs survived showing her in lace kebaya, fashionable in the Dutch East Indies around the turn of the century (Figure 9.3). However, note that the picture was taken in the private setting of a garden, at ease with her female companions, while Mrs Lee Choon Guan and Helen Yeo were public figures always under the limelight. This indicates a public-private division between the fashion styles. There were also photos of Dr Lee Choo Neo in the Chinese ensemble of jacket and skirt. But there is no extant image of her in cheongsam.

What explained the Nyonyas' embrace of Chinese fashion? If the sarong and kebaya were deemed unmodern and 'out-of-date' as indicated by the newspaper article, what made these Nyonyas choose Chinese fashions over those of the West which were also gaining currency among forward-looking young girls in the British colony around the same time? Why did Mrs Lee Choon Guan and Helen Yeo Hee Neo not dress in Western fashion like their husbands, even during their European trips? And what did these changes in wardrobe reveal about changes within the Peranakan community, and the gendered differences between Babas and Nyonyas?

Straits-Chinese Reform: Re-Sinicization of Nyonyas

China-born women were a rarity in Southeast Asia before the 20th century. In 1864, there was only one Chinese woman to 15 men in British Malaya who sought employment as indentured laborers.[26] Many early female immigrants were mostly young girls sold into prostitution by transoceanic traffickers to capitalize on the sexual and emotional needs of a young restless male population.[27] These women continued to dress in the Qing dynasty Han Chinese style robes, long jackets, skirts and trousers, sometimes matched with the Manchu style flower-pot shoes (Figure 9.4). Some Babas, during their education or business trips in China, also acquired wives to bring back to Singapore. Some of them had bound feet, and their Chinese outfits were starkly different from the local Nyonya wives who dressed in the native baju panjang matched with kasut manek (Figure 9.5).

Chinese immigration into Southeast Asia accelerated as the Qing dynasty, beset by a series of civil and territorial fights exacerbated by frequent natural disasters, approached its waning years.[28] Chinese Peranakans in Singapore gradually became marginalized by the expanding migrant population from south China. In 1891, approximately 50,000 Peranakans in the Straits Settlements were outnumbered by 175,000 newcomers from China; and by 1931, about 68 percent of ethnic Chinese in British Malaya were China-born.[29] The new immigrants were collectively known as 'sinkeh' – a term meaning 'new guests' in the Chinese dialect Hokkien to distinguish them from earlier migrants and Chinese Peranakans.

To the Straits Chinese, the sinkehs were not strictly speaking cultural others or complete strangers, for many shared the same ancestral roots back in China. Outwardly, Babas also retained Chinese attire, at least in public spaces, and many kept the queue hairstyle mandated by Manchu rulers in China. Sarong could be their casual wear in the comfort of their homes, but rarely would the Babas be seen in public in Malay costumes. In the concluding years of the 19th century, it was not uncommon to see some Babas pose for photographs in official Mandarin robes following their purchase of official titles from Chinese authorities.

The mixed ethnicity and existential ambiguity of the Peranakans were thrown into sharp relief when the exponential increase in sinkeh population began to impinge on the traditionally privileged position of the Peranakans in British Malaya. The Babas had been occupying a higher social stratum, assuming a mediating role between dialect-speaking sinkehs, English-speaking colonial masters, and Malay-speaking local population. Over time, some entrepreneurial sinkehs began to successfully make inroads into an economic monopoly previously controlled by the Straits Chinese. Being able to communicate better with Chinese authorities, and having closer connections with local guilds and clan

Figure 9.4 Portrait of a Chinese lady, most likely a prostitute. Her Han Chinese long jacket and trousers were matched haphazardly with a pair of Manchu style flower-pot shoes, probably to enhance her exotic sexual appeal. Lee Brothers Studio Collection, courtesy of National Archives of Singapore, c.1890–1910.

organizations, sinkeh merchants possessed additional leverage for striking business deals, sometimes bypassing the Straits Chinese altogether. Moreover, the rise of nationalism among overseas Chinese toward their motherland, coupled with anti-colonial and anti-imperialist sentiments, meant that spaces for ethnic ambiguity and political maneuvering were rapidly diminishing. Peranakans were under increased pressure to take a stand for an unadulterated racial make-up and a position of political affiliation. Anxieties over their identity and survival in uncertain times propelled leaders of the Straits Chinese to embark on a socio-cultural reform program which aimed at reinforcing the image of their people as ethnic Chinese who spoke English and pledged unquestionable loyalty to the British crown. This way, the leaders hoped that their community could secure British protection while avoiding antagonism with their Chinese brothers. They launched the

Figure 9.5 Family portrait of a Chinese Peranakan family in Singapore. The seated woman in baju panjang was most likely the mother of the male family head who was dressed in the traditional Chinese magua and boater hat. The two seated ladies on each side were most likely Nyonya wife in baju Panjang and kasut manek (beaded slipper) on the right and China-born wife with lotus feet on the left. Lee Brothers Studio Collection, courtesy of National Archives of Singapore, c. 1900–1920.

Straits Chinese Reform at the turn of the century, and their ideas and agendas were primarily put forth in the reform's mouthpiece, the *Straits Chinese Magazine*. Song Ong Siang was a key reform advocate, and one of the editors of the magazine.

The reform was patriarchal in nature, and spearheaded by a handful of English-educated Babas whose education also included Chinese literary and philosophical classics.[30] The Nyonyas, on the other hand, were mostly illiterate, confined to the domestic realm, and associated almost entirely with other Nyonyas and servants of heterogeneous backgrounds throughout their lives. The only public announcements of their 'Chinese-ness' were during rites of passage such as weddings and funerals, during which times they donned the voluminous Chinese wedding dress, and the robe of old age in the last years of their lives.[31] Abhorrence of Peranakan indigenous cultural heritage, falsely identified in the 20th century as exclusively Malay, was clearly put forth by the reform's main advocate, Lim Boon Keng: 'Due to the constant influx of Malay blood, every Baba family bears the marks of decay such as extravagant habits, distaste for work, eccentricity, and recklessness'.[32] Since the 'Malay' blood came primarily from the maternal side, and indigenous influence ostensibly displayed in the fashion sense of the womenfolk, the Nyonyas bore the main brunt of the criticism as an affront to their community and hindrance to progress. Educating the Nyonyas was therefore a key component of their reform agenda. And by educating, they meant re-sinicizing:

We should encourage our girls in every possible way to give up the Malay language and revert to the Chinese tongue. We should also strongly recommend our young maidens to return to the Chinese style of dress and coiffure . . . No one possessing a keen appreciation of the beautiful will ever hesitate to make a choice between the Malayan sarong and baju with the concomitant slippers [the kasut manek], and the dainty silk garments of China with their variety of tasteful colours and attractive cuts.[33]

Clearly favouring the Chinese style over the Southeast Asia dress sense, the Baba leaders promoted a re-sinicization program for their female counterparts who were more outwardly 'Malay' than the Babas. In the process of formulating a new ethno-political identity suitable for their community, there seemed little or no room for any form of 'Malay-ness' in the vision of the reform leaders who reduced mixed-racial hybridity to a pure ethnicity of being Chinese. Political allegiance to the British was to be pronounced by their proficiency in the English language. In terms of dress, the Baba leaders also set out to reform menswear by liberally selecting elements from the European and Chinese sartorial styles, in the hope of creating a 'genuine product of the Straits Chinese'.[34] The proposal, however, remained on paper and was never implemented. With regard to the Nyonyas, the male leaders did not prescribe any concrete guidelines other than a general distaste for their native costumes and an explicit urge to take up the Chinese fashion. The onus therefore was left with the Nyonyas themselves.

Experimenting with Chinese Fashion

Textual and visual evidence suggest an ascendency of Chinese fashion with a concomitant decline of fashion trends emanating from urban centers in Java in early 20th century Singapore. However, the sartorial switch did not take place overnight, nor was the transformation completed quickly. In the process, a period of experimentation engendered some exciting hybrid styles that became ephemeral moments in the history of Nyonya fashion.

Baju Shanghai

The first transient style was a hybrid Chinese ensemble of long jacket and skirt. It was given a localized name, baju shanghai in British Malaya, and baju peki in the Dutch East Indies.[35] The variation in name did not point to any stylistic differences in the respective colonies, nor to the Chinese city of origin where the fashion was inspired. Having no standardized name for this new hybrid style, the Peranakans combined a generic Malay word for blouse – baju – with the name of a well-known Chinese city to refer to this Southeast Asian modified Chinese ensemble. Until now, there is no standard definition for baju shanghai or baju peki, for there was no fixed way of mixing and assembling an array of diverse stylistic elements.[36] It is also often confused, and sometimes used interchangeably with the samkoon outfit (discussed later) which I posit is a closer imitation of the contemporaneous 'new culture attire' in China.

The baju shanghai is a hybrid outfit of a mélange of embellishments from different sources onto a Chinese ensemble of long jacket and skirt. The jacket has a Mandarin collar and side opening to the right fastened with knotted frog buttons. It is matched with an ankle-length pleated or paneled skirt. The tubular silhouette was similar to the late Qing robes for Han Chinese in Figure 9.4. The most pronounced difference was the added layers of Western embellishments such as lace trimmings, flounces, and appliques to both the jacket and the skirt. In addition, where common fabrics for Qing robes were silk, damask and satin, extant photos show Nyonyas wearing baju shanghai made from fine cotton which would defray the heat and humidity in Singapore. Similarly, the Victorian and Edwardian lace, ruffles and trimmings with broderie anglaise of European women in Singapore were also used generously in Nyonya baju shanghai fashion.[37] These features were seen randomly applied onto the Chinese ensemble, which the Nyonyas completed with Western style leather shoes. However, engagement with Chinese and European dressing trends did not mean a complete retreat of Nyonya stylistic elements. The traditional sanggol persisted, as did the Nyonyas' predilection for flamboyant displays of jewelry (Figure 9.6). Such a discordant array of styles produced a cross-cultural multi-layered look, which was, in essence, a continuation of the historical multidirectional citation in nearly all aspects of the Peranakan culture. This new hybrid outfit indicated an initial attempt on the part of the Nyonyas to expand their daily wardrobe to include Chinese attire beyond ceremonial dresses, modified to their liking.

The baju shanghai was most likely the work of local tailors responding to the tastes of well-to-do Nyonyas who had more exposure and contact with European colonial masters and China-born wives within their households.[38] From photographic evidence, it appears it was most popular in the 1910s, but did not last beyond the early 1920s. The ostentatious baju shanghai was but a transient trend symbolizing an early experimentation with modernity and with wearing a new identity in life. As with any new fashion, young people were at the forefront of the conversion. In Figure 9.6, the four young Nyonyas were dressed in the typical baju shanghai style with black leather shoes. The girls on the extreme left and right wore jackets decorated with an extra layer of what looked like broderie anglaise flounces that ironically resembled the Qing dynasty cloud shoulder in shape.[39] Their Nyonya stylistic features, however, were still evident. The two elderly Nyonyas in the center were dressed in baju panjang with iconic beaded slippers. All of them had their hair done in the traditional Nyonya sanggol.

Samkoon / Sam Kun / Koon Sah

While the silhouette and hemlines of baju shanghai highly resembled that of late Qing robes for Han Chinese women, a further simplified version of the jacket/skirt outfit took over the heavily-embellished look of baju shanghai as the new trend among prominent Nyonyas in Singapore in the 1920s. Known locally by its various dialect transliterations of the upper body garment (sam/sah) and skirt (koon/kun), the samkoon, samkun, or

Figure 9.6 The young Nyonyas were dressed in baju shanghai. The influence of Western embellishments was clearly shown in the liberal use of lace trimmings especially on the shoulder pads. The older Nyonya and the female matriarch were dressed in traditional baju panjang whose dull colours were appropriate for their age. Lee Brothers Studio Collection, courtesy of National Archives of Singapore, 1900–20s.

koon sah was a close imitation of the contemporaneous Chinese fashion. After the collapse of the Manchu Qing regime in 1911, which brought more than two thousand years of dynastic imperial rule to an end, China underwent a turbulent time as the nation and its people searched for a new sense of being. The issue of dress was of immense political and cultural import as the new attire for the new era under a new regime (a republican government) should signal a complete break from the imperial past, at the same time being representative of a dignified people in the face of foreign encroachment. This meant that a wholesale adoption of Western attire was not an option, while reviving an ethnic Han Chinese costume from previous eras was also out of the question.[40]

Similar to the Peranakans, but for different reasons, the Chinese nation underwent an explorative phase for a new outlook of its people. The queue, which represented submission to Manchu rulers, had to go; the practice of foot binding which symbolized more than a thousand years of the oppression of women had to end. Before the cheongsam (or qipao in Mandarin) became an iconic look for modern Chinese women in urban centers, a minimalist version of the jacket-skirt ensemble was made popular by reform-minded students. Jackets were significantly reduced in bagginess, and became more fitted to the body. The previous tubular sleeves which often extended to the back of the hands were shortened to quarter-length, some with bell-shape openings. The pleated skirt, sometimes called skirt with a hundred folds (bai zhe qun) or horse-face pleated skirt (mamian qun, a front flat panel that resembled the face of a horse) now assumed a restrained A-line shape. The hemlines of both jacket and skirt were shortened, with that of the skirt slightly below the knee, exposing the wearers' ankles to the public gaze. Mary-Janes with stockings or black cotton striped shoes with ankle-length white socks completed the look. Stripped of all accessories and decorative elements, a light blue or white colour cotton jacket with black skirt was adopted as the uniform for female students in many schools. This austere student look gained immense popularity after the 1919 May Fourth New Culture Movement in Peking in which female students took to the streets along with their male classmates. Thereafter, this minimalist sober outfit was dubbed the 'new culture attire', or wenming xinzhuang, and became synonymous with progressive female intellectuals. Lin Huiyin (1904–1955), a Chinese architect and poet, was one of the best-known female figures during Republican China (1911–1949). She was among the Chinese public intellectuals to receive Rabindranath Tagore in China in 1924, serving as his interpreter. Photos from the trip showed that Lin stood side-by-side with the Nobel Laureate in stylish, dark colour 'new culture attire', completed with black stockings, striped leather heels, and a pair of white gloves.

In Singapore, this trend was copied by forward-looking and fashion conscious Nyonyas. Not an exact replica of the 'new culture attire', samkoons in Singapore were made in various prints and fabrics. Its main difference from baju shanghai was a leaner silhouette, with a significant reduction in embellishments. Though much lighter in terms of adornment, it was still considered showy compared with the sober look of the Chinese intellectuals. Mrs Lee Choon Guan chose to dress in a samkoon outfit for her trip to London in 1918. She was the first Straits Chinese woman to be conferred Member of the Order of the British Empire (MBE) for her charitable efforts during WWI. In a photo taken during the trip, she was seen to complete her look with a pair of pointed, high-heeled shoes with stockings, and a string purse, but continued to do her hair in the sanggol style.[41] Instead of a long straight tubular silhouette, the jacket of the samkoon outfit had a slightly cinched waist to accentuate the figure, while the skirt had a neat A-line cut. However, when compared to the 'new culture attire' popular in urban centers in China, the hemline for samkoon tended to be longer and rarely went above the calf. This might be indicative of a more conservative outlook for Nyonyas in Singapore than the female intellectuals in China. Photographic evidence indicates that the samkoon was a popular style in 1920s Singapore. As more Straits Chinese women adopted the samkoon, and with the consistent streamlining of accessories, it became increasingly harder to distinguish the native Nyonyas from sinkeh women when the trends gradually turned toward a closer imitation of the Chinese fashion.

'Shanghai Gown' – Cheongsam

The term 'Shanghai gown' used in the newspaper article was commonly employed in local print media to refer to cheongsam before its Cantonese name became the standard usage for the dress in overseas Chinese communities. It referred to the one-piece figure hugging dress, known in Mandarin Chinese as qipao, now quintessentially recognized as a symbol of China. The term 'Shanghai gown' aptly referenced the metropolis where this new fashion took root and shot to fame. Its origin lay in the Qing dynasty when the robe was worn by both men and women, with a range of insignias that distinguished gender, rank, and stature. In fact, its genesis was given a feminist overtone when the novelist Zhang Ailing (aka Eileen Chang, 1920–1995) famously attributed its origin to an egalitarian impulse by women who pushed for gender equality.[42] This androgynous feature was also embedded in its Cantonese name, for 'cheongsam' is a the gender-free term literally meaning 'long robe'.[43]

The 1930s was the golden age for cheongsam in China. Shanghai tailors, incorporating Western techniques, improved the flat look of early cheongsam to be more three-dimensional to accentuate the figure.[44] Women in urban centers, from female revolutionaries to wealthy housewives and prostitutes, adopted the fashion. In Singapore, Chinese immigration continued to stream into the island. The sinkeh population expanded to include more women beyond girls sold into servitude in brothels or rich households as domestic servants. Literate women joining their husbands or relatives in Singapore entered the workforce as clerks or teachers, bringing the latest fashion from China with them. Shanghai movies were screened in Singapore, and copies of its first women/fashion magazine, the *Young Companion* (Liangyou huabao), were circulated in the local market. As such, Nyonyas were never insulated from fashion trends in China. In a photograph taken in the mid-1920s, Mrs Lee Choon Guan and two other ladies seated in the front row were dressed in the early style of cheongsam with A-line silhouette and bell-shaped quarter sleeves (Figure 9.7).[45] One of them had a short bobbed hairdo, while Mrs Lee had by this

Figure 9.7 Mrs Lee Choon Guan, third from the left. Photograph taken at Tan Cheng Lock's seaside villa at Klebang, Malacca, mid-1920s. Source: Peter Lee, 'Cross-dressing chameleons', *The Peranakan*, 1 (2013) 9.

time given up her Nyonya sanggol for a short permed wave trendy at the time, a sign of her literacy and progressiveness. As the cheongsam's popularity continued to increase, there was a consistent reduction of Nyonya stylistic remnants in favour of trends from China. Helen Yeo attended a public event in 1936 in a fashionable cheongsam with a permanent short-wave hairstyle and a hand clutch. Her photograph appeared in the local newspaper *Straits Times* (26 January 1936, 19): with no traces of her earlier Nyonya fashion style, she appeared as a fashionable modern lady referencing Shanghai style in the 1930s.

Given their social status and public exposure, we may surmise that prominent Nyonyas like Helen Yeo and Mrs Lee Choon Guan consciously dressed to support the agenda of the Baba-led reform in constructing an ethnic-stable image for the Strait Chinese community. Accompanying their husbands, who were leaders of the community, to formal public functions, their carefully deliberated outfits naturally came under the media spotlight which made them recurring figures in the local press. Newspaper reports, sometimes accompanied by photographs, often included a line of two on their outfits which read like 'Lady Helen Yeo appeared in a blue silk Shanghai dress', or 'Mrs Lee Choon Guan dressed in her usual dazzling diamond-stud chong sham'.[46]

'Jacket and Trousers' – Samfoo

A third Chinese outfit adopted by Straits Chinese women was the jacket and trousers referred to as samfoo, which became ubiquitous casual wear for Chinese women in Singapore.[47] Samfoo was the Hokkien transliteration for an ensemble that comprised a blouse/jacket (sam) and loose-cutting trousers (foo/fu). Women's trousers had a long history in China. Manchu women in particular wore trousers to facilitate their horse-riding lifestyle. It was also customary for Han Chinese women to match long jackets with trousers (see Figure 9.4). The labouring classes, such as domestic workers and young girls before marriable age, wore samfoo because of its practicality (see Figures 9.7 and 9.8).[48] The two-piece outfit was usually made from the same piece of fabric. A low Mandarin collar fastened to the right with knotted buttons made the attire characteristically Chinese. Slits were sometimes cut at each side of the blouse up to waist area to facilitate ease of movement. Together with the practicality of the trousers, samfoo was comfortable to wear and therefore explains the 'general preference for the jacket and trousers, both as indoor and outdoor wear'.

Conclusion

Based on the 1938 newspaper article, examples discussed in this chapter reveal how Nyonyas gravitated toward Chinese fashion during the early decades of the 20th century. Prominent Nyonyas, in particular, demonstrated a conscious effort to forge a Chinese identity out of their ethno-cultural make-up by consistently reducing their Nyonya stylistic references while keeping abreast of the Chinese fashion. This offers an alternative narrative of the Nyonya wardrobe to beyond the essentialization of sarong kebaya.

Figure 9.8 The two young girls on each side were dressed in samfoo, while the older lady seated in the middle was in a clean, minimally embellished samkoon. Note the pair of gelang kaki on the ankles of the girl on the right, which announced her Nyonya identity. Lee Brothers Studio Collection, courtesy of National Archives of Singapore, c. 1920.

Nyonya fashion is shown to have a history no less dynamic than that in the West. This chapter demonstrates that the evolution of Nyonya fashion observes a logic of its own predicated on the malleability and vulnerability of the community's creole origin. In the same way that their Southeast Asia indigeneity is being highlighted today in response to the urge for self-distinction in a global world, the Chinese element in their ethno-cultural make-up was emphasized a century ago in response to volatile geopolitics. This high degree of versatility is a salient character of Nyonya fashion.

The chapter also has implications for the present. Deeply held assumptions about non-Western cultures embedded in dominant fashion discourses have found expression in the exoticization and feminization of the presentation of Peranakan culture. In addition, museums have to comply with orthodox State discourses of racial harmony in which political controversies and unsavory internal histories of discrimination are to be avoided. While Peranakan culture has been successfully repackaged into a national heritage that serves the domestic need for self-distinction and for bringing in tourist money, it has also inadvertently reinforced the East-West binary that locks Peranakan culture in a perpetual effeminate persona symbolized by Nyonyas in sarong kebayas. New questions of authenticity and accuracy, the traditional, the historic, and the folkloric in relation to Peranakan fashion need to be asked by challenging both colonial conceptualizations and Statist approaches.

Notes

1. The author would like thank Professor Louise Edwards for reading an early draft of this paper, and Peter Lee for his invaluable feedback and assistance in acquiring image reproduction. Gratitude also goes to Dr Erica de Greef and Dr Sarah Cheang for their editorial work.

2. Legend has it that a Ming Dynasty princess, Hang Li Po, married a Malacca Sultan in the late 15th century. Her entourage of five hundred later intermarried with the locals, and her children became members of the royal family, and Muslim. This story was recorded in the Malay Annals (*Sejarah Melayu*), but it cannot be verified as there is no mention of this in Chinese records. Though the arrival of a Chinese princess as the progenitor of the community has largely been discredited, the legend nonetheless holds sway in people's imagination.

3. Baba is a designation for male Peranakan, Nyonya (sometimes also spelt as Nonya) is the designation for female Peranakan.

4. Examples include the Baba Nyonya Heritage Museum and State Chinese Jewelry Museum in Malacca, and Pinang Peranakan Museum in Penang. Unlike the Peranakan Museum in Singapore which is state-sponsored, and the Baba House being managed under the National University of Singapore Museum, the establishments in Malaysia are smaller in scale and privately run. They are former residential houses of Peranakan families turned into for-profit museums, and managed by the families' descendants. The collections, no less resplendent than those in Singapore, are nonetheless more dispersed. Malaysia's racial demographics account for the lack of interest on the part of the government, which would prefer to avoid being seen as favoring the Chinese at the expense of the Malay majority. For a discussion of the cultural heritage projects in Singapore and Malaysia, see Karen M. Teoh, 'Domesticating Hybridity: Straits Chinese Cultural Heritage Projects in Malaysia and Singapore', *Cross-Currents: East Asian History and Culture Review*, 5 (1) (2016) 115–146.

5. Batik shirts and kebaya are the national costumes for men and women in Indonesia, associated with nationalistic movements in the second half of the 20th century. They are also widely accepted as *the* costume for Chinese Peranakans in island Southeast Asia. This chapter, however, will demonstrate that the fashion of Peranakan women has been more diverse and fluid than the singularly fixed style of the sarong kebaya.

6. Christine Ong Kiat Neo, *Nyonya Kebaya: Intricacies of the Peranakan Heritage* (Singapore: Christine Ong Kiat Neo, 2011); Datin Seri, *Nyonya Kebaya: A Century of Straits Chinese Costume* (Singapore: Tuttle, 2012); Peter Lee, *Sarong Kebaya: Peranakan Fashion in an Interconnected World, 1500–1950* (Singapore: Asian Civilization Museum, 2014); E-pnn Debra-jean Ng, *The Nyonya Kebaya : Understanding its Characteristics and Social Significance*, (Hong Kong: University of Hong Kong Libraries, 2018); Christine Ong Kiat Neo, *Nyonya Kebaya: Peranakan Heritage Fashion*, (London: Transnational Press London, 2019).

7. Wing Meng Ho, *Straits Chinese Beadwork and Embroidery: A Collector's Guide*, (Singapore: Marshall Cavendish Editions, 2008); Hwei-Fe'n Cheah, *Phoenix Rising: Narratives in Nyonya Beadwork from the Straits Settlements* (Singapore: National University of Singapore Press, 2010).

8. Peter Lee, *Sarong Kebaya: Peranakan Fashion in an Interconnected World, 1500–1950* (Singapore: Asian Civilization Museum, 2014).

9. For discussion of auto-exoticism in fashion, see the introduction of José Teunissen and Jan Brand, *Global Fashion, Local Tradition: On the Globalization of Fashion* (Warnsveld: Terra, 2006).

10. 'Hands or Forks – Sarongs or Jacket or Gown, What Chinese Think', *Singapore Free Press and Mercantile Advertiser*, 2 February 1938, 3.

11. These are the three port cities along the Straits of Malacca – Penang, Malacca, and Singapore. They were merged together in 1826 as the Straits Settlements, and administered by the British East India Company. 'Straits Chinese' is a politicized term for Peranakans, specifically referring to Chinese Peranakans residing in the British colony of Malaysia. It is also sometimes written as 'Straits-born Chinese'. 'Peranakan' is in fact a pan-Southeast Asia category that denotes all people of foreign-indigenous mixed racial heritage. Besides Chinese Peranakans, there are also Chitty/Chetti Peranakans (between foreign Tamil males and indigenous women), and Arab Peranakans (between foreign Arab males and indigenous women). The two appellations, Straits Chinese and Peranakans have been used interchangeably.

12. For a discussion of the impact of Social Darwinism on fashion theory, see Linda Welters and Abby Lillethun, *Fashion Theory: A Global View* (London: Bloomsbury, 2018), 33–34.

13. Tzu-hui Celina Hung, '"There Are No Chinamen in Singapore": Creolization and Self-Fashioning of the Straits Chinese in the Colonial Contact Zone', *Journal of Chinese Overseas*, 5 (2) (2009) 257–290.

14. These were usually Anglicized Babas who received an English education and were Christians.

15. Peter Lee also argues against this phenomenon: *Sarong Kebaya*, 30.

16. Another likely reason could be that other races all have a highly identifiable outfit associated with their ethnic identities – cheongsam for Chinese, sari for Indian, and corseted dress for Europeans. The sarong kebaya was therefore given a Malay identity to represent the vastly diverse population of island Southeast Asia.

17. Peter Lee and Alan Chong, 'Mixing Up Things and People in Asia's Port Cities'. In Alan Chong, Richard Lingner and Clement Oon, Eds. *Port Cites: Multicultural Emporiums of Asia 1500–1900* (Singapore: Asian Civilization Museum, 2016) 31–41.

18. An effort to amend the imbalance was an exhibition by Peter Lee in 2008 at the Peranakan Museum, titled 'Junk to Jewels', which looked at humble objects from ordinary Peranakan families.

19. His father hired a Methodist missionary teacher, Miss Sophia Blackmore, who arrived in Singapore in 1887.

20. The one instance she wore sarong kebaya during her adult life was during the mourning period for her husband, who died in 1924.

21. Baju panjang is a hip- or knee-length tunic worn over a sarong. 'Baju' is a generic word for blouse in Malay, and 'panjang' means long. It is a style that precedes sarong kebaya. Having no buttons or any kind of fastening, a set of three brooches is used to pin baju panjang and later the kebaya.

22. Peter Lee, *Sarong Kebaya*, 260.

23. It is a hairstyle that pulls all hair up tightly into a bun at the top or back of the head, decorated with hairpins or flower garlands.

24. For a visual depiction of gelang kaki, see Figure 9.8.

25. Note that the character 'neo' – '娘' in Chinese – appears in the names of all three Nyonyas discussed here. It is a term that denotes young ladies as well as women who have entered motherhood. It was a Fujian tradition for naming girls that goes far back to imperial years, and a common practice when naming Nyonyas. Dr Lee Choo Neo was the aunt of Lee Kuan Yew, Singapore's first prime minister.

26. Gretchen Liu and Singapore National Heritage Board, *Singapore: A Pictorial History 1819–2000* (Singapore: Archipelago Press published in association with the National Heritage Board, 1999) 84.

27. See James Francis Warren, *Ah Ku and Karayuki-San: Prostitution in Singapore, 1870–1940* (Singapore: NUS Press, 2003).

28. The Qing dynasty fought a series of wars with Britain (first and second Opium Wars 1839–1842, 1856–1860), and with Japan (1894–1895) to cite a few examples. Widespread drought created conditions for the rise of the infamous Boxer Rebellion (1899–1901).

29. Teoh, 'Domesticating Hybridity', 121.

30. Baba Malay is a creole language blending Malay and the Hokkien dialect, the combination of which varies by geographical location. In Penang, *Hokkien* features more heavily, while in Malacca it is Malay. Since many Peranakans in Singapore originally came from Penang and Malacca, the Baba Malay spoken in Singapore has a roughly equal mix of both.

31. Nyonyas dressed in the Chinese robes for old age, the baju tua, on her 61st birthday, and every decade thereafter. Like the wedding costumes, robes for old age were also ordered by local agents to be shipped from China. Peter Lee, 'Crossing Dressing Chameleons', *The Peranakan*, 1 (2013) 6.

32. Lim Boon Keng, 'Race Deterioration in the Tropics', *Straits Chinese Annual* (1909) 5.

33. Soh Poh Thong, 'Concerning our Girls', *Straits Chinese Magazine*, 11 (1907) 143.

34. Lim Boon Keng, 'Straits Chinese Reform', *Straits Chinese Magazine*, 3 (1908) 58.

35. 'Peki' refers to Peking, the capital city of Qing Dynasty China (1644–1911).

36. Discussions of this transient style are sparse and at times confusing. It is often only mentioned in passing along with other more well-known and recognizable styles. For brief discussions of baju shanghai, see Peter Lee, *Sarong Kebaya*, 259–260; and Wessie Ling and Simona Serge-Reinach, Eds. *Fashion in Multiple Chinas: Chinese Style in the Transglobal Landscape* (London: Bloomsbury, 2018) 223.

37. For a concise overview of Singapore sartorial history through old photographs, see Fashion Designers Society (Singapore), *Costumes through Time, Singapore* (Singapore: National Heritage Board and Fashion Designers Society, 1993).

38. The 'modern colony' gallery at the Singapore National Museum has a baju shanghai dated to the 1910s on display. It is clearly stated as a work of Shanghainese tailors in Singapore who married elements from the East and West into one outfit.

39. 'Cloud shoulder/collar' was a common decorative element in the costumes of Han Chinese women that emphasized the shoulder and neck with extra embroidery and sometimes detachable outer layers. It was also commonly employed in Peranakan wedding gowns.

40. For a detailed study of sartorial changes in republican China, see Antonia Finnane, *Changing Clothes in China: Fashion, History, Nation* (New York: Columbia University Press, 2008).

41. See portraitsofthestraits.wordpress.com/2013/10/2 showing photos that were collected in the 1923 edition of *One Hundred Years of Chinese in Singapore* written by Song Ong Siang. Refer to Figures 9.1 and 9.2 for local renditions of the jacket and skirt outfit.

42. Zhang Ailing, *Gengyi Ji [Chronicle of Changing Clothes]*, https://baike.baidu.com/item/%E6%9B%B4%E8%A1%A3%E8%AE%B0 (accessed 12 July 2020).

43. For close study of the style, see Hazel Clarke, *The Cheongsam* (Hong Kong: Oxford University Press, 2000); and Finnane, *Changing Clothes in China*, Chapter 6.

44. See for example Y. Liu, 'Westernization and the Consistent Popularity of the Republican Qipao', *International Journal of Fashion Studies*, 4 (2) (2017) 211–224.

45. This early style of cheongsam was commonly known as the Beijing style (jingpai) for its flat two-dimensional cut as opposed to the later three-dimensional and figure-flattering Shanghai style (haipai).

46. 'Chong sham' was an early spelling of cheongsam in the early newspapers of Singapore. The more accurate transliteration of the Cantonese pronunciation – cheongsam – began to be used in the local print media in the 1950s.

47. Sometimes also spelt as samfu.

48. For a brief description of the jacket-trousers outfit in China, see Valery Garrett, *Chinese Clothing: An Illustrated Guide* (Hong Kong: Oxford University Press, 1994) 78–79, 87–89, 108–109.

SECTION III
GLOBAL DESIGN PRACTICES

INTRODUCTION TO SECTION III
TAKAGI Yoko

As the authority of a Euro-American dominance within the fashion system is being threatened and new solutions need to be found to address the global problems of environmental destruction by fashion production, younger designers are emerging to innovate in the industry. These designers observe the new realities of globalization and rethink what fashion design means without necessarily being bound by Western values. Their approaches are interdisciplinary, ethical and sometimes can be qualified as social activism. The fashion education sector is also changing its curricula and combining theory and practice to respect more diverse histories and the contexts of other cultural traditions rather than simply applying these as ethnic elements to be used as inspiration without understanding their complexity. Ethical and socially conscious fashion has become a popular theme at symposiums and within academic publications.

This final section reflects on design processes that do not necessarily conform to the Western notion of 'The Fashion System', and explores how new globalization flows have led to new values in the field of fashion design practices, and provides new approaches to fashion education. In this section, we share examples of fashion designers of mixed backgrounds and geographical roots, but also of fashion curation and fashion education, each using non-Eurocentric approaches in order to respond creatively in rethinking global fashion.

With a series of vignettes drawn from their fieldwork, Malika Kraamer and Osuanyi Quaicoo Essel introduce fashion creators of the Volta and Central Regions in Ghana, Africa, highlighting the presence of posters in the Ghanaian fashion design process. Despite the emergence of the internet and social media, fashion posters in Ghana continue to play an influential part in the creative process between fashion creators and their customers and form part of the complex bespoke fashion system.

Through their analysis of the work of two young fashion designers, Gosha Rubchinskiy (Russia) and Ma Ke (China), Hazel Clark and Alla Eizenberg propose that, going forward, the agents in the process of reconstructing fashion will not necessarily be those who are firmly entrenched in the Western fashion system, nor will they necessarily draw from hackneyed visual references. Through both case studies, they provide evidence for designers who originate from and reside in nations which are currently considered antithetical to fashion's creative and conceptual direction, and whose references privilege underrepresented elements of their respective cultures.

As a curator for the exhibition The Future of Fashion is Now that took place in Rotterdam, José Teunissen analyses how new forms or approaches to globalization are driving the current changes in the fashion system, and the need to redefine both fashion and luxury. Designers are seeking renewed and meaningful relationships with society and culture, reflecting altermodern 21st century values, by taking an interdisciplinary, explorative design approach shaping new values and definitions of what a more inclusive Fashion Luxury might entail.

In the final chapter in this section, Jennifer Hughes introduces the non-Western concepts of ma and wabi-sabi that she used with her fashion and textile students at UCA Rochester. Via this alternative pedagogical approach, students were stretched and encouraged to experiment in more dynamic ways and to explore wider perspectives, to look beyond their own cultural borders, addressing ecological concerns, migration, social and gender issues.

CHAPTER 10
CREATIVE COLLABORATIONS BETWEEN CONSUMERS AND FASHION DESIGNERS: THE ROLE OF FASHION POSTERS IN URBAN AND RURAL GHANA

Malika KRAAMER and Osuanyi Quaicoo ESSEL

Introduction

Fashion in Ghana plays an important role in the socio-cultural life of Ghanaians. Men and women take great pride in their sense of style and fashionable dress. Thousands of fashion designers, seamstresses and tailors produce made-to-order ensembles of high aesthetic quality ranging from haute couture, middle-class dress to street fashion. Due to this bespoke nature of most of Ghana's fashion systems, hundreds of new designs trickle into her fashion markets on a daily basis. Consumers not only have many options to choose from, but also often actively participate in creating new styles. Many of these designs are catalogued and published in fashion posters that are widely distributed and found in almost every tailoring shop across the length and breadth of the country.

In existing studies on Ghanaian fashion cultures, the focus is often on metropolitan high-end fashion designers of which many operate internationally. This chapter, which is part of a wider project on fashion systems in Ghana, complements those studies by discussing what the majority of Ghanaians wear and the role of fashion posters. Although the literature on posters in Africa has been growing in the last 30 years, attention given to the fashion poster has been scarce. This study draws critical attention to a fashion system beyond the often-perceived dominant global city networks, and explores aspects of a system that does not currently have its main references in European fashion trends but is nonetheless international, as the fashion posters are widespread throughout West Africa and also influence the special-occasion wear of Ghanaians in the diaspora. This chapter begins, therefore, with a series of vignettes drawn from our fieldwork, introducing some fashion creators of the Volta and Central Regions, and highlighting the presence of posters in the Ghanaian fashion design process.

Vignette 1: Hamidu Tenni and Pat Glauh-Yeh

Walking through the city of Ho, one can find a fashion atelier on each corner. Hamidu Tenni, for instance, is well-known for making fashionable clothing for both men and women. For three years, she has had a shop in one of the top spots in Ho where she employs one seamstress and trains five apprentices. Ho is the capital of the Volta Region of Ghana. Her atelier is full of fashion posters bought at different times (Figure 10.1). The fashion posters support the customers in selecting a preferred outfit and give the shop an attractive look. Although apprenticed in Ho for two years, she moved to Accra and had a shop in Madina where she started in 1996. Seven years ago, she returned to Ho. Next to her is the atelier of Pat Glauh-Yeh, a lecturer at the fashion department of Ho Technical University, who sews mainly for upper-middle and middle class customers and teaches several apprentices in her atelier. Hamidu managed to retain customers from Accra and even has some Ghanaian customers living in the UK. Pat counts many university staff, office workers and well-to-do businessmen and women among her clientele, and also receives orders from abroad.[1]

Hamidu has been using fashion posters since she was apprenticed and uses them continuously. These posters facilitate the creative interactions with customers that characterize Ghanaian fashion: 'You tell them to choose the styles they want. It makes it easier to find a style'. 'Sometimes they do not know exactly what they want, and they look at the posters; or the posters help to find a specific style'. She uses the 'freehand'

Figure 10.1 Hamidu Tanni, a fashion creator flanked by her apprentices in her shop in Ho, December 2018. © Photo Malika Kraamer.

cutting method and creates outfits based on her perception of her customers' preferences. Some of her clients, especially younger university students, bring their own smartphone photos of celebrities, or snapshots taken from magazines, Instagram or the street to communicate to her their desired outfit. With her customers in Accra and abroad, she mainly sends them photos and they send photos back until desired fabric, cut, and embellishments are agreed. Usually the agreed outfit differs from the design and fabric used on the poster, magazine or photo. Hamida buys the posters from Ho market, or Makola market in Accra. She bought six posters in 2018. When buying a new poster, she keeps in mind the posters she already has, along with what she believes her customers' desires are.

Vignette 2: Dzifa Edith Kuleke

Dzifa Edith Kuleke (Figure 10.2) has trained dozens of apprentices over her career of 25 years in Agotime-Kpetoe, a district town close to the Togolese border and well-known for the production of kente cloth. She meets her clients, sometimes at her atelier but mainly at the market, bringing the fashion posters along. A decision for an outfit is often only reached after a lively discussion with the customer, in which the fashion poster helps in making clear what the precise requirements are from the client. In this communication, she makes suggestions as much as the customer. She is only able to buy a few new posters once a year.[2]

Figure 10.2 Dzifa Edith Kuleke (seated), a fashion creator in Agotime-Kpetoe, December 2018. © Photo Malika Kraamer.

Figure 10.3 Kwesi Otabil, the fashion creator in Winneba. 2019. © Photo Osuanyi Quaicoo Essel.

Vignette 3: Daniel Kwesi Otabil

Daniel Kwesi Otabil (Figure 10.3), a creative fashion designer whose shop is located at the Winneba Market, has been working actively in the bespoke fashion environment of Winneba Municipality for 15 years. He designs and constructs menswear ranging from shirts and trousers to masculine Ghanaian classics. Otabil has trained more than 12 apprentices on the job, some of whom are working in their own tailoring shops. His clientele are of different social classes and ages, and include lecturers, students, organizations and clubs. He testifies that:

> [The] Majority of my clients come with their designs on their smartphones; some select their designs from the fashion posters and magazines displayed in my shop, while some prefer that I create new designs for them. Sometimes, the clients suggest changes on the designs selected from the fashion poster as well as that of the designs on their smartphones.

Vignette 4: Wofa Kurabi

Wofa Kurabi, a tailor who works in Awutu Bawjiase town in the Awutu Senya East District of the Central Region of Ghana, has provided active tailoring services to the community for about 21 years. Specializing in menswear, he has trained apprentices who have established their own tailoring shops. Kurabi confirms that though some of his clients come with designs on their smartphones, more than half of them select their preferred designs from the fashion posters displayed in his shop. Occasionally, some of the clients ask him to design new styles that would suit them.[3]

These scenarios of bespoke fashion culture exemplify the uniqueness of Ghana's fashion system as well as the creative and interactive collaboration that characterizes such a system. The creative collaboration between the clients and fashion creators contributes to the realization of new designs, with fashion posters as a ubiquitous source of design inspiration.

This chapter discusses the networks of people who contribute to the diffusion and consumption of bespoke fashion for middle- and low-income people, the vast majority of Ghanaians, in two rural and regional urban centres in Ghana. It examines the factors that shape consumer choices of designs and styles, preferences of fashion designers, seamstresses and tailors and editorial preferences of fashion poster designers. It then analyses the creative collaborations between consumers and designers, the facilitative roles of fashion posters in this encounter and other factors shaping this process.

We use the term fashion creator as a general inclusive term for fashion designers, seamstresses, dressmakers and tailors. All these individual terms are used in fluid, time shifting, and at times contested understandings. For example, Nelly Hagan-Deegbe, the internationally renowned creative director of Duaba Serwa, feels that we should not speak of haute couture in Ghana as it lacks the infrastructure, and prefers to refer to herself as a dressmaker.[4] At the same time, most ateliers for bespoke fashion dotted throughout the cities and villages use the word fashion designer as part of their shop's title.

We argue that bespoke fashion production workshops in regional centres and rural areas contribute significantly to the great variety of outfits in Ghana. Each encounter between a fashion creator and client is a creative collaboration in which fashion posters continue to play a major role. Furthermore, this creative discourse is not just shaped by fashion creators and their understanding of their customers' preferences, but also the clients' ideas of the latest fashions and their own personal tastes, the editorial choices of fashion poster producers and, to a much lesser extent, of editorial teams of fashion magazines.

Overview of Ghana's Fashion Scenes

Ghanaians take great pride in their sense of style and fashionable dress in every occasion in life. As in other West African countries, 'clothing is the major visual aesthetic practice' and a cultivation of and passion for fashionable body display is common.[5] Casually, many wear the same garments as in the rest of the world, namely suits, jeans, sneakers and dresses, often (partly) assembled from second-hand clothing that has flooded the Ghanaian market. Special-occasion wear, and a growing proportion of daily and office wear, may be machine-made, hand-tailored or wrapped carefully around the body. Ghana has a wealth of continuously changing textile and dress traditions, such as kente, fugu and kaba fashions

Figure 10.4 Kaba fashion composed of Kente fabric designs. Designed and produced in 2018 by Thomas Boakye of Kantamanto, Accra. © Photo Osuanyi Quaicoo Essel.

Figure 10.5 Samples of fashion found in tailoring shops in Swedru and Winneba, Ghana in 2019. © Photo Osuanyi Quaicoo Essel.

(Figures 10.4 and 10.5). Kente is a colourful hand-woven textile used for wrappers or garments tailored in Southern Ghana, while fugu are smocks mainly produced in Northern Ghana. Kaba are blouses with matching skirts for women made from woven, printed, batiked or tie-dyed materials that are made locally and/or imported from every corner of the world. Hand-tailored shirts for men are also made with these fabrics.

In Ghana, it is standard practice that customers bring their own fabrics to a designer, although it is possible to ask the dressmaker to source the materials. Some designers, working for the high-end of the market, source high-quality materials worldwide, but this is a rather small segment of the market concentrated in Accra and Kumasi, the second largest city in Ghana. Aisha Obuobi, creative director of Christie Brown, for instance, produces haute couture and limited ready-to-wear collections. In the last 10 years there has been a tremendous increase in ready-to-wear availability in the shopping malls of Accra and Kumasi and specialist shops of some high-end fashion designers. Since the late 1990s, many cheap materials, especially from China, India and Korea, have saturated the market, including cheaper versions of so-called 'African-print' textiles.[6] With the influx of Southeast Asian cheap fabrics in the late 1990s, the local machine-printed textile industry declined further.[7] In recent years, the Ghanaian government has established several garment firms in Accra and Tema to boost the fashion industry.[8]

Historical Ghanaian Fashions

Fashion-consciousness is nothing new in Ghana. For example, in Figure 10.6, we see an early 19th century drawing of a colourful Asante festival. Festivals play, and have played for centuries, a major role in many Ghanaian royal and aristocratic courts, and they are also, among many other social functions, a fashion show of the newest designs in locally made kente, smocks, adinkra prints and other hand-made cloths. As cut and uncut garments, kente should also be seen as mainly a bespoke fashion, as they are more often produced on commission, so that design innovation lies at the heart of this tradition.[9]

Furthermore, the archival records of European merchants of the 17th to 19th century, who traded European and Indian textiles and accessories for a range of African goods and enslaved Africans, shows many complaints indicating that they could not keep up with the changing fashions and requests for dress and fashion items along the West African coast.[10]

Tailored customized clothing produced in Ghana using sewing machines can be traced back to the 19th century, but hand-sewn tailored smocks and trousers have been around throughout West Africa since at least the 8th century.[11] European tailored clothes had been imported and sold at coastal 'factories' since the Portuguese built the Elmina fort in 1482 (the first trading post built on the Gulf of Guinea). In the 19th century, European missionaries and African-Brazilian returnees introduced sewing machines and the making of machine-tailored clothing.[12] George Aruna Nelson, descendant of

Figure 10.6 A display of Asante Ghanaian pomp and pageantry. Illustrator: T. E. Bowditch, Engraved by R. Havell & Son. 1818.

these African-Brazilian returnees, founded Scissors House in 1854, the first tailoring shop in Accra.[13] In the Volta Region, one of the requirements for conversion to Christianity was the wearing of tailored dress. Missionary wives trained young women to sew clothes for themselves and their children from imported Western materials.[14] When working in the Volta Region, a Pietist missionary of the Norddeutsche Missiongesellschaft noted the strong local fashion consciousness. In 1894, he rather surprisingly commented (framed in the racist tone common among Europeans of that time): 'Their ideal is and this is what they [Ewe ethnic converts working for the mission] work for: *Beautiful clothes* and good food . . . Or in a free hour they ask me to look at my photograph album . . .'[15]

The people of Ghana practised bespoke fashion that has evolved over time and which continues to be relevant in their lives today. Fashion cultures differed from place to place; local innovations, regional and international trends, disseminated through elaborate networks of textile and garment trades, all influenced people's choices in what to wear.

Understanding Poster Cultures

Within the extensive literature on popular culture in Africa, writing on visual media forms and in particular on posters is relatively new even though these posters have been produced in large quantities throughout the continent and play diverse roles in African society.[16] Posters have been popular collectors' items, finding their way to archives and museums worldwide, such as the National Museum of Ethnology (Museum Minpaku), Osaka, Japan, and it is therefore not surprising that many of these publications discussing posters rely on literature collections.[17] These focus predominantly on political posters, public information posters (for instance health and education), advertisements for new video-film productions and religious movements, and posters with a commercial goal.[18] This latter genre includes posters for new hairstyles and fashion styles, and they are often referred to as 'almanachs', 'calendars', or 'calendriers'.[19]

It is unclear when posters first appeared in Ghana but public education and health posters, political party campaign posters as well as posters featuring new fashions and hairstyles have been around since at least the 1950s.[20] Wendelin Schmidt asserts that the printed poster in general in Africa originated in the 1960s, and as she writes mainly on Ghanaian, Nigerian and Beninoise posters, this is presumable also the case for Ghanaian posters.[21] Suzanne Gott, more specifically, places the widespread use of fashion posters in the late 1990s in Ghana, when they replaced the practice of displaying completed commissions of the latest kaba fashions on colourfully painted fashionable-lady plywood hangers produced by local sign painters.[22] In the early 1990s, seamstresses also displayed mock-ups of current kaba blouse styles, made from sturdy paper bags.[23] This practice clearly changed the process of choosing a style. Giorgio Miesher also situates the beginning of the fashion poster in the early 1990s, and regards the fashion posters introduced by Akosombo Textiles Limited in 1972 as the forerunner to the modern poster.[24] This sounds plausible as fashion posters are still often called fashion calendars in Ghana, but they might have already been produced before the 1990s. Several designers remembered their use in the early 1990s, however, none of the people that we interviewed were working in the 1980s, and a more exact history of the early development of fashion posters is yet to be written.

Interviewing Fashion Creators

The vignettes with which we opened this chapter were drawn from a pilot study that we conducted in 2018 and 2019 among tailors, dressmakers and designers on the one hand, and fashion poster producers and sellers on the other. We interviewed 30 fashion creators from city centres and rural communities in the Central Region and the Volta Region. Winneba, one of the municipal centres in the Central Region (c. 60,000 inhabitants), is noted for its fishing communities, masquerade festival (fancy dress) and local ceramics. Bawjiase, which is about 50 minutes' drive to Accra, is a town located in the Awutu Senya East district of the Central Region of Ghana.[25] Ho (c. 70,000 inhabitants) is the Volta Region's regional capital and economic hub. Agotime-Kpetoe, one of the main weaving centres of kente in the Volta Region, has around 37,000 inhabitants.[26]

We used participant and direct observations to further understand the creative relationships between clients and designers, and the role of fashion posters in this interaction. We also interviewed two of the most popular fashion poster producers in the Greater Accra Region. While it is often assumed that the pace of dispersal of fashion, the variety of fashion practices and number of fashion businesses is greater in cities than in rural areas, our experiences suggest that the fashion systems in Ghana operate in more complex and dense ways. As much of the literature focuses on the elite markets and capital cities, we focused on regional and rural areas and the production of fashion for the lower- and middle-class segments in the market in an attempt to contribute further in decolonizing Eurocentric as well as African fashion discourses.[27]

Creative Encounters

Fashion networks in Ghana, like elsewhere in Africa, with its mainly informal and small-scale productions, intertwine culture and economics, creative power and economic oppression. It is 'a world of creative power, not only in the objects and meanings it produces but also in its modes of exchange between producers and consumers'.[27] These creative encounters in the myriad economic arrangements of tailoring establishments ultimately shape the kaleidoscopic fashion styles found on the streets throughout Ghana.

Fashion posters and magazines serve as albums from which some clients select their preferred design. The posters are pasted or hung in the tailoring and dressmaking shops to attract potential clients. Even though mobile phones and social media play an increasing role in the creative process between designers and customers, especially among younger people, fashion creators continue to patronize these posters.

Clients' Patronage of Designs in Posters

Many clients visit tailoring shops with no particular dress style in mind. Most of the time, they bring their own fabric, but refer to the posters (and magazines) to choose a design. Sometimes they buy material from the atelier, or ask the fashion creators to source the material. Clients often seek design advice from the fashion creators. They in turn base their advice on the surface and structural decoration details of the clients' fabrics, the body type of the customer and the occasion the dress style is meant for. Hardly any of the customers approach the fashion creators with sketches of their dress styles to be sewn. However, whether clients select their designs from social media or fashion posters, they often suggest modifications of their chosen designs, such as resizing of parts, or repositioning of pockets, collar, and notions.

Age and purchasing power play a role in the importance of fashion posters in the creative process. In the capital Accra, where a larger part of the population uses smart phones, fashion posters are especially found in the low-income neighbourhoods.[28] However, even in these neighbourhoods, when there is access to power, smartphones and the internet, youthful clients rely more on what is trending on social media to select their dress styles. They frequent social events with their phones and take shots of interesting dress styles to build a mini-image gallery on their phones. They also take shots from electronic and print media, and on the street. Many fashion designers do the same, as well as building up image galleries through the pictures sent to them, and snaps they take of their own sewn outfits.

The creative interaction between designers and clients is a proper dialogue in which modifications are negotiated. Sometimes this is predominantly based on one design, whether from social media or posters, but more often creating a new outfit based on several elements of different outfits. The designer is expected to advise, and clients endorse their trust in repeat visits and recommending a designer to others.

Purchasing Fashion Posters

The ways in which fashion creators use fashion posters in their creative interactions with clients includes their selection of preferred printed posters out of the hundreds released. It is clear that location matters in terms of accessibility to posters. In the major metropolitan areas, such as Accra and Kumasi, some individuals and small groups of fashion creators select their own designs to be produced in posters. However, the majority of creators in Accra, Kumasi, Winneba and Ho buy them from markets and itinerant sellers. In Winneba, the designers purchase these posters from itinerant merchandisers who come from Swedru, a nearby urban centre, 25 minutes away by car. These itinerant poster traders carry in their hands numerous posters on hangers for display and marketing. In the two rural centres in which we conducted research, people either travelled to larger towns to get these posters, or were buying them from occasional itinerant traders. In Winneba and Ho, designers do not produce their own posters. However, in Bonwire, a town of around 10,000 people which is one of the main centres for hand-woven kente weaving in the Ashanti Region, some tailors and seamstresses, through the local branch of their fashion association,[29] regularly order posters with the newest fashion styles – in particular the latest fashion in kabas and mens' shirts – made in kente.[30]

As well as their own preferences, fashion creators buy posters with their particular customers in mind. When interviewed, the main reason fashion creators gave for choosing particular fashion posters was the number of innovative or new designs featured, as it is the dominant feature that clients are looking for. Designs on posters that the fashion creators considered as conventional or obsolete did not encourage them to buy. Other factors that influenced the fashion creators' selection of posters were creativity, simplicity and aesthetic appeal of the fashion designs, decorative finish of the outfits, the overall look of the poster, the extent the poster fits with the perceived taste of their customers, and how well new posters add to the existing body of posters acquired during the lifespan of a designer's business. Sometimes the suitability of the slogans on the posters, shaped by social happenings and events, also influenced purchasing decisions.

Characteristically, bespoke fashion emphasizes individual styles. Individuals crave to look distinctive in what they wear. A fashionable classic or trend may be subjected to subtle changes in terms of colour choice, cuts, fabrics type, or decorative finishing techniques to give it contemporary uniqueness in appearance. However, the aesthetics of fashion in the Ghanaian context goes beyond the colour schemes, cuts, decorative detailing and general look or appearance of the fabric to be worn. The editorial choices of poster producers also shape the creative encounter, albeit in more complex ways than one would expect.

Poster Producers

The production of these fashion posters and magazines in Ghana is a creative venture that also contributes to the circulation of new fashion trends and styles. First, good posters are characterized by simplicity, boldness, legibility and attractiveness. This means that for a poster to communicate its intended message well, it must possess these features to draw the attention of its audience. In the case of the fashion poster, picture quality, the modelling of fashions (including tailoring to fit), and stylistic placement of the pictures are crucial to the success of the entire poster (Figures 10.4 and 10.5).

Most fashion posters are produced by individual publishers/printers, but some fashion magazine companies also produce posters. They select their designs from specific fashion designers and edit them for production. The great majority of fashion posters are sold wholesale in one particular lane in Kantamanto Market, central Accra.[31] One of the fashion poster designers and producers, Thomas Boakye (Figure 10.7), has been in business for the past 18 years and also designs fashion posters for neighbouring countries including Nigeria, Cote d'Ivoire and Togo. He purchases fabrics of high aesthetic value and creates designs that would appeal to customers. He illustrates or describes the design to his tailor-machinists who construct the garments. The design is tailored to fit a model after which a photoshoot is done. The images are then edited to create the posters.

Figure 10.7 Thomas Boakye, fashion poster designer, in his shop full of stacks of fashion posters. Kantamanto Market, Accra, 2018 © Photo Malika Kraamer.

Boakye pointed out that he is part of a fashion poster/magazine association that regulates the number of fashion posters produced by members per month. Each member of the association is bound to produce a maximum of two fashion posters in a month. After the fashion posters are done, they print in thousands to test the market, and increase production based on patronage. One stunning feature of these fashion posters is their seemingly simple yet complex naming system. The naming system is characterized by slogans, aphorisms, proverbs, titles of trending/popular songs, and titles of popular local or foreign operas aired by Ghanaian television stations, among others. For example, a poster named 'Ahenepa nkasa' (Precious beads make no noise) (Figure 10.4) is an Akan proverb that warns against boastfulness or pride. It also connotes intrinsic and extrinsic beauty. Ascribing such interesting names to posters that feature fashion designs reveals the premium they place on the designs featured.

Like posters, fashion magazines can be found in almost every fashion atelier that also has posters, but their use is less frequent, especially outside Accra. They are more expensive, meaning many ateliers only have very few, and fashion posters are easier to use in the dialogue between fashion creator and client. Some of the current Ghanaian fashion magazines are *Glitz Africa* magazine, *Krobia Fashion*, and *Adehyie Magazine*. *Krobia Fashion* have been making posters since at least the early 1990s, with African-print fashion outfits to counteract the influence of second-hand clothing. They now produce posters and magazines to promote African wear. They work with a small team of fashion and graphic designers, photographers and magazine production personnel. The whole team is involved in the final selection of designs. *Adehyie* also made posters at first, but shifted completely to making magazines. Their team of freelance fashion designers, who provide the designs and fabrics and use in-house models for their photoshoots, target middle- and upper-class customers and strive to influence their purchasing decisions. 'We look at the colour schemes, the religious festivities, the fabric type, and the available fabrics on the Ghanaian market to create'.[32] Trending locally and foreign produced fabric types, social festivities, and the latest fashion cuts and embellishments largely inform the editorial teams of the two magazines in their creation of new dress outfits for publication.

The advent of the smartphone, more than the fashion magazines, has affected fashion poster producers as it has challenged them to release more unique and innovative designs to satisfy the tastes of buyers.[33] However, most consumers do not use smartphones in opposition to posters, but rather simultaneously in creating the outfit they envision.

From the fashion behaviour of consumers, fashion creators, and fashion posters/ magazine producers, a cyclical system works to promote fashion business in a bespoke environment. The print and electronic media, social gatherings and clients' own imaginations contribute to fashion designers' creation and dissemination. Posters/ calendars dominate, in the case of Ghana, since they are found in almost every tailoring/ dressmaking shop, even in the remotest village. The internet also contributes and the dissemination process is facilitated by availability of and accessibility to image-based information communication technologies (ICT) and a power supply. The multiple channels of image dissemination make fashion diffusion uniform across many demographics and increase the consumption rate once accepted.

Conclusion

Fashion posters in Ghana continue to play an influential part in the creative process between fashion creators and their customers and form part of the complex Ghanaian bespoke fashion system. The case study we present here is a clear example of the complex nature of many African fashion systems and the rich facets of African creativity. It helps to rethink fashion globalization discourses and shows that the dichotomy between urban and rural areas is much more complex than often theorized. Although major trends and styles clearly originate in the main metropolitan areas including Accra and Kumasi, which in turn are in an ongoing and complex relationship with trends elsewhere in the world, the bespoke nature and creative use of fashion posters means that there is a continuous invention of new styles and individual tastes by the plethora of designers in rural and regional urban centres.

Consumer preferences are key in fashion creation and production, and contribute to the sustenance of bespoke fashion. These preferences and the desire to be individualistic give anchorage to custom-tailored creation in contrast to mass-produced clothing. The fashion posters have become handy tools in bespoke fashion advertising that shape and inform the fashion choices of consumers and are still of great importance even though smartphones have opened up another way of communicating consumer preferences.

The limited amount of analysis of Ghanaian and other African fashion posters in the existing literature is surprising given their prominence of use. It is perhaps related to the way that most studies of Ghanaian and other West African fashion systems focus on *haute couture* and high-end, often globalized, fashion markets, which is exactly that segment of the market that does not use these posters.[34] Ignoring fashion posters implicitly includes traces of Eurocentric and/or colonial analytical models and does not do justice to the complexity within fashion systems in different parts of the world.

Notes

1. Personal communication with Hamidu Tanni, Ho and Pat Glauh-Yeh, Ho, December 2018.

2. Personal communication with Edith Kuleke, Agotime-Kpetoe, December 2018.

3. Personal communication with Wofa Kurabi, Winneba, December 2018.

4. Personal communication, Nelly Hagan-Deegbe, September 2019.

5. L. W. Rabine, *The Global Circulation of African Fashion* (Oxford: Berg, 2002) 27; K. T. Hansen, 'Introduction'. In K. T. Hansen and D. S. Madison, Eds. *African Dress: Fashion, Agency, Performance* (London: Bloomsbury, 2013) 1.

6. The Ghanaian fashion industry is largely made up of small-scale fashion creators established as sole proprietor businesses (Figure 10.1 and 10.3). In 1995, only 72 medium-/large-scale garment manufacturing companies were registered with the Ministry of Trade and Industry (down from 138 in 1979); most of them are concentrated in Accra and Tema. V. O. Ampofo, *Ghana's Textile/Garment Industry* (Ghana: Industrial Development and Investment Division, Ministry of Trade and Industry, 2011).

7. O. Q. Essel, 'Deconstructing the Concept of "African print" in the Ghanaian Experience', *Africology: The Journal of Pan African* Studies, 11 (1) (2017) 37–51.

8. A. M. Amankwah, W. Baidoe and C. A. Chichi, *Ripple Effect of a Vibrant Fashion Industry on Graduate Unemployment* (Kumasi: Department of Industrial Art, Kwame Nkrumah University of Science and Technology, 2014); B. E. Dzramedo and R. Dabuo, 'Challenges and Sustainability of Smock Weaving within the West Gonja District of the Northern Region', *Ghana Journal of Science, Technology and Development*, 3 (1) (2015) 36–43.

9. M. Kraamer, 'Origin Disputed: The Making, Use and Evaluation of Ghanaian Textiles', *Afrique: Archéologie & Arts* 4 (2006) 53–76.

10. C. E. Kriger, *Cloth in West African History* (Lanham: Altamira Press, 2006); M. Kraamer, 'Thomas Clark's West African Textiles: Abolitionism and Kente Cloth in the Early Modern African World'. In B. Marin-Aguilera and S. Hanß, Eds. *In-Between Textiles* (forthcoming).

11. Kriger, *Cloth in West African History*; Q. O. Essel and E. R. K. Amissah, 'Smock Fashion Culture in Ghana's Dress Identity-Making', *Historical Research Letter*, 1 (2015) 32–39; D. Heathcote, 'Hausa Embroidered Dress', *African Arts* 15 (2) (2009) 12–19, 82, 84.

12. African-Brazilian returnees are called Tabom people in Ghana. They have settled on the shores of West Africa since 1836.

13. 'The Business of Street Fashion in Accra', http://accradotaltradio.com/2014/04/the-business-of-street-fashion-in-accra/ (accessed on 26 April 2020).

14. B. Meyer, 'Christian Mind and Worldly Matters: Religion and Materiality in Nineteenth Century Gold Coast', *Journal of Material Culture*, 2 (3) (1997) 328.

15. Monatsblatt der Norddeutsche Missionsgeschelschaft 1894, 19, in Meyer, 'Christian Mind and Worldly Matters', 328.

16. K. Barber, *Readings in African Popular Culture* (Bloomington, IN: Indiana University Press, 1997); K. Barber, *A History of African Popular Culture: New Approaches to African History* (Cambridge: Cambridge University Press, 2018); J. Fabian, *Remembering the Presence: Painting and Popular History in Zaire* (Chicago, IL: University of Chicago Press, 1997); A. Mbembe, 'The "Thing" & its Doubles in Cameroonian Cartoons'. In K. Barber, Ed. *Readings in African Popular Culture* (London: James Currey; Bloomington: Indiana University Press, 1997), 151–163; S. Newell, *Readings in African Popular Fiction* (Oxford, London and Indiana: James Currey, International African Institute and Indiana University Press, 2011); J. Ogude and J. Nyairo, Eds., *Urban Legends, Colonial Myths: Popular Culture and Literature in East Africa* (Trenton: Africa World Press, 2007); Gadzakpo, 'Street News: The Role of Posters in Democratic Participation in Ghana'. In H. Wasserman, Ed. *Popular Media, Democracy and Development in Africa* (London: Routledge, 2010) 105; G. Miescher, L. Rizzo, and J. Silvester, Eds. *Posters in Action: Visuality in the Making of an African Nation* (Basel: Basler Afrika Bibliographien, 2009) 6.

17. e.g. South African History Archive, *Images of Defiance: South African Resistance Posters of the 1980s* (Johannesburg: STE Publishers, 1991); W. Schmidt, 'Mass Media and Visual Communication', *Third Text*, 19 (3) (2005) 307–316; G. Miescher and D. Henrichsen, *African Posters: A Catalogue of the Poster Collection in Basler Afrika* (Basel: Basler Afrika Bibliographien, 2004); Miescher et al., *Posters in Action*.

18. See for instance L. Fourie, 'South African Election Posters: Reflecting the Maturing of a Democracy', *Communication*, 34 (2) (2008) 222–237; Gadzakpo, 'Street News'.

19. Schmidt, 'Mass Media and Visual Communication', 27–42.

20. Gadzakpo, 'Street News', 107.

21. Schmidt, 'Mass Media and Visual Communication'.

22. S. Gott, K. S. Loughran, B. D. Quick and L. W. Rabine, Eds. *African-Print Fashion Now. A Story of Taste, Globalization and Style* (Los Angeles, CA: Fowler Museum Publications, 2017) 143–144.

23. ibid., 143

24. Akosombo Textiles Limited, owned by the Cha Textile Groups since 1970, was established in Ghana in 1967. For marketing proposes, in 1971 they started to organize fashion shows. The target market was Ghanaian young people in particular, and it gradually became a household name without ever advertising in the local press. Producing fashion calendars, starting in 1972, was another marketing strategy. S. F. Miescher, 'Bringing Fabrics to Life: Akosombo Textiles Limited of Ghana'. In S. Gott, K. S. Loughran, B. D. Quick and L. W. Rabine, Eds. *African-Print Fashion Now. A Story of Taste, Globalization and Style* (Los Angeles, CA: Fowler Museum Publications, 2017) 87–95.

25. Osuanyi Quaicoo Essel conducted interviews and observations in Winneba, his place of work, and Bawjiase, his hometown.

26. Malika Kraamer conducted interviews and observations in Ho and Kpetoe. She has been coming to these two places for over two decades and lived there for more than three years. Kwarshie Evans from Agotime-Kpetoe and Xorla Adabla from Ho supported her in this research.

27. L. W. Rabine, *The Global Circulation of African Fashion* (Oxford: Berg, 2002) 5.

28. More young customers in Winneba than in Ho reported the use of social media, possibly as the Volta Region is relatively less wealthy than the Central Region.

29. There is an umbrella association named Ghana Tailors and Dressmakers Assocation. There are branches of this association in almost every district. Separate from that, fashion poster producers also have an association.

30. Personal communication, Prince Agyeman, Bonwire, August and December 2018.

31. Kantamanto Market is the largest second-hand clothes market, and is adjacent to Makola Market, the largest point of trade in the city. One lane has several fashion poster producers. Kantamanto is a community in itself, full of shoes, hand-me-down clothes, footwear, vehicle spare parts and home décor, all arranged in large piles and displays with almost no space left to spare.

32. Personal communication, Owusu, Accra, 2018.

33. Personal communication, Thomas Boakye, Accra, 2018.

34. A notable exception is N. Sylvanus, *Patterns in Circulation: Cloth, Gender, and Materiality in West Africa* (Chicago, IL: University of Chicago Press, 2016).

CHAPTER 11
STATE OF FASHION: SEARCHING FOR THE NEW LUXURY
José TEUNISSEN

Introduction

Due to the digitalization and globalization of fashion at the start of the 21st century a new generation of fashion designers has come to rise, who no longer need to move to established fashion centres to start a global career and to gain global recognition. Through web shops, blogs, social media and local Fashion Weeks they are able to establish a global business from anywhere. As a result, the fashion discourse has slowly started to change into a more decolonial,[1] inclusive narrative and practice.[2]

As stated in my previous exhibitions and research, this new generation of fashion designers are operating from a new and engaged vision.[3] Being aware of the current social and environmental issues of the current fashion system, they have started to fundamentally rethink and redefine the fashion system by implementing new values and new imaginations that are more inclusive and informed, decentred, using sustainability, local economy, craft revivals and new micro-narratives as key drivers. With increasing amounts of newcomers having a non-Western background, the fashion discourse is opening up to include new voices, and different values and aesthetics which are not part of the conventional values and notions of the dominant Western fashion history, and to welcome the intertwining of this discourse with conceptualism, modernism and post-modernism. Instead, this new generation is taking an approach in line with what curator and scholar Nicolas Bourriaud coins 'altermodernism', a new aesthetic with a more inclusive value-system because of globalization. 'From the understanding that the universal master narrative of modernism is obsolete, as well as the idea of judging each work according to the codes of its author's local culture implies the existence of viewers who have mastered each culture's referential field, we need to imagine and learn to decode any global language preferable without judgement'.[4] A globalization that according to the anthropologist Arjun Appadurai has resulted in a new concept of imagination no longer portrays/presents an ephemeral and glamourous phantasy, but an organized field of social practices, a form of work (in the sense of both labour and culturally organized practice).[5]

My findings are based on the research I have undertaken, as a curator, for the exhibition *The Future of Fashion is Now* that took place from October 11, 2014 until January 18, 2015 in Museum Boijmans van Beuningen in Rotterdam, addressing how globalization was driving the current changes in the fashion system then. Here I showcased how sustainable thinking, digitalization, a new approach to materials and craft became drivers for change whilst embedding speculative ideas for a better future reflecting new values – via new narratives and new stories – as well as by embedding more inclusive identities, and political activism.

The exhibition, *State of Fashion: Searching for the New Luxury* (Arnhem June 1 – July 26, 2018) started as a further exploration of this disruptive transition to the fashion system. Via an open call supported by the Prince Claus Fund, we invited designers from all over the world to participate and to share ideas that offer new perspectives on these fashion themes.[6] The selection of the panel as well as further research informed the selection of the final 50 contributors to the exhibition and deepened the themes of the exhibition. This chapter focuses on the exhibition themes *interrogating* what fashion luxury means in this moment of time, where we are aware of both big societal challenges and the scarcity of our resources, and with what kind of luxury we want to surround ourselves in the 21st century. In more theoretical terms, the exhibition (and this chapter) explored what 'fashion luxury' means in a context where we are re-defining the fashion discourse and fashion system in light of globalization, de-colonization, de-Westernization and the urgent need for more responsible consumption.

Radicant Identities

In *The Radicant* (2009), Nicolas Bourriaud addresses globalization in the context of aesthetics, questioning how globalization is affecting our life *forms*.[7] Essential to him is to re-think the Western concept of modernity into what he coins altermodernity, referring to a more inclusive aesthetic born out of global and decentralized negotiations and heterogeneous discourses, which are *polyglot*.[8] Different from postmodernism, altermodernism does not concern itself with the past, origins and 'authentic' and 'national' identity, but with the future: premised on the destination rather than the source. 'What I am calling altermodernity thus designates a construction plan that would allow new intercultural connections, the construction of a space of negotiation going beyond postmodern multiculturalism, which is attached to the origin of discourses and forms rather than to their dynamics. It is a matter of replacing the question of origin with that of destination. Where should we go?' states Bourriaud.[9]

In essence, altermodernism is a translation-oriented modernity that – unlike the modernism of the 20th century that cultivated a Western colonial language of progression – is seeking compromises in singular discourses, to enable disparate elements to function together. As such Bourriaud offered an adequate framework to describe current developments in the fashion system, originally a Western capitalist phenomenon,[10] opening up for more inclusive, non-hierarchical conversations re-defining universal social and aesthetic values as well as addressing current challenges.[11] In Bourriaud's terminology, every artist and every author (and every fashion designer) becomes a translator accepting the idea that no speech bears the seal of any sort of 'authenticity', but is entering a world of subtitling, establishing a path in a multicultural landscape.[12]

The so-called altermodern designers understand how to actively re-think and reshape our classical notions of identities explored by the conventional fashion and art system. They are addressing issues such as globalization, de-colonization, political, social and economic systems in an open dialogue, whilst using traces of heritage, craft and values of their own cultural and social origins in a space where those elements come together in non-hierarchical ways.

As a result, these changes have an effect on the role of the designer in our contemporary culture. It is no longer the star designer who dominates the fashion system, but the designers who are embodying 'the figure of the immigrant, the exile, the tourist and the urban wanderer'.[13] As we will see described in the examples in the subthemes here below, fashion designers are taking up different roles, not putting themselves in the centre as the creative genius, instead taking a supporting and collaborative role bringing together skills, ideas, narratives, heritage, artisans, and engineers to create a sustainable, inclusive, ethical future. Living in a globally connected and culturally globalized world, the designers create new paths and practices whilst integrating their local cultural backgrounds into the future using problem-solving thinking approaches. 'With at once dynamic and dialogical signification, the adjective "radicant"[14] captures this contemporary subject, caught between the need for a connection with its environment and the forces of uprooting, between globalization and singularity, between identity and opening to the other'. states Bourriaud.[15] By definition, they do not depend on a single root for their growth but advance in all directions on whatever surfaces present themselves by attaching multiple hooks as ivy does.[16] Radicant here means setting one's roots in motion, staging them in heterogeneous contexts and formats denying them the power to completely define one's identity, translating ideas, transcoding images, transplanting behaviours, exchanging rather than imposing.[17] Exploring these new constructions of 'fragmented' identity, designers require new forms of presentation. They are not only producing garments and products anymore, but they invite the consumer to accompany them throughout the entire design and thought process, presented by means of *micro-narratives* and *future scenarios* showing the process.

Imagination in the Post Nation-State

Through an anthropological lens, Arjun Appadurai prognosticates in *Modernity at Large* (1996) that the nation-state has entered a terminal crisis, because the system is poorly equipped to deal with the interlinked diaspora of people and images that mark the here and now. Considering media and migration as its two major, and interconnected, diacritics he explores their joint effect on the *work of imagination* as a constitutive feature of modern subjectivity.[18] According to him, electronic media have decisively changed the wider field of mass media, because they offer new resources and new disciplines for the construction of imagined selves and imagined worlds. 'The image, the imagined, and the imaginary – these are all terms that direct us to something critical and new in global cultural processes: the imagination as a social practice', states Appadurai.[19] The same applies to fashion, where one of the distinctive forces is that it is able to create new worlds and manages to tempt us to immerse ourselves within them. Designers and labels are increasingly using this force of the imagination as a space of contestation in which individuals and groups seek to annex the global into their own practice of the modern.[20]

The Failure of the Current Fashion System

More and more it has become clear the current fashion system is outdated, still operating within a 20th-century model that celebrates individualism and consumption with a focus on 'the new' and the 'star designer'.[21] On the one hand, designers and big brands experience enormous pressure to produce new collections at an ever-growing pace, leaving less room for reflection, contemplation and innovation. On the other hand, there is the continuous race to produce at even lower costs and implement more rapid life cycles, resulting in disastrous consequences for society and the environment.[22] As a result, the classical luxurious dream of escapism into a world of glamour and Parisian elegance as traditionally represented in fashion magazines and luxury brands has ended. More and more designers coming from different continents are exploring new ways to redefine fashion as luxury underlining the values of the 21st century and the Millennial and Gen Z generations, who ride a bicycle instead of owning a car, prefer a 'shared economy' over property and possession and embody environmental awareness. As conscious consumers, they want to know how things are made, as well as what the ethical impact is of what they are buying. Working from their pocket and intensively using social media, they are shifting the traditional boundaries between public and private life, 'blurring' the conventional 'urban landscape' and the place of the flâneur as pivotal to fashion. 'Globalization has shattered the stable hierarchy of centre and periphery, the neat distinction between the city and non-urbanized areas has faded, the mobility of people has immensely increased, and the means of communication (especially social media) have become places for social life', states Patrizia Calefato in *The End of Fashion*.[23] It makes clear that the system as we know it does not function anymore.

The Need to Re-Define Fashion and Luxury

In *How Luxury Lost its Luster* (2007), Dana Thomas describes how during the late 1980s small family-run fashion luxury businesses slowly turned into big luxury goods holding companies. It was the moment where a longstanding focus on the artisanship and exclusivity of these brands turned to a focus on enlarging profits by making them accessible for the masses, focusing on handbags, accessories and cosmetics whilst outsourcing their fashion production to developing nations. This has led to an inferior quality and a non-transparent supply chain. The same story – in a slightly different way – applies to fast fashion chains and many high street brands whose aim is to reduce costs as much as possible by outsourcing production to nations where wages are lowest. In recent years, the devastating effects of this outsourcing policy have become visible, with Rana Plaza[24] as an iconic example.

As a result, traditional fashion luxury values seem no longer appealing to (especially) the younger generations – now the biggest consumer market in luxury. 'Less interested in outward displays of status they buy luxury primarily to please themselves', states Diane Primo in *Forbes*, based on a Deloitte report *What Makes Millennials Spend More?* (2017).[25] Although the majority of Chinese Millennials still prefer to buy a premium brand, the majority of UK, Italian and US Millennials do not show interest anymore in the status of a premium brand. Remarkably, almost 40% of Chinese Millennials do make sure the brand is ethical and sustainable before they purchase, which is much more than the 20% of UK and Italian Millennials. Although Chinese Millennials still appreciate luxury brands, their sustainable and ethical awareness is almost as high as that of the US Millennials (48%) (Deloitte, 2017). The recent success of the Gucci Equilibrium programme – Millennials and Gen Z already account for nearly 50% of Gucci's total sales– demonstrates clearly the need for a committed, ethical approach to business and *new fashion luxury* values such as *purpose*, *authenticity* and *passion*.[26] Oskar Metsavaht

Figure 11.1 'Manifesto' 2018. State of Fashion: Searching for the New Luxury. Photograph: Eva Broekema.

(Osklen) and Stella McCartney have already proven that a sustainable (conscious and ethical) approach is commercially viable for a luxury brand. In 2011 Franca Sozanni proposed in *Vogue* Italy that luxury fashion should be approached more from the lens of art and design, adding artistic value as experimentation, research and innovation to the values of what fashion luxury might offer.[27] Purpose, ethics, research and innovation (digital and material), as well as experimentation in the context of art and design, have brought a new range of values and drivers to the table, which might be able to inform new definitions of a 21st-century concept of fashion and luxury.

With a manifesto of nine hashtags and five subthemes, *State of Fashion: Searching for the New Luxury* tried to capture in more detail and depth what these new definitions and directions of 'new luxury' in fashion might entail (Figure 11.1). The nine hashtags of the manifesto refer to a series of concrete actions, solutions and directions that fashion brands and consumers are currently exploring to gain a more ethical, purposeful innovative engagement with fashion. In addition, the five subthemes clustered and underlined new principles, insights and opportunities informing directions and values for the future of fashion luxury. The themes not only refer to the fashion product on a design and aesthetic level, they also involve changes to the fashion system involving new and different values, new designer roles in manufacturing and design processes, as well as new micro-narratives and new business models.

Subtheme 1: New Imaginations

The first theme refers to a new design aesthetic, underlining that imagination is no longer referencing the conventional ephemeral, glamorous fashion history but is shaping new and more responsible, socially connected worlds. The latest campaign of sustainable pioneer Stella McCartney formed such a cornerstone of a new visual identity and concept, imagined for her work in sustainability. The film, made by Viviane Sassen, conveys the symbiotic nature of humans, nature and animals; it explores the idea that to fully protect and care for ourselves we must also nurture the world we live in, as we are one and the same. The words of Maria Barnas' poem 'To Nurture, To Nature' – specially conceived for the project – are recited over the film.

Through Sassen's abstract visual language demonstrating ideas about abstraction and objects in relation to their often incongruous surroundings, Stella McCartney finds a new way to engage in sustainability conversations. Perfectly illustrating the cutting-edge sense and original imagination, whilst avoiding any references to the classical fashion dream of elegance, they build in purpose and ethics around sustainability (Figure 11.2). In addition, the visionary work of the Japanese designer Yuima Nakazato, inspired by new technologies, integrates laser cutting techniques and body scanning with traditional samurai buttoning principles, and displays an interesting hybrid of heritage and craft in combination with state-of-the-art technologies.

Eco-fashion designers VIN + OMI (2004) combine Chinese and English backgrounds and call themselves an ideology instead of a brand. They primarily focus on the

Figure 11.2 'Stella's World of Sustainability' 2017 Viviane Sassen for Stella McCartney, The Netherlands/UK. Photograph: Eva Broekema.

Figure 11.3 'Freedom' a/w 2017–2018 Yuima Nakazato, Japan. Photograph: Eva Broekema.

development of unique sustainable textiles. The origins of each fabric have a social programme built around them. For example, areas of river or ocean in need of cleaning up from plastic waste were identified, and VIN + OMI initiated a clean-up project to collect the plastic, which was then turned into rPET fabric. Until now, they have produced and patented 12 unique fabrics. As such, they use their company primarily as a driver of sustainable change and an activist tool.

All the examples described so far are shaping sustainable stories and innovative products by using new technologies as well as ethics and a political agenda with imagination (Figure 11.3). Precisely these changes have taken the fashion imagination from a glamorous ephemeral fantasy towards an imagination that relates to fashion as a social and embodied practice. The imagination is today a staging ground for action, and not only for escape.[28]

Subtheme 2: The Product and the Maker in the Spotlight

The internet has made it possible to make all the layers within the production chain visible. It allows us as consumers to make better-informed and more conscious choices when consuming fashion. However, this is not the only benefit. Access to more information can shape new, horizontal relationships between us, and the producers of our garments. With a better understanding of the skills and craftsmanship that go into the creation of a garment (a knowledge that many of us have lost), the artisans involved in making our clothes gain not only our recognition, but also better financial rewards, and intermediaries like shops, producers and marketers (the so called middle men) disappear.

11.11/eleven eleven, a label established by the Indian entrepreneurs Mia Morikawa (1983) and Shani Himanshu (1980), are bringing the journey of kala cotton and khadi denim, from seed to stitch, into focus in their Khadi Way project. Each product within this collection is handmade from start to finish. *11.11/eleven eleven* garments have a product code that traces the human imprint on the product and helps to connect the maker and wearer. The project contributes to environmental sustainability by using organic materials and recycled waste materials. Kala is one of the few genetically pure cotton species left in India, and one of the only species of pure old world cotton that is still cultivated on a large scale without requiring external input from farmers. The project also contributes to social sustainability by cherishing values such as traceability, transparency and local craftsmanship. The product in their approach becomes the materialization of a novel relationship between consumer and the artisan, which is shifting the focus from the 'star designer' to the value of the artisanship, cultural origins and traces behind it whilst putting them in a new global context of ethical sustainability.

Vivienne Westwood Bags are 'handmade with love' in Nairobi in Kenya, produced in collaboration with the Ethical Fashion Initiative (EFI) of the International Trade Centre, and highlight a comparable story. EFI is a joint body of the United Nations (UN) and the World Trade Organization (WTO), currently supporting the work of thousands of micro-producers from marginalized African communities. The NGO empowers

216

informal manufacturers and craftspeople to enter the international value chain, providing an income for some of the poorest people in the world. This promotes the growth of sustainable business instead of aid dependency, and creates stability among these communities. 'This is not charity, this is work', states Westwood in *State of Fashion: Searching for the New Luxury*. Instead of teaching the workers traditional Western styles and techniques, Westwood started to design bags building on existing craft traditions, using recycled canvas, reused roadside banners, unused leather off-cuts, and recycled brass that is produced in the Kibera slum (Nairobi's biggest), where discarded metal like padlocks and car pieces are collected and then melted down (Figure 11.4).

Taking a conscious, social responsibility approach, this project explores a fair and transparent system where respect for local craft and cultural heritage is driving the aesthetics and the design of the bags. Traces of local heritage and the highlighting of

Figure 11.4 'Handmade with Love' a/w 2011–2012. Vivienne Westwood in collaboration with the Ethical Fashion Initiative and UN. United Kingdom. Photograph: Eva Broekema.

artisans – radicant identities – have become an integral part of fashion's value, story and imagination, including more cultural diversity and more inclusiveness in a meaningful and hybrid system. Cultural heritage in this project is the starting point to Vivienne Westwood and *11.11/eleven eleven* reflecting cultural values with relevance for future 'pluriversal' fashion systems.[29] In terms of Bourriaud, you could say they act as 'semionauts' – defined as creators of paths in a landscape of signs – whilst integrating different cultural backgrounds in future, and problem-solving thinking approaches.[30] In order to find a universal language, designers act here as *translators* 'accepting the idea that no speech bears the seal of any sort of "authenticity": we are entering the era of universal subtitling'.[31]

Subtheme 3: New Business Models

Digitalization has opened radical new business models, creating opportunities to change and innovate the fashion system. Biannual collections, big investments and compulsory catwalk shows are no longer conditions for a successful fashion business. Through web shops, blogs, social media and local Fashion Weeks designers are able to establish global businesses from anywhere, as well as contribute to the current critical fashion discourse to re-think the system. Fundamental new ways of producing and selling have been developed such as circular production and upcycling that also have led to more equal collaborations, horizontal networks, consumer involvement, and to more inclusive, environmental- and people-friendly businesses. Maven Women, displayed at *State of Fashion: Searching for the New Luxury*, is an online clothing company that designs, manufactures and releases new products with the help of a worldwide community of members. Members co-design and crowdfund the designs into existence within a matter of weeks. This new system helps the fashion system to transform from a push market where 40% of the garments are not sold, into a made-to-measure market via a far more sustainable business model where clothes will be made strictly according to demand and on a much more locally produced basis. In addition, the direct involvement of the consumer in the design process increases the agency of the consumer, as well as resulting in a more engaged connection to the product. This project underlines how we can become co-creators in a culture where the real seat of agency is not the consumer but the producer and the many forces that constitute production.[32]

A second example from the *State of Fashion: Searching for the New Luxury* exhibition is Matti Liimatainen (1983), a Finnish fashion designer who specialized in conceptual and computational design, who creates ready-to-assemble garment construction kits by using a custom CAD/CAM system for his label 'Self-Assembly'. All the products are made with a special seam that allows them to be assembled by hand without any tools or machinery. The products are delivered as loose, packed components, which need to be joined together prior to wearing. Some of the garments can also be amended. The most essential aspect about the design process of Self-Assembly and the foundation of the design method is that products are not ready-to-wear but ready-to-assemble. Self-Assembly is an example of personalized luxury with more agency offered to the consumer, and a focus shifting from the product towards the processes and stories of making. As such, it shows similarities with new practices such as upcycling, recycling, and cradle-to-cradle principles that are changing the design practices and aesthetics, as well as the business models, of the fashion system, and are resulting in consumption that is more conscious.

Subtheme 4: Fashion Design for a Better World

For too long innovations in fashion have been led primarily by functional and economic drivers where the latest business innovation – fast fashion — has made fashion the second most polluting industry and detached it from its socio-cultural role of criticism, condemnation, protest, and progressivism that it had in the 20th century.[33] Recent initiatives have shown that fashion has opened up its scope, by regarding the discipline not only as a field of production or as a market and using its design capabilities to shape diverse socio-cultural contributions. The 'Conscious Contemporary Craft: Connecting Communities' project, for example, is a collaborative initiative that involves the community of San Patrignano, supported by Fondazione Zegna, together with participants from the London College of Fashion's (LCF) 'Making for Change' project. San Patrignano, located in Northern Italy, is a community promoting the rehabilitation of young people affected by substance abuse. Supported by Fondazione Zegna, San Patrignano enables young individuals to transform themselves through education and the acquisition of artisanship.

'Making for Change' is LCF's training and manufacturing unit based at HMP Downview women's prison. The project aims to increase well-being and reduce reoffending rates amongst participants by equipping them with professional fashion-related skills and qualifications within a supportive environment. This project promoted the effectiveness of two social facilities, namely a therapeutic community and a prison. Working with menswear designer and LCF graduate Bethany Williams, women in the weaving workshop of San Patrignano used traditional handlooms to create innovative textile samples from industrial waste materials, textile fibres, plastic tapes and electrical wires. These textile samples in turn inspired LCF students to design garments and accessories reflecting contemporary issues, including what it means to 'protect', 'migrate', 'protest' and 'survive' (Figure 11.5). Six garments incorporating fabrics woven at San Patrignano have been produced at LCF's workshops and displayed at *State of Fashion: Searching for the New Luxury*. The collaborative project illustrated how fashion can be used as a cultural and symbolic value-driven force where craft, heritage and design can open dialogues with women about disclosing their sense of lost, forgotten or unknown value, whilst at the same empowering them.

A comparable project also shown at the exhibition was *Dress for Our Time* (2014) by Professor Helen Storey, an artist, designer, and researcher at LCF's Centre for Sustainable Fashion. Storey uses the power of fashion to communicate and act upon some of the world's most complex issues, such as climate change and the mass displacement of people. A dress was created from a decommissioned UNHCR (United Nations High

Figure 11.5 'Conscious Contemporary Craft: Connecting Communities' 2018. Fondazione Zegna/San Patrignano and Making for Change at London College of Fashion (UAL), Italy/United Kingdom. Photograph: Eva Broekema.

Commission for Refugees) refugee tent that once housed a displaced Syrian family at Za'atari Camp in Jordan. It was given a second life. The public art installation explored the unbreakable bond of humanity and represented the importance of nurturing and protecting all people and the need for safeguarding generations to come. Based on this installation, Storey led some follow-up projects working with refugees in the camp responding to their living challenges using crafts and design to engage with them and to explore with those who have lost everything, the basic (and overlapping) values of life and garment making.

Subtheme 5: Interdisciplinarity

Finally, cross-disciplinary collaboration and research and the merging of technical science and fashion are prerequisites for creating a more sustainable and resilient future. This has led to practices where designers take a much more collaborative approach with engineers and scientists from scratch, knowing that material experiments can lead to new opportunities, shapes and functions for fashion, whilst also challenging the status quo. Using new materials made from algae, fruit residue, and other celluloses, designers are showing how scientific technologies are leading to new design applications. Trained as an anthropologist as well as a footwear designer, Catherine Willems is looking into alternative footwear that is sustainable for both the environment and the body. By hybridising the craftsmanship and knowledge from indigenous footwear in combination with biometrics and the technology of the bodyscan and 3D printing techniques, she is developing unique, 3D-printed sandals informed by the design of an indigenous sandal. The intellectual property of the community has been respected, as they will get paid royalties with each 3D-printed version.

Where Bourriaud defines altermodernity as a future in art 'to be constructed on a global scale, through cooperation among a multitude of cultural *semes* and through ongoing translations of singularities',[34] one could add the importance of a multidisciplinary approach. Here artists, designers and scientist work together using a multitude of cultural and scientific semes in order to be able to address current, complicated societal challenges.

Conclusion

At this moment in time, designers are seeking a renewed and meaningful relationship to society and culture reflecting 21st-century values. By taking an interdisciplinary, explorative design approach, they are shaping new values and new definitions of what fashion luxury might entail in more inclusive terms. Five exhibition subthemes highlighted some of these new directions of the fashion system. It is clear that imagination is no longer being employed as a materialised fantasy, a form of escapism – as evoked in conventional Western fashion glamour – it needs a *purpose* and is a 'staging ground for action creating ideas of neighbourhood in a post-national society'.[35] As a result, fashion designers are shifting priorities from a focus on fashion as a short-term ephemeral product towards a much more resilient product development that contributes to solving the big societal change reflected in new values.

For more than a century, fashion was very much about *representation* and the *new*, where the new meant that it was in tune with and demonstrating the zeitgeist. Within the 21st century, the product is no longer outdated as soon as it has been launched on a catwalk, but gains more value during its lifecycle. In essence, the value of *new* (as the repetition of the same but different) has been replaced by a set of different values. Besides the value of *innovation* materialized in digital innovative products, there is the value of *patina*,[36] the value of micro-narratives based on local heritage and artisanship; the value of purpose and the value of *re-use*, *repair* and *recycle* in business models, shown in transparent and traceable and socially inclusive products.

Finally, designers are exploring new aesthetics and a new design language that are no longer searching for an authentic national style or are being expressed in terms of regional craftsmanship. Today's fashion designers bring together a collection of heterogeneous elements to which they impart meaning in an ever-changing context, 'in the infinite text of world culture'.[37] Intrinsically, they bring together fragments of identity acquiring meaning in the context of the *project*, in which the focus is not only on the product but also on the process and story behind it.[38] This results in an artistic fashion practice and fashion system that includes pluriversal voices and narratives to break through the hegemony of a primarily Western fashion history or modernity.[39]

In this post-Western context, artists and designers are converting their cultural background and stories into a universal visual language – in a translation that is very often a process – that is comprehensible to everyone. All this has led to a new, open and more inclusive and pluriversal definition of fashion as 'a desirable dress at a given moment and place',[40] whereby its desirability is based on a wide range of values, whether social, political, nostalgic, or based on exclusivity, modernity, innovation or nationalism.[41]

Notes

1. Where the conventional fashion system, developed and defined during the industrialization and democratization of the early 19th century, was very Western oriented – defining other dress cultures as non-fashion and exotic – the new fashion discourse refers to a more inclusive aesthetic born out of global and decentralized negotiations amongst heterogeneous discourses and cultures.

2. José Teunissen, 'On the Globalization of Fashion'. In Jan Brand and José Teunissen, Eds. *Global Fashion, Local Tradition* (Arnhem, Utrecht: Centraal Museum, 2005) 8–23; José Teunissen, 'Deconstructing Belgian and Dutch Fashion Dreams: From Global Trends to Local Crafts', *Fashion Theory*, 15 (2) (2011) 137–215; Lise Skov, 'Dreams of Small Nations in a Polycentric Fashion World', *Fashion Theory*, 15 (2) (2011) 137–157. José Teunissen, *The Future of Fashion is Now*, Jan Brand, Ed. (Rotterdam: Museum Boijmans Van Beuningen, 2014); José Teunissen, 'State of Fashion: Searching for the New Luxury', *Issuu* (2018), https://issuu.com/stateoffashion/docs/stof_07_2018_catalogus_interactive_, (accessed 12 July 2019).

3. Teunissen, 'On the Globalization of Fashion'; Teunissen, 'Deconstructing Belgian and Dutch Fashion Dreams'; Teunissen, *The Future of Fashion Is Now*; Teunissen, 'State of Fashion'.

4. Nicolas Bourriaud, *The Radicant*, trans. James Gussen and Lili Porten (New York: Lukas and Sternberg, 2009) 29.

5. Arjun Appadurai, *Modernity at Large* (London: Minnesota Press, 1996) 3–5.

6. To widen the scope of State of Fashion 2018, the Sonsbeek & State of Fashion Foundation organized an open call for projects in collaboration with the Prince Claus Fund. Designers and concept developers from all over the world were invited to share ideas that offer new perspectives on the fashion system and on the way we deal with the things that surround us. The call resulted in 97 applications from 22 countries. Thanks in part to the network of scouts from the Prince Claus Fund, but also through international contacts mobilised by the curator and the organization, as well as social media, we were able to reach participants in Asia, Africa and South America. The selection for the open call was made with the help of an international expert panel, consisting of: Joumana El Zein Khoury (Prince Claus Fund), Corinna Gardner (Senior Curator of Design & Digital, V&A Museum), Dr Hakan Karaosman (Expert – Enhancing Transparency and Traceability of Value Chains in Garment Industries, United Nations Economic Commission, Politecnico di Milano), Han Nefkens (Han Nefkens Foundation), Johan Maris (Control Union).

7. Bourriaud, *The Radicant*, 7.

8. ibid., 43.

9. ibid., 40.

10. Elizabeth Wilson, *Adorned in Dreams: Fashion and Modernity* (London: Virago Press, 1982) 17.

11. Walter Mignolo and Rolando Vasquez consider modernity inseparable from coloniality. Therefore, decolonial aesthetics to them is 'not modern, postmodern, or altermodern, but rather the multitemporal movement of those who look and have looked to rebuild the world from the ruins of the modern/colonial system, with all the specifics of what this may look like in a given time and space'. However, the designers I describe in my contribution are all part of and contributing to the existing fashion system, where they try to open up the narrow value system by adding pluriversal stories and narratives. Walter Mignolo and Roland Vasquez, 'Decolonial AestheSis Dossier', *Social Text Online* (2013), https://socialtextjournal.org/periscope_article/the-decolonial-aesthesis-dossier/ (accessed 12 July 2019).

12. Bourriaud, *The Radicant*, 44.

13. ibid., 51.

14. Bourriaud calls this form of identity a radicant, like a plant that sends out roots from its stem and propagates in order to keep re-creating its identity. Here identity is constructed as a series of fragments that tell the story together. ibid.

15. ibid.

16. ibid.

17. ibid., 22.

18. Appadurai, *Modernity at Large*, 3.

19. ibid., 31.

20. ibid., 4.

21. Lidewij Edelkoort, *Anti-Fashion: A Manifesto for the Next Decade* (Paris: Trend Union, 2014); Calefato Patrizia, 'Fashionscapes'. In Adam Geczy and Vicky Karaminas, Eds. *The End of Fashion* (London: Bloomsbury, 2019), 32–45.

22. Teunissen, 'State of Fashion', 13.

23. Calefato, 'Fashionscapes', 31–32.

24. On 24 April 2013, an eight-story commercial building, Rana Plaza, collapsed just outside Dhaka. The building contained five clothing factories: most of the people in the building at the time were garment workers. Over 17 days of search and rescue, 2,438 people were evacuated, more than 1,100 people died, and many more were left with lifelong debilitating injuries.

25. Diane Primo, 'What Can Luxury Brands Learn from Gucci about the Millennials', Forbes, 2 November 2018, www.forbes.com/sites/forbesagencycouncil/2018/11/02/what-can-luxury-brands-learn-from-gucci-aboutmillennials/ (accessed 12 July 2019).

26. Gucci Equilibrum has started an ambitious program around sustainability based on an aim to help deliver the UN Global Goals as well as the Paris Climate Agreement. A program where women empowerment, diversity, inclusion and social responsibility are key, as well as scouting start-ups and innovations in tech and natural materials. Ibid.

27. Franca Sozani, 'What is the Meaning of Luxury', in *Vogue Italy*, 5 March 2011, www.vogue.it/en/magazine/editor-s-blog/2011/03/march-5th (accessed 12 July 2019).

28. Appadurai, *Modernity at Large*, 7–10.

29. Walter Mignolo, 'Delinking', *Cultural Studies*, 21 (2) (2007) 500.

30. Bourriaud, *The Radicant*, 39.

31. Ibid., 44.

32. Appadurai, *Modernity at Large*, 42.

33. Jennifer Craik, 'Globalization'. In Adam Geczy and Vicky Karaminias, Eds. *The End of Fashion* (London: Bloomsbury, 2019) 133.

34. Bourriaud, *The Radicant*, 39.

35. Appadurai, *Modernity at Large*, 7.

36. Calefato, 'Fashionscapes', 32; Appadurai, *Modernity at Large*, 76.

37. Bourriaud, *The Radicant*, 39.

38. Teunissen, *The Future of Fashion is Now*, 18.

39. Following Mignolo's concept of decolonialism, we need to step out of the global capitalistic fashion system. 'For decolonization to be fully operative, we must create alternatives to modernity and neo-liberal civilization. We must begin to imagine such alternatives from the perspectives and consciousnesses unlocked in the epistemic, ethical and political domain of the geo- and the bio-political loci of enunciation and of action. Such alternatives are not mere fantasies or the imagining of another utopia. Liberation and decolonization are currently being enunciated (in writing, orally, by social movements and intellectuals, by artists and activists) from nodes in space-time (local histories) that have been marginalized by the temporal and spatial colonial differences. Although silenced in mainstream media, multiple fractures are creating larger, spatial epistemic breaks (e.g. geopolitics of knowledge) in the overarching totality of Western global and universal history that from Hegel to Huntington was successful in negating subjectivities from non-Western, non-capitalist, non-Christian nations'. Mignolo, 'Delinking', 492.

40. Joanne Entwistle, *The Fashioned Body* (Cambridge: Cambridge Polity Press, 2000) 1.

41. Angela Jansen and Jennifer Craik, Eds. *Modern Fashion Traditions* (London: Bloomsbury 2016) 8.

CHAPTER 12
MAKING THE ORDINARY FASHIONABLE: NEW SARTORIAL LANGUAGES FROM RUSSIA AND CHINA
Hazel CLARK and Alla EIZENBERG

Introduction

> In today's world, the real fashion is not those vain beautiful body coverings, but finding the extraordinary in the ordinary.[1]

Across the 20th century, the politics, histories and cultures of Russia and China resonated with one another and in addition the dress of both countries served as 'inspiration' for Western fashion designers. As we know, this referencing drew in particular on spectacular and extraordinary garments from Imperial Russia (e.g. Yves St Laurent's 'Russian' collection 1976/7) and China (e.g. Christian Lacroix, Frontière Chinoise F/W 1992/3). In the late 20th century, a similar aesthetic was adopted by some emerging Chinese and Russian designers and brands as a form of self-orientalization. The motivation for the choice was both market-driven and reflective of the political climate. We can cite, for instance, the establishment of the brands Shanghai Tang, and Blanc de Chine in Hong Kong in the early 1990s prior to the return of the British colony to mainland China. While their visual identities differed from one another, each presented nostalgic interpretations of China's past, at a time that the global fashion system was also engaging with orientalism, coincident with Hong Kong's handover to China.[2] Similarly, with the liberal policies introduced by Michail Gorbachev, the West could experience first-hand the richly ornate creations of Slava Zaitsev, the only fashion designer to gain any recognition outside of the country in the Soviet post-war era. In the 1960s the French press dubbed Zaitsev the 'Red Dior' and after his show in Paris in 1988, *Vogue* referred to him as 'the czar of Soviet fashion'.[3] Zaitsev is known for his ostentatious use of Russian traditional floral motifs based on Pavlovo Posad scarves, red and gold Hohloma patterns, and furs produced to the standards of haute couture, recalling tales of Russian riches.

In the second decade of the 21st century, historical and cultural points of reference from both China and Russia, continued to provide inspiration for indigenous designers working both inside and outside of those countries. Recently, Russian designers Ulyana Sergeenko and Vika Gazinskaya became regulars at the Paris haute couture and ready to wear fashion weeks, with designs referencing Imperial Russian and folk dress. Similarly, Chinese haute couture designer Guo Pei has gained substantial international attention, in the press and with exhibitions, for sumptuous and spectacular handmade gowns featuring conventional Chinese motifs and colours. In the United States her renown began with her work being featured in the *China through the Looking Glass* exhibition at the Metropolitan Museum of Art (2015), and the spectacular dress worn by singer Rihanna to the annual Met Ball. The exhibition clearly and intentionally reflected an orientalist gaze, and was not representative of the greater diversity of fashion design that has emerged from Russia and China in the 21st century. The role of this chapter, therefore, is to add knowledge and understanding of other designers working 'beyond the West' and apart from orientalist tropes. In focusing on Chinese Ma Ke and Russian Gosha Rubchinskiy, we demonstrate how each engages with aspects of their own cultural backgrounds. In doing so, they contribute to the global fashion discourse by employing strategies which acknowledge and value the ordinary and the everyday, as we outline in the following paragraphs, beginning with some background to their work in fashion.

Considering Ma Ke and Gosha Rubchinskiy

Ma Ke began her career as a fashion designer in 1996, with the brand Exception de Mixmind, while Gosha Rubchinskiy started working as a designer and photographer a decade later. Exception was intended by Ma Ke to be 'the first Chinese designer brand'[4] aimed at 'fashion-conscious middle-class consumers'.[5] One of its objectives was to challenge the Western definition of female beauty that Ma Ke considered was being perpetuated by the fashion industry.[6] The brand developed a relaxed aesthetic favoring unstructured shapes, natural and muted colours, textured fabrics and knits, which have been referred to as 'sustainable style',[7] and produced garments intended to transcend distinct fashion seasons. Gosha Rubchinskiy is similarly known for an understated sartorial style[8] that is deeply rooted in Soviet and early post-Soviet streetwear aesthetics. His collections, abundant with sweatshirts, t-shirts, and jeans, have often incorporated the logos of Western brands with Cyrillic script and Soviet symbols. With 'their focus on the everyday and the banal' his designs have been described as having an 'affiliation with youth culture rather than an allegiance to fashion'.[9] By the designer's own account his 'frames of reference are a lot bigger than just designing clothes'.[10]

Rubchinskiy started his creative career by taking photographs of young Moscow skateboarders, whose sense of community and energy became central to the images he produced. The dress and embodiment of the young Russian skaters has continued to be a reference in his photography and fashion. Rubchinskiy calls the teenagers 'who wear his clothes on the catwalk and off, Gosha boys',[11] suggesting the importance of their commonplace attitude to the integrity of his message. By identifying with skateboarding as an everyday practice, Rubchinskiy has achieved what might be termed a 'glocal'[12] effect. Through the connection with skateboarding, the clothes worn by the Russian skaters resonate with young people internationally, highlighting the popular agency of fashion, in common with music and sport, to 'bring people together'.[13] Ma Ke likewise has come to focus her work more around ordinary and collective practices, albeit with different points of reference. In 2006, she left Exception de Mixmind, despite the brand's commercial success, to establish Wuyong ('Useless'), a studio in Zhuhai, Guangdong Province, with the aim of conserving the traditional skills seen as 'useless' in a rapidly modernizing China. There she has continued to employ craftspeople to spin, weave, sew and naturally dye fabrics, while also challenging and developing her own creative practice.[14] For Ma, Wuyong represents a world completely and refreshingly insulated from the commercial fashion system and it has provided the focus of her work going forward, practically and philosophically.[15]

Our investigations of both designers have led us to recognize similarities in their perspectives on their work, if not in their designs. Each draws from the varied, but also ordinary and everyday, practices indigenous to their own country's complex culture and history. We highlight some parallels between the history and politics of Russia and China in the 20th century, notably the political impact of Communism and totalitarianism on how people dressed. Rubchinskiy and Ma Ke are both alive to the concerns of the contemporary world, such as climate change, massive migration and displacement, and cultural responses to social inequalities framed by Arjun Appadurai's observation as 'a congeries of large-scale interactions'.[16] Appadurai notes how interactions are facilitated by the advancement of technological capabilities to produce and disseminate images, 'in which the world of commodities and the world of news and politics are profoundly mixed', creating what he calls *mediascapes*.[17] Previously existing categories of local/global, or center/periphery disintegrate, and the distinctions between the real and imagined become inherently blurred, allowing the emergence of new expressions to originate from less familiar geographical locations and cultural perspectives. We consider that Rubchinskiy and Ma Ke's practices, informed by particular, but often overlooked, aspects of their cultural backgrounds, represent this tendency, and thus contextualize them against wider global fashion interests and concerns. What makes the designers' cases compelling and unites them, as we discuss in this chapter, is how they have addressed but also distanced themselves from market-driven concerns to develop their own particular fashion discourses. Their forms of creative expression and media include exhibitions, performances, films, photography, and writing, through which both Ma Ke and Rubchinskiy offer the potential for new sartorial languages to emerge from Russia and China, based on their respective interests in the ordinary and the everyday. But before we discuss and analyze their work in more detail, we will introduce the structuring of our argument relative to the ordinary and the everyday.

The Ordinary and the Everyday

In framing our argument from the perspective of 'the ordinary' we are building upon Buckley and Clark's investigation of fashion and everyday life,[18] and in particular the understanding that 'within fashion's discourses, the truly "ordinary" remains elusive'.[19] Acknowledging, as they do, interest in the everyday by scholars from a range of disciplines (including Lefebvre; de Certeau; Sandywell; Highmore) we draw in particular in this chapter from the work on the everyday of Michel de Certeau. From de Certeau's argument for the role of 'ordinary language' in everyday life, we argue for the existence of an 'ordinary language' of fashion. Thus the definition of 'fashion' is extended beyond the commodity, to encompass fashion's social, cultural, symbolic and political roles. What makes de Certeau's notion compelling is the distinction he makes in a power discourse between 'strategies' and 'tactics'. He attributes 'strategies' – 'the calculus of force-relationships' – to the dominant discourse.[20] This term can be applied to the political institutions in Russia (as part of the Soviet Union) and China during totalitarian times, as well as to the fashion system in the context of Western cultural hegemony. 'Tactics', on the other hand, are the practices intended to manipulate 'the imposed spaces' and 'belong to the other'.[21] Writing of the Soviet Union, Djurdja Barlett has noted, for example, how 'fashion tactics introduced the political into socialist everyday life [as] a performing device enabling women to negotiate official strategies'.[22] For de Certeau 'many everyday practices (talking, reading, moving about, shopping, cooking etc.)' and of course for us dressing and self-fashioning, are in fact tactical in character. His 'poetic ways of "making do" (*bricolage*)'[23] also highlight how consumers (in regard to fashion in particular) 'reappropriate everyday objects, actively and indeed subversively transforming them as part of their own highly personal identity project'.[24] Buckley and Clark further develop this idea, noting that while 'making do' with everyday culture, people have also been 'making with', that is creatively 'transforming and inventing by appropriating and re-deploying'.[25] They also note how some groups of people, teenagers in particular, have 'refused fashion per se to create their own "identities" in opposition to an increasingly homogeneous consumer market'.[26]

Developing further Buckley and Clark's time period and focus, we consider how in the 21st century the ordinary and the everyday became a greater focus of attention for the work of a number of fashion designers internationally. It was, for instance, manifested in workwear references in menswear designs in the first decade of the century (such as those created by Junya Watanabe). The parallel continues with the increase in the number of collaborations between well-known fashion designers and sportswear brands[27] to produce what became referred to as 'high-low' fashion. Recognized designer brands such as Raf Simons and Kenzo also included everyday items such as sweatshirts and hoodies in their high-end collections. Later, brands such as Hood by Air, Vetements, and Off-White introduced fashion strictly built on the aesthetics of the ordinary. Yet what we are presenting, comparatively, in discussing the work of Rubchinskiy and Ma Ke, is not only designs that are responding to a fashion trend, but work which also represents a deeper engagement with the historical and political transformations that took place in their respective countries in the 20th century. We propose that these two designers stand out, and can be considered together, due to the particularity of their references, which draw upon intrinsically mundane and everyday aspects of their countries and cultures which have previously been excluded from fashion. They are also affiliated, in a broader sense, with the parallel historical and political transformations within their respective nations. Each in their own way draws upon their backgrounds to expand the discourse of fashion in content and in form – that is through what they produce and how they present their ideas, including the broad range of media they employ.

Transformations

The Bolshevik Revolution of 1917 brought a radical change into every aspect of life in Russia, as well as creating a break in the already complex relationship of the country with the West, due to ideological and political tensions. At first, sartorial practices and fashionable dress remained a focus of attention in the newly born Socialist state, but with Stalin's rise to power in the late 1920s, fashion, one of the prominent features of bourgeois life, was condemned and any interest in it was considered anti-Socialist. The new regime thought that the Soviet people needed their own sartorial identity, which was in sync with proletarian ideals. 'A new functional aesthetics was hastily introduced, as well as a new concept of woman. She was socially perceived as a worker dressed in a practical work uniform, as the new states privileged class over gender'.[28]

Comparatively, in China, the development of an embryonic fashion industry was sanctioned by the May Fourth Movement of 1919.[29] Later, the political synergies between China and the Soviet Union had a sartorial impact. In the 1940s and 50s, Chinese women adopted the 'Lenin suit' in parallel to the ubiquitous Sun Yat-sen suit being worn by the majority of men.[30] Uniform dressing became even more marked during the Cultural Revolution (1966–1976). Contemporary accounts document how women whose dress was considered bourgeois could be subject to physical attacks by the politically fervent Red Guards. Yet, despite the lack of variety in dress, many accounts of the time reference clothing's symbolic qualities. Chinese scholar Peidong Sun has argued that the 'silent and subtle' modifications that many individuals made to their garments could be seen as 'a cultural practice of everyday resistance'.[31] The longevity of items made by hand during the period has also been commented upon. Writing in the 1990s, Wu Xiaoping recounts how in returning to a remote mountain village near the city of X'ian that she had visited during the Cultural Revolution, she discovered a sweater for which she had donated the wool, still being worn over 22 years later.[32]

From the 1960s, with the discreet approval of the regime, 'women in [Russia] found alternative ways to acquire pretty and fashionable dresses, whether they made their own clothes, purchased them on the black market or at private fashion salons'.[33] In China by comparison, uniformity of dressing continued through the 1970s. The launch, in 1979, of the first fashion magazine during China's Reform period reflected not only the opening up of China's contact with the rest of the world, but the importance of fashion in that process.[34] The fall of the Soviet Union in 1991 was a further marker in the historical trajectory of both countries. In Russia, 'the socialist dream had been cancelled, but in its place there was to be another utopia, a consumerist paradise, buttressed by liberal democracy at home'.[35] The same sentiments could also be applied to China. This was followed in Russia by post-socialist 'nostalgia [that] became a defense mechanism against the accelerated rhythm of change and economic shock therapy'.[36] Rubchinskiy and Ma Ke both had first-hand experience of the transition of their countries into the new realities, where both nations placed the fashion industry and garment making at the forefront of production and the development of consumer culture. We are proposing that each of the designers were influenced in their particular attitudes to fashion by the national cultural and political changes they experienced during their own lifetimes, allied to the wider context of global fashion.

We note that Ma Ke was born in 1971, in the middle of the Cultural Revolution in China, a time when many intellectuals were sent 'to the country' to work with farmers and the proletariat. While we do not know the situation of Ma Ke's family during this period, it may be significant to her later work that she was born in Jilin Province in the far north east of China, next to the border with North Korea. For Rubchinskiy, born in 1984, it was the turbulent 1990s in Moscow that provided an ongoing frame of reference for his work, 'with all the poverty and disorder', explains the designer, 'there was a feeling of something big and positive coming'.[37] The everyday experiences of most of the population during this period were characterized by economic instability, and the potential danger posed by criminal gangs roaming the streets. But it was also distinguished by the powerful energy and excitement created by the discovery of Western cultural products, including fashion, and even extending to toys, bright and stylish, often carrying their brand logos. Rubchinskiy recalls that it was 'like an explosion, where thirty to forty years of culture were experienced in a few years'.[38] What Rubchinskiy implies by culture here refers to the products of creative industries existing under the model of Western liberal capitalism, in particular popular outpourings in the form of music, fashion, and movies that were expressive and subversive, but still intrinsically connected to and compliant with the rules of commerce. Living through this period as a child and later as a teenager, the dramatic changes happening around him and the natural transitions associated with being a teen congealed into a vivid memory characterized mostly by the intensity of emotions, which have continued to constitute a central drive in Rubchinskiy's creative practice.

Given the political histories mentioned above, it can be argued that the aggressive withdrawal from the Western aesthetic and cultural discourse, and the scarcity of resources characterizing Soviet and Chinese life under Communism, had a profound effect on the relationship between people and objects, in our case clothes. In this context, the important observation made by Simmel on fashion, which he described as a continuous struggle between the need to belong and a drive for individualization,[39] becomes even more acute. In Socialist times, the sartorial construction of the self had to navigate not only individual psychological complexities, but also do so within the clearly defined institutionalized constraints privileging collectivity and uniformity. This de facto reduced a sartorial wardrobe into a group of *ordinary items*, a term that well-described the only clothes that were available for legal consumption under the Socialist and Communist regimes.

It can be argued that Rubchinskiy's ability to construct narratives with limited and often overtly banal items of clothing relates to the tactics developed during the Soviet epoch characterized by scarcity and aesthetic oppression which became cultural capital for some. His collections consistently include leather jackets, 'badly fitted' tailored pants, and a large variety of sportswear styles all intermixed into a look reminiscent of the transitional years of 1990s Russia (Figures 12.1 and 12.2). During this time, sportswear became a status symbol in the form of highly coveted Western goods, that according to the designer everybody, including young boys and their parents, were wearing for any occasion.[40] Ignorant of the original function and meanings of those clothes, people

Figure 12.1 Gosha Rubchinskiy, F/W 2017. Courtesy Gosha Rubchinskiy.

Figure 12.2 Gosha Rubchinskiy F/W 2016. Photograph: Victor Virgile. Getty Images #506462562.

combined dressy pants with sweatshirts, leather jackets with track pants, and button-down shirts with windbreakers, developing disparate styles of their own that allowed them to negotiate their sense of self in the fast-changing surroundings. This experience had a profound impact on the designer's sensibilities for the ordinary and, by some accounts, the 'ugly',[41] and informed his ability to construct meaningful messages with the familiar and the mundane.

Ma Ke is also drawn to the ordinary, albeit in a different form and content from Rubchinskiy. She values traditional Chinese crafts, both as a point of reference for her own designs and discourse and in terms of the objects produced, without glamorizing the harshness of her country's history and, for many, its present. She has drawn from the ordinary to produce what Hui has described as 'dirty fashion', for example, by smearing dirt and earth on the garments displayed and on the faces of the models in her *Wuyong/The Earth* collection, which is discussed further below. Hui interprets this as a symbolic choice to endow a garment 'with a sense of history and memory, turning it from a garment that forgets to a garment that remembers'.[42] He determines the very ordinariness of dirt in Ma Ke's work as representing 'slowness, duration, permanence and history'.[43] While Ma Ke is not the first designer to expose her creations to dirt – we can cite for example, the work of Hussein Chalayan (Spring/Summer 1995; Spring/Summer 2002) – she is the first *Chinese* designer to have done so. She has been described as seeing the role of the fashion designer as part of 'society's conscience', someone who retains traditional skills and imparts Chinese cultural memories. In reconceptualizing traditional materials, using indigo dyes, cottons and embroideries, the elaborate, deconstructed garments she designs retain cultural memories of the minority peoples of China, while also employing an international fashion language.[44]

Fashion as Expanded Practice/s

The interest in the ordinary expressed by Ma Ke and Rubchinskiy is not the only element that unites the designers. Transcending the commercial realm of material objects, the world of commodities, designer names and brands, their representational practices constitute a rich variety of creative outputs, including image-making, film, performance, and writing. They are not alone in broadening the fashion discourse through their work, as Jessica Bugg has noted:

> ... there can be clearly articulated alternative strategies for fashion design and communication that are concept and context based, rather than being driven by commerce, the market and trends [which are found at] the intersection of fashion with fine art and performance disciplines.[45]

Our proposition is that Ma Ke and Gosha Rubchinskiy are developing concept- and context-based tactics that are 'alternative' to the overarching commercial strategies of the fashion system (including as manifested in China and Russia), and are informed by their cultural origins from two countries which are not seen as places of creative imagination within global fashion. To do so they are both employing the broader range of creative methods and outputs to which Bugg refers. Patricia Calefato has commented on 'the opening of new scenarios' in fashion in the 21st century that, while being 'rooted in fashion or their surroundings, translate fashion beyond itself'.[46]

Ma Ke has utilized performance, film, photography and exhibition since she first showed *Wuyong/The Earth* during Paris Fashion Week, Autumn/Winter 2007. That collection was staged in a high school sports stadium, where non-professional models stood on elevated light boxes dressed in enveloping garments made from used fabric (Figure 12.3). The performance disrupted the traditional seating hierarchy of the fashion show, demanding for example that the audience moved amongst the pieces, thus aligning it to the international fashion avant-garde (for example, the performance element in the Hussein Chalayan Fall/Winter 2000 show). Her show received very positive press

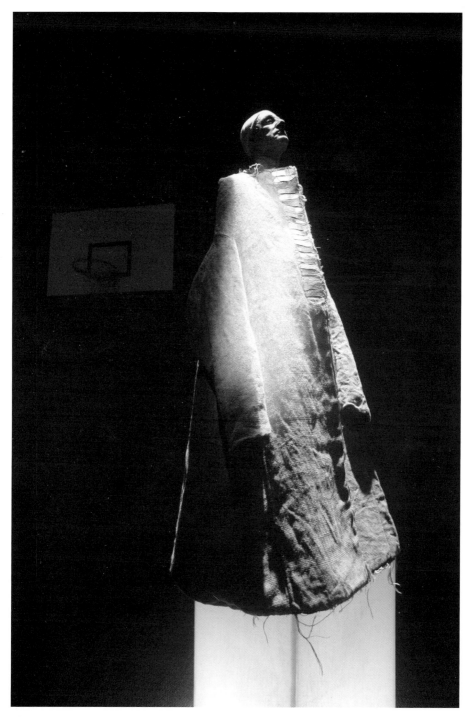

Figure 12.3 Ma Ke, *Wuyong/The Earth*, performance during Fall/Winter 2007/8 Paris ready to wear collections, presented in a school sports stadium, February 25, 2007. Getty #73425311.

attention and resulted in invitations to exhibit in museums around the world, including a re-staging at the Victoria and Albert Museum in 2008, as part of the *China Design Now* exhibition. A second show in Paris followed soon after. In July 2008, 'Luxurious Qingpin' ('simplicity') was performed in the gardens of the Palais Royal. Set to the voice of a Mongolian singer, a group of yoga practitioners of different ages and races, wearing simple loose clothing, danced slowly and meditatively to the rays of the setting sun, and two seamstresses from her studio worked at a traditional loom and spinning wheel (Figure 12.4). It gained her the praise of Didier Grumbach, then chair of Chambre Syndicale de la Haute Couture, who described her as a 'real talent', noting how she chose to show her more minimalist creations abroad, with China having to settle for the 'more banal' pieces sold under the Exception label (which she had already left).[47] Ma Ke effectively relinquished her commercial engagement with fashion to experiment with a range of media, venues, contexts and collaborations.

For Rubchinskiy, diverse creative practices are even more intertwined with one another, as photography, film-making, fashion, and performance are in constant interaction, constituting a cohesive narration at the center of which is the community of Russian skateboarding teens. Their being in the world, their attitude and energy, is what ignites Rubchinskiy's creative process.[48] They also form the cast that models his clothes in carefully choreographed performances, often involving non-traditional activities like a choir singing (Fall 2018) or working out for an hour in a disused gym in Moscow's suburbs (Spring 2010). In common with Ma Ke, Rubchinskiy has chosen sites for his fashion shows

Figure 12.4 Ma Ke, *Wuyong* performance for Fall/Winter 2009 Paris haute couture collections, in the garden of the Palais Royal. Getty #81812244.

outside of the conventional fashion locations, often opting for places associated with youth, clubbing, or sports, which resonate with the garments he has designed, their sources of reference and their intended wearers. He has shown his collections in a stadium (2008), gyms (2009, 2010), a rave club (2017), and a Centre for Youth Culture (2017). The spectacles have been energetic and made even more powerful in conveying the sense of a gang, a tribe, or a community that emerges from the powerful interaction of the fashioned bodies with the selected spaces. As he has often commented, 'The kids who inspire me are the goal of my work'.[49] 'For me, it's more like a performance. I wanted to show only this community of boys, and the collection [was] made only for them'.[50] Adrian Joffe of Comme des Garçons, who since 2012 has provided an operational support to Rubchinskiy, sees him less 'as a fashion designer', than as 'a recorder of things'[51] or 'a storyteller'.[52]

Yet, it is photography that is at the core of Rubchinskiy's creative practice, his reference base, and the narration device. Five published photobooks: *Transfiguration* (2012) released in conjunction with the eponymous film; *Crimea / Kids* (2014); *Youth Hotel* (2015); *The Day of My Death* (2016) (also accompanied by the film produced in collaboration with Renata Litvinova and Lotta Volkova); and *Perfume Book* (2017), are a testament to his unique practice. Different from the common use of imagery in fashion that is created in the post-production stages to communicate the final outcomes, for Rubchinskiy, photographic documentation stands at the foundation of each project. This is in accord with Gilles Lipovetsky's observation that the fashion image has long transcended the object. 'The center of attention is no longer the clothing', notes Lipovetsky, 'but the photograph and what it symbolizes',[53] and it can be argued that Rubchinskiy's photographic work provides a clear illustration of this statement. With his focus on Russian youth, Rubchinskiy's images manage to convey the emotion that the designer experienced with his subject, which 'yields an image with specific suggestive powers that can direct the viewer into a specific and known feeling, state or place within himself'.[54] Rubchinskiy deploys the full potential of photography and not only in the documentary images of young men, but also in their juxtaposition with images of Soviet-looking landscapes of monotonous concrete apartment blocks, Communist monuments, or as in *Transfiguration* with Russian Orthodox icons and works of art. 'Indeed', suggests Roberts, 'fashion may be little more than the means to an end for Rubchinskiy, a way for him to stage performances . . . around the images he creates'.[55]

Documentation has similarly formed part of Ma Ke's interests and practice. One of the better-known outcomes is her collaboration with Chinese filmmaker Jia Zhanke on the award-winning documentary *Wuyong (Useless)* (2007). The message of the film is clear and preempts the direction of her 2009 manifesto, that the greater mass-production of commodities has changed lives in China – and not always for the better. In the film she expresses her belief that handmade objects can facilitate more lasting and emotional connections for people. It is an interest that led her to travel to remote mountain areas of China in Gansu province in the north east and Sichuan in the south west. The trips resulted in the exhibition *My Land, My People* (2011 and subsequently) which comprises photographs, objects and written ethnographies. It documents the lives and living conditions of the local residents who rely on very few material possessions, but treasure highly what they possess, materially and psychologically. Many clothing items would typically have been handmade and then patched and re-patched, as is illustrated by a man's jacket that had been worn for over 15 years. For Ma Ke, the items demonstrate the potential for longer and more emotional relationships with objects, garments in particular, which also reflect China's recent past. As we have already noted, in some remote areas of the country, clothing items had retained a longevity which recalls the practices of preserving and repairing that were instituted during the Cultural Revolution. Ma Ke has subsequently sought to preserve and draw attention to ubiquitous and utilitarian objects by staging exhibitions of Chinese folk arts and handcrafts at Wuyong Living Space, which she opened in Beijing in 2014. Her work has also been included in international exhibitions, including the architecture biennale in Venice (Figure 12.5).

An engagement with the profoundly local, and seemingly peripheral, which is 'uncontaminated' by the urban intensity of the big megalopolises, is also present in Rubchinskiy's work. After four seasons presented on the international stage, Rubchinskiy returned to show his collections in Russia, where the choice of locations (Kaliningrad Fall 2017, Yekaterinburg Fall 2018) and the cast of models represented less familiar aspects of the vast country. 'It is a portrait of Russia', stated Rubchinskiy after the Fall 2017 show, 'if you think about Russia, you think about politics. It's more interesting for me to invite you here and show you what Russia is, rather than showing you in Paris'.[56] Substitute China for Russia and these words could also apply to Ma Ke. Through their

Figure 12.5 Ma Ke, *Wuyong/The Earth* shown in the China pavilion of the 15th International Architecture Biennale, Venice, 2016, curated by Chilean architect Alejandro Aravena. Getty Images #534383230.

focus on community and an admiration of the kinship of tightly-knit groups of youth for Rubchinskiy, and of families for Ma Ke in *My Land, My People*, both are making statements about the local and the intimate. As Rubchinskiy notes, 'it's easy for international brands to talk about culture with a broad brush . . . but culture is created in local communities . . . I want to prove that you can show international ideas but in a small Russian city'.[57] Journalist Lou Stoppard describes his work, stating it merits consideration, [and] demands that you reflect and ponder'.[58] The approach underlines Rubchinskiy's view of fashion as a platform for communication, which he considers a 'medium where you can do different things',[59] which could also apply to Ma Ke.

A number of further comparisons can be made between Rubchinskiy and Ma Ke, not least the fact that neither designer is, or aspires to be, part of the international 'star system' of designer names and identities, yet each is undoubtedly known and respected in their home countries. Since 2013, for instance, Ma has designed outfits for China's first lady Peng Liyuan to be worn on trips overseas, demonstrating her standing as a fashion designer and her social and cultural capital in China. She has also shared her informed and ethically concerned fashion practice through lectures and prestigious international events. In October 2009, she presented her manifesto, *Design with Conscience, Live with Simplicity* to the Icograda World Design Congress, which was being held to coincide with the first design week in Beijing. Her manifesto is part autobiography and part polemic, the latter informed by Chinese and Western thinkers. It is framed by what can be learned from ordinary and everyday aspects of life, which are rapidly vanishing in China, especially in rural areas. As a result, she describes her infatuation with handmade things since childhood, and her adaptation to a 'slow life'[60] when she chose to move from the city to Zhuhai. She issued these in a manifesto, the content of which brings to mind that published six years later by Lidewij Edelkoort, one of the world's most famous fashion forecasters, *Anti_Fashion: Ten Reasons Why the Fashion System is Obsolete*.[61] Like Ma Ke, Edelkoort criticizes aspects of the very system which sustains her, fashion, its star designers, the cult of celebrity, the valuing of individualism above community, all of which she sees as informing fashion education. It is damning, but also, as Christopher Breward has noted, it 'captures the spirit of our times and suggests that the concept of fashion, as it has existed for the past two decades, is ripe for reconstruction'.[62]

Crossing Boundaries

If fashion is (always) 'ripe for reconstruction' then through our analysis of the work of Gosha Rubchinskiy and Ma Ke we propose that, going forward, the agents in this process will not necessarily be those who are firmly entrenched in the Western fashion system, nor will they necessarily draw from hackneyed visual references. Rubchinskiy's and Ma Ke's case studies provide evidence for designers who originate from and reside in nations which are currently considered antithetical to fashion's creative and conceptual direction, and whose references privilege underrepresented elements of their respective cultures.

In tandem, their work resonates with and responds to some of the wider concerns that fashion and societies in general are addressing in the 21st century, which have also been the focus of a range of scholars. The 'global and cultural flows' or '-scapes'[63] characterizing the contemporary cultural climate, and applied to fashion by Vicki Karaminas and Patrizia Calefato,[64] prove helpful in consolidating and in summing up our argument. As transportation and communication technology has brought people and physical objects closer, the advances of media, characterized by the unprecedented presence of images, signs, and bodies, has created 'communities with "no sense of place"'.[65] In this contemporary context 'the imagination has become an organized field of social practices, ... a form of negotiation between sites of agency (individuals) and globally defined fields of possibility'.[66] It is a possibility, we would agree with Karaminas and Calefato, which facilitates the development of the concept of fashionscapes, as represented by our two designer case studies, both in their places of location, and in the range of media that they employ in their broader definition of 'fashion'. For Calefato, fashionscapes are the 'stratified, hybrid, multiple, and fluid disposition of imageries of the clothed body of our time'.[67] Fashionscapes relate to the complexities described by Appadurai through the lens of 'the body and its way of being in the world, of its representations, its masking, its disguises, its measures, and its conflicts with stereotypes and myths'.[68]

Conclusion

As stated in the introduction to this chapter, Gosha Rubchinskiy and Ma Ke are breaking down the stereotype of the designer working 'beyond the West'. By refuting the more extraordinary aspects of their nation's histories and cultural backgrounds in favor of the ordinary and the everyday, they are not only contributing to the international fashion discourse, but are also challenging the established primacy of particular locations and cultures in the global fashion system. This is more than simply their nationalities being outside those highlighted in the prevailing Western-based fashion discourse (at a time when China is already developing its fashion capacity in terms of production and consumption). Thus their 'decolonizing' of fashion moves beyond a discourse based largely on place, to one also focused on fashion's relationship to culture and values. While both designers are conscious of the global fashion system, and popular culture, their work offers the potential for expanded practices of design from beyond the West that present new values and ways of dressing and appearing which are not determined by the existing 'fashion system' and related premises of neoliberalism. By referencing their cultural and historical backgrounds and understanding and employing their imagination as forms of fashion tactics, Rubchinskiy and Ma Ke, and other fashion practitioners beyond the West, become a new form of fashion tacticians who challenge existing (Western-generated) fashion strategies. In that sense they begin to effectively decolonize fashion as they 'contest and sometimes even subvert the imagined worlds of the official mind and of the entrepreneurial mentality that surround them'.[69]

Notes

1. Ma Ke, 'Design with Conscience, Live with Simplicity' (unpublished speech). Icograda Beijing Conference, 28 October 2009.

2. Hazel Clark, 'Fashioning "China style" in the twenty-first century'. In Eugenia Paulicelli and Hazel Clark, Eds. *The Fabric of Cultures: Fashion, Identity and Globalization* (Oxford: Routledge, 2009) 177–193.

3. Liana Satenstein, 'Meet Russia's Very Own Christian Dior, Legendary Designer Slava Zaitsev', *Vogue*, 2017, www.vogue.com/article/russian-designer-vyacheslav-slava-zaitsev-profil (accessed 1 October 2019).

4. Ma Ke, 'Design with Conscience, Live with Simplicity', 1.

5. Bao Mingxin and Lu Lijun, 'A Brief History of Chinese Fashion Design'. In Hongxing, Zhang and Lauren Parker, Eds. *China Design Now* (London: V&A Publishing, 2008) 108.

6. Ma Ke, 'Design with Conscience, Live with Simplicity', 1.

7. https://irenebrination.typepad.com/irenebrination_notes_on_a/2016/06/venice-architecture-china-pavilion-ma-ke.html (accessed 30 December 2018).

8. Alexander Fury, 'Gosha Rubchinskiy: Fall 2016 Menswear', *Vogue*, 2016, www.vogue.com/fashion-shows/fall-2016-menswear/gosha-rubchinskiy (accessed 20 September 2019).

   Anders Christian Madsen, 'From Russia with Love: We Meet Gosha Rubchinskiy and His Gang', *I-D Magazine*, 2017, https://i-d.vice.com/en_uk/article/j5mxwp/from-russia-with-love-we-meet-gosha-rubchinskiy-and-his-gang (accessed 3 May 2017).

9. Alexander Fury, 'For Gosha Rubchinskiy, Sweatshirts, T-Shirts, and Jeans Are the Coolest Things in Fashion', *W Magazine*, 2016, www.wmagazine.com/story/for-gosha-rubchinskiy-sweatshirts-t-shirts-and-jeans-are-the-coolest-things-in-fashion/ (accessed 15 March 2017).

10. William Oliver, 'Go Go Gosha', *Dazed Digital*, 2010, www.dazeddigital.com/fashion/article/6436/1/go-go-gosha (accessed 20 September 2019).

11. Fury, 'For Gosha Rubchinskiy, Sweatshirts, T-Shirts, and Jeans Are the Coolest Things in Fashion'.

12. Graham H. Roberts, 'Angels with Dirty Faces: Gosha Rubchinskiy and the Politics of Style', *Journal of Extreme Anthropology*, 1 (3) (2017) 34, https://journals.uio.no/index.php/JEA/article/view/5564 (accessed 27 November 2017).

13. Anastasiia Fedorova, 'Gosha Rubchinskiy: Inside his Vertically Integrated Youth Universe', *032c*, 2016, https://032c.com/Gosha-Rubchinskiy-interview?curator=FashionREDEF (accessed 22 October 2019).

   Fury, 'For Gosha Rubchinskiy, Sweatshirts, T-Shirts, and Jeans Are the Coolest Things in Fashion'; Madsen, 'From Russia with Love: We Meet Gosha Rubchinskiy and His Gang'.

14. Ma Ke, 'Design with Conscience, Live with Simplicity', 2.

15. ibid.

16. Arjun Appadurai, *Modernity at Large* (Minneapolis, MN: University of Minnesota Press, 1996) 31.

17. ibid., 35

18. Cheryl Buckley and Hazel Clark, *Fashion and Everyday Life: London and New York* (London and New York: Bloomsbury, 2017).

   Cheryl Buckley and Hazel Clark, 'Conceptualizing Fashion in Everyday Lives', *Design Issues*, 28 (4) (2012) 18–28.

19. Buckley and Clark, 'Conceptualizing Fashion in Everyday Lives', 18.

20. Michel de Certeau, *The Practice of Everyday Life* (Berkeley and Los Angeles, CA: University of California Press, 1988) xix.

21. ibid.

22. Djurda Barlett, 'Can Fashion Be Defended?' In Djurda Bartlett, Ed. *Fashion and Politics* (New Haven, CT: Yale University Press, 2019) 21.

23. de Certeau, *The Practice of Everyday Life*, xv.

24. Roberts, 'Angels with Dirty Faces: Gosha Rubchinskiy and the Politics of Style', 3.

25. Buckley and Clark, *Fashion and Everyday Life: London and New York*, 9

26. ibid., 10

27. Yohji Yamamoto collaboration with Adidas named Y-3 launched in 2002; Alexander McQueen collaboration with Puma launched in 2006.

28. Djurda Bartlett, *Fashion East: The Spectre That Haunted Socialism* (Cambridge, MA: Massachusetts Institute of Technology, 2010) 5.

29. Antonia Finnane, 'Between Beijing and Shanghai: Fashion in the Party State'. In Valerie Steele, Ed. *Paris, Capital of Fashion* (London and New York: Bloomsbury Publishing, 2019) 137.

30. Antonia, Finnane, *Changing Clothes in China, Fashion, History, Nation* (New York: Columbia University Press, 2008) 205.

31. Jin Li Lim, 'Wang Guangmei's Crimes of Fashion: The Politics of Dress in China's Cultural Revolution'. In Djurda Bartlett, Ed. *Fashion and Politics* (New Haven, CT: Yale University Press) 75.

32. Xiaoping Wu, 'Down to the Countryside'. In Lijia Zhang and Calum MacLeod, Eds. *China Remembers* (Hong Kong: Oxford University Press, 1999) 133.

33. Bartlett, *Fashion East: The Spectre That Haunted Socialism*, 243.

34. Finnane, *Changing Clothes in China, Fashion, History, Nation*, 255.

35. Graham H. Roberts and Anna Louyest, 'Guest Editors' Introduction: Nostalgia, Culture and Identity in Central and Eastern Europe', *Canadian Slavonic Papers/Revue Canadienne des Slavistes*, 57 (3–4), (2015) 175, www.tandfonline.com/doi/full/10.1080/00085006.2015.109073 0 (accessed 5 October 2019).

36. Svetlana Boym, 'From the Russian Soul to Post-Communist Nostalgia', *Representations*, 49 (1995) 164, www.jstor.org/stable/2928753 (accessed 18 September 2019).

37. Fedorova, 'Gosha Rubchinskiy: Inside his Vertically Integrated Youth Universe'.

38. Fedorova, 'Gosha Rubchinskiy: Inside his Vertically Integrated Youth Universe'; Fury, 'For Gosha Rubchinskiy, Sweatshirts, T-Shirts, and Jeans Are the Coolest Things in Fashion'; Madsen, 'From Russia with Love: We Meet Gosha Rubchinskiy and His Gang'.

39. Georg Simmel, 'Fashion'. In Daniel Leonhard Purdy, Ed. *The Rise of Fashion* [1901] (Minneapolis, MN: University of Minnesota Press, 2004).

40. Oliver, 'Go Go Gosha'.

41. Calum Gordon, 'How Did Gosha Rubchinskiy Become So Big, So Quick?' *Highsnobiety*, 2016, www.highsnobiety.com/2016/03/14/gosha-rubchinskiy-op-ed/?curator=FashionREDEF (accessed 15 September 2019).

42. Calvin Hui, 'Dirty Fashion: Ma Ke's Fashion "Useless", Jia Zhangke's Documentary Useless and Cognitive Mapping', *Journal of Chinese Cinemas*, 9 (3) (2015) 258.

43. ibid., 259.

44. Lauren Parker, (2008) 'Shanghai: Dream City', in Zhang Hongxing and Lauren Parker, Eds. *China Design Now* (London: V&A Publishing, 2008) 97.

45. Jessica Bugg, 'Fashion at the Interface: Designer – Wearer – Viewer', *Fashion Practice*, 1 (1) (2009) 10.

46. Patrizia Calefato, 'Fashionscapes'. In Adam Geczy and Vicki Karaminas, Eds. *The End of Fashion: Clothing and Dress in the Age of Globalization* (Bloomsbury: London, 2019) 38.

47. www.lesechos.fr/03/11/2008/LesEchos/20292-051-ECH_la-chine-cherche-ses-marques.html (accessed 30 December 2018).

48. Oliver, 'Go Go Gosha'; Fury, 'For Gosha Rubchinskiy, Sweatshirts, T-Shirts, and Jeans Are the Coolest Things in Fashion'.

49. Joerg Koch, 'Gosha Rubchinskiy', *032c*, 2010, https://032c.com/gosha-rubchinskiy/ (accessed 15 September 2019).

50. Fury, 'For Gosha Rubchinskiy, Sweatshirts, T-Shirts, and Jeans Are the Coolest Things in Fashion'.

51. Vikram Anatoliy Kansara and Anastasiia Fedorova, 'How Comme des Garçons Grew Gosha Rubchinskiy', *BoF*, 2016, www.businessoffashion.com/articles/bof-exclusive/comme-des-garcons-gosha-rubchinskiy-dover-street-market-london. (accessed 29 September 2018).

52. Fury, 'For Gosha Rubchinskiy, Sweatshirts, T-Shirts, and Jeans Are the Coolest Things in Fashion'.

53. Gilles Lipovetsky, 'More than Fashion'. In Gilles Lipovetsky et al., Eds. *Chic Clicks* (Boston, MA: The Institute of Contemporary Art, 2002) T8.

54. White cited in Allan Sekula, 'On the Invention of Photographic Meaning'. In Victor Burgin, Ed. *Thinking Photography* (London: Macmillan, 1992) 101.

55. Roberts, 'Angels with Dirty Faces: Gosha Rubchinskiy and the Politics of Style', 21.

56. Madsen, 'From Russia with Love: We Meet Gosha Rubchinskiy and His Gang'.

57. Vikram Anatoliy Kansara, 'BoF Exclusive: How Gosha Rubchinskiy and Adidas Are Refashioning Football' *BoF*, 2017, www.businessoffashion.com/articles/bof-exclusive/gosha-rubchinskiy-adidas-kaliningrad-globalization-localization (accessed 15 September 2019).

58. Lou Stoppard, 'Lou Stoppard Reports on the Gosha Rubchinskiy Show', *SHOWstudio*, 2015, http://showstudio.com/collection/gosha_rubchinskiy_paris_menswear_s_s_2016/lou_stoppard_reports_on_the_gosha_rubchinskiy_show (accessed 22 January 2019).

59. Fury, 'For Gosha Rubchinskiy, Sweatshirts, T-Shirts, and Jeans Are the Coolest Things in Fashion'.

60. Ma Ke, 'Design with Conscience, Live with Simplicity', 5.

61. Li Edelkoort, *Anti_Fashion: A Manifesto for the Next Decade* (Paris: Trend Union, 2015).

62. Christopher Breward, 'Foreword'. In Heike Jenss, Ed. *Fashion Studies, Research Methods, Sites and Practices* (London: Bloomsbury, 2016) xvii.

63. Appadurai, *Modernity at Large*, 33.

64. Calefato, 'Fashionscapes', 32.

65. Meyrowitz 1985 cited in Appadurai, *Modernity at Large*, 29.

66. Appadurai, *Modernity at Large*, 31.

67. Calefato, 'Fashionscapes', 33.

68. ibid.

69. Appadurai, *Modernity at Large*, 33.

CHAPTER 13
BODY MAPPING: CROSS-CULTURAL INFLUENCES IN THE STUDIO
Jenny HUGHES

Introduction

As a practising textile artist and lecturer at University for the Creative Arts (UCA) specializing in fashion design, I strive to instil a sense of 'critical adventure' in fashion and textile students. I encourage them to question their own understanding, break down perceptions, re-invent and deconstruct stereotypes, and re-map fashion to try to move away from well-worn Eurocentric perspectives.

My chapter is a case study of the work of pre-degree fashion/textiles pathway students at UCA Rochester, United Kingdom, documenting their experience of fashion and experimental textiles within the studio, via multidisciplinary, issue-based work exploring cross-cultural narratives, 2018–19. The pre-degree course comprises students from the Foundation and Extended Diploma in Art and Design who have completed their A Level studies and intend to go on to study at degree level. There are also some mature students from the Access to Higher Education course. The pre-degree course encourages students to experiment and build their conceptual creative and technical skills and build an inventive portfolio of work. Stage 1 is the Exploratory stage where students work on a series of rotation projects within fine art, fashion/textiles, visual communication, 3D design and moving image and photography to help them decide where their focus will be in Stage 2. Stage 2 is the Specialist pathway where students work on more specific projects relating to fashion/textiles and build their conceptual design, technical and contextual understanding over a series of focused projects. Stage 3 is the Confirmatory stage where students devise research and evolve a final major project focusing on their specialist interest.

I will focus on the students' creative experiences through five documented workshops and projects in the fashion/textiles pathway. These were designed to enhance European students' knowledge of, and questioning of, the meta-narrative of 'Global Fashion'. In short, we see how a group of students begins to identify and contest the more and less visible boundaries that permeate fashion systems around the world.

As they begin to explore the specialist fashion and textile projects, students are introduced to the work of Yohji Yamamoto, Rei Kawakubo, Junya Watanabe and Jun Takahashi. Japanese design history and aesthetics are used as a key way to challenge the students and encourage them to look beyond the European way of designing. Emerging Japanese fashion in the 1980s sought to deconstruct European aesthetics and to encourage people to reconsider their Western ideas of beauty. The avant-garde 1980s designs of Yamamoto and Kawakubo heralded the grunge movement of the 1990s and continue to challenge fashion aesthetics today. 'The void is important', stated Kawakubo in 1985.[1]

Students sometimes find these concepts and aesthetic principles difficult to integrate within their studio practice at the outset. But they gradually free themselves and move away from more Eurocentric fashion perspectives.

Students begin by exploring the work of Yamamoto and Kawakubo in relation to the aesthetic concepts of 'wabi-sabi' and 'ma' practiced within Japanese culture.

- wabi-sabi – accepting transience and the innate beauty of imperfection as a conceptual springboard for design and construction.
- ma – exploring the space/gap between the body and clothes.

Wabi-sabi is a philosophy linked to Zen Buddhism. For me, it expresses the beauty found in imperfection and transcience; the beauty of the modest, the humble, the unconventional. Wabi-sabi is the aesthetic appreciation of the evanescence of life ... the need to tread lightly on the planet. As such it chimes with contemporary ecological concerns. Wabi-sabi is often assigned a vagueness, a blurry or attenuated quality; referencing a simplicity, an emotional warmth. For example, the ephemerality of cherry blossom; its presence felt for a mere seven days.

In 1982–3, Kawakubo is said to have manifested these aesthetic qualities when she apparently sabotaged the computer program of a textile loom to create holes and ladders in her collection for Comme des Garçons. She demonstrated a refusal to be dominated by technology, and a need to show the human touch at work in the creative process. Making clothes is, in essence, about relating flat fabric to a 3D figure in the form of the human body. In keeping with ma, designers who keep to the structure of kimono can be free from European couture methods which continue to give a 3D form to fabric by using curved lines and darts to fit to the body.

In practice, ma is an assemblage of rectangles, simply draping cloth over the body; echoed in Issey Miyake's APOC concept of 1976. Complementary elements of origami can be also seen in the work of Kawakubo (Autumn/Winter 2012) and Junya Watanabe for Comme de Garçons (Autumn/Winter 2016). Students are encouraged to adopt this approach in the studio from the outset. 'Superfluous space between garment and body, referred to as ma, is more than a void, rather a rich space that possesses incalculable energy ... only when worn do they take on the final form'.[2]

Within the studio environment, students explore concepts of ma through the work of Yamamoto. We reference the traditional Japanese kimono as 'a study of the space between the garment and the body', a subtle interplay between two- and three-dimensional space. Questions are posed to the student cohort concerning the relationship between body and clothes.

Students may struggle initially with some of the aesthetic concepts and contextual underpinnings described above. But as the term proceeds, they evolve their studio practice and their understanding of the possibilities of creative and critical adventure.

Figure 13.1 Emily Saunders Memento project: an example of student work from the specialist stages showing the influence of ma; art deco inspirations combine with dramatic pattern cutting using a futuristic monochrome screen-printed textile.

They work individually and in small groups to devise experimental designs and constructions. They learn to take risks in the studio, to 'unlearn' their pre-conceived ideas around fashion. Students are encouraged to challenge scale, to contrast, to experiment with minimal colour, and to create surface tensions.

The pre-degree course at UCA takes place over one academic year and is comprised of three stages. First is the Exploratory stage where students experiment with the main specialist areas within art and design in a series of week-long fast-paced studio projects. This gives the student a taste of each specialist area and equips them with a conceptual and creative skillset for the Stage 2 specialist pathway projects. Stage 3 concludes with the Final Major Project as students develop an extended independently researched creative project.

Project 1: Planet Organic

The first studio project, Planet Organic, takes place in the Exploratory stage of the course. It keys into the aesthetic idea of wabi-sabi. It expresses the beauty within imperfection, the impermanent, the incomplete, and references the natural world. Students take part in an experimental fashion workshop to create a series of dynamic designs. Working intuitively using calico and pins they respond to the creative challenge of producing draped designs on the mannequin.

The focus is on asymmetry, organic form and a juxtaposition of scale and texture. Students are encouraged to recreate their sketches and drawings of organic forms in fabric in a playful, irreverent manner. After sketching and photographing five alternative designs, the student sews up the most successful one by hand. Surface texture is explored through fabric manipulation and hand and machine stitching. The fashion/textiles studio is thus seen as a place of creative energy, openness and experimentation.

In this project, we also look at the work of Yamamoto who has inspired generations of fashion students to explore asymmetry, deconstruction and a more abstract approach to design. His shredded garments continually challenge, and visualize the edgy, anti-authoritarian and imperfect aesthetic favoured by young people. His aesthetic is echoed in those of Watanabe and Jun Takahashi as they wrap/envelop the body. After material and contextual experimentation, students move on to combine draping, deconstruction and structuring to create a wearable garment. This exercise challenges students' perceptions of 'fashion'.

Final project outcomes reflect the asymmetrical emphasis of wabi-sabi. They also echo the work of Yamamoto who tore, frayed, cut and stretched fabric to reference fabric history and memory, responding to quotations such as: 'A good garment is one that allows you to live well and grow old well in its company'.[3] Sustainability and history are referenced here too.

Colour palette for the initial Planet Organic project is limited to white/cream, as preferred by Kawakubo and Yamamoto.

Figure 13.2 Planet Organic: design sheet by Jess Loxton showing experimental fashion design. Jess instinctively combined sculptural form and fine graphic skills to evolve a sensitive design sheet exploring the process using coffee and tea staining combined with drawing.

Project 2: Map Manipulation

In this project, students explore maps as a source of inspiration. Maps offer enormous potential for interesting shapes, structure, pattern, print, colour and colour combinations. Patterns themselves can be seen as maps to be followed with instructions. Students work with various cartographic artefacts: old, worn and stained maps, UK Ordinance Survey sheets, street plans, Google Earth images, astronomical charts and constellations, and/or architectural blueprints. Maps are considered in a political, cerebral, geographical sense. We also look at psychogeography – an exploration of urban environments that emphasizes playfulness and 'drifting' – as a theoretical stimulus for design concepts and ideas. Here, we reference Guy Debord's *Theory of the Dérive* (1954) and the work of Julie Mehretu. The project is essentially a shape-finding exercise. Students re-draw and re-define fashion systems exploring ma, the concept of the space between the body and clothing. Referenced again is Kawakubo, who refuses to define and explain her clothes. She is often quoted as having said: 'The meaning is there is no meaning'.[4]

Kawakubo is seen as a very private person whose deeply personal, self-reflective narratives manifest in her work: 'Each collection is an expression more of what I am feeling at the time, my inner sentiments, my doubts, my fears and my hopes'. Kawakubo's

'Abstraction and introspection confound our ideas of fashion and its interpretation . . . in turn prosaic and descriptive, poetic and expressive.'[5] At first, students may find Kawakubo's approach confusing, even confused. But through deeper engagement, they come to appreciate her challenging of fashion orthodoxies, and gain more confidence in expressing creative visions of their own.

Experimentation and dynamics of scale are encouraged as students explore shape, mark-making and texture in their design sheets using acetate, layered drawing and collage to work directly and intuitively. To develop the skills and confidence to complete their project outcomes, they learn pattern making and surface-decoration techniques that echo the flat-pattern constructions of the Japanese avant-garde designers they have been studying while working with the concepts of mapping described above.

Enhancing this more playful and abstract approach to design development and investigation, students also experiment with the dynamics of scale. Pattern making and actual construction often divides the student cohort. Some individuals gravitate to the technical and creative challenge, others feel more comfortable in pure design. The importance of pattern-making skills is emphasized from the outset. Students gain confidence through developing and constructing ambitious abstract patterns to push their creative design knowledge in the spirit of the avant-garde creations of Kawakubo and Yamamoto. 'I like to work with space and emptiness' Kawakubo has stated.[6]

Figure 13.3 Mapping Manipulations: final outcomes exploring ma by Jess Loxton (13.3a) and Grace Moore (13.3b).

Project 3: Memento Re-Making History

This project explores historical and cultural references relating to a specific period chosen by the student, engaging with the aesthetic of wabi-sabi through garment distressing, deconstruction and re-working. In the studio, experiments with Draping on the Stand serve as a design starting point. Through intensive historical research, and experimenting with fabric manipulation, students evolve their own vintage-inspired designs. They extract design references from historical collections to help them inform and generate ideas for design, construction and colour, with Yamamoto again as a strong influence.

We recognize that designers take inspiration from the world around them – from memories, cultural references, chance meetings, a fragment of embroidery, or a discarded ticket found in the street – many random references and traces of the past and present. As an example, we look at the work of Yves Saint Laurent who is well known for his particular fascination with Asian art and culture. Saint Laurent used his collections, for example Haute Couture Autumn/Winter 1994, to construct his own imaginary vision of the East as a dreamlike realm of luxury and delight. He initially drew on Asian inspiration while working on the Dior collection in 1958, using Japanese silk brocade embroidered with gold thread, and stated 'The marvellous thing is that the dream and the reality are one. It is just one short step from the dream to the real'.[7]

We balanced the European positioning of Yves Saint Laurent with the writings of Tanizaki: 'I have said that lacquerware decorated in gold was made to be seen in the dark; and for this same reason were the fabrics of the past so lavishly woven of threads of silver and gold'.[8] We also consider Japanese textile designs. These suggest a vivid connection with nature which is seen as gentle and devastating in turn; an ally to be tamed and controlled. Japanese literature and history are used to reference the symbolism of the pine tree, the cherry blossom, bamboo red maples, and plum trees.

Another guide for our Memento project is Yoshida Kenko, the 14th century writer of 'Essays in Idleness'. Kenko said: 'In everything no matter what it may be, uniformity is undesirable. Leaving something incomplete makes it interesting and gives one the feeling there is room to grow'.[9] This enables us to start the project by considering the key themes of asymmetry and juxtapositions of scale and texture. Next, students develop, sketch and photograph five alternative draping designs. They sew up the most successful of these by hand, using vintage fabrics, embroideries, fragments of lace and pre-loved garments that they have sourced. If required, staining with coffee, Quink ink and tea is used to give cotton, muslin and silk an antique finish.

Pattern pieces are separated and inventively reassembled, and an unfinished aesthetic is achieved through details such as raw edges, using machine and hand stitching to create surface texture and structure. In the final wearable garment, students have combined techniques of draping, deconstruction and fabric manipulation. Through ageing and distressing fabrics, deconstructing and unravelling, students explore the aesthetics

Figure 13.4 Memento inspired design by Lucy Godley exploring fabric manipulation referencing wabi-sabi, to emulate Elizabethan dress.

Figure 13.5 Memento: deconstructed dress by Rob Wignall.

of wabi-sabi and the beauty in imperfection as a way of working with their chosen time period.

Project 4: Multiples in Nature

Within this project, fashion students explore the 'Pattern Magic' system of pattern making as created by Tomoko Nakamichi.[10] Learning focuses on experimental design development, asymmetry, scale and texture with reference to the natural world. Students again explore wabi-sabi aesthetics within textiles experimentation. A reference point is Yamamoto's reflections on the dislocation and alienation felt in mass consumption and globalization in this digital age: 'They don't realise the meaning of an object . . . like stone or trees . . . they consume everything . . . they think they can buy everything . . . that is very sad'.[11]

Experiments with heat-set shibori, and creating Pattern Magic sections in multiple forms, stimulate the students to take their creative ideas further. A playful approach to scale, texture and surface decoration is encouraged among students within the studio as they explore various construction formats following the instructions of Nakamichi.

Figure 13.6 Multiples in Nature: design sheet by Jess Loxton using a mixed media collage technique.

We also look at the Kimono, which literally means 'thing to wear' and has proved inspirational for many cultures and periods. As Akiko Fukai observes, 'The 1920s dresses of Madeleine Vionnet, her extremely simple, linear garment patterns, were completely different from the complex curves of traditional Western dressmaking. They have much in common with kimono ... the West had moved beyond its initial superficial interest in the kimono's exoticism to appreciate it on a deeper level'.[12] Growing in confidence and learning more construction skills, students gain a clearer understanding of Japanese fashion and textiles, and of the tactile and haptic, as alternative viewpoints.

Project 5: Final Major Project

For their self-generated final project within Stage 3 of the course, students begin to address ecological concerns, and migration, social and gender issues. Design experiments move beyond Eurocentric/ethnocentric discourses within fashion to explore dynamic cultural hybrids to weave an alternative future. Through students' questioning and re-framing issues and perspectives deemed 'global', their outcomes become more politically, socially and ethically engaged.

To evolve their designs, students initially make detailed drawings and fashion/textiles visuals. To create samples, they work with techniques including digital printing, silkscreen printing, stitching, knitting, weaving and fabric manipulation. In their independent studies, students are encouraged to explore a wide range of Western and non-Western references and techniques. We present the notion of 'hybrid', whereby many diverse references come together. And we delve into the fluid, cross-cultural nature of contemporary design and art, as practiced by the likes of Grace Wales Bonner, Tchai Kim, Nick Cave and Manish Arora.

Examples include Iris van Herpen's 'Ludi Natura' Spring/Summer 2018 collection which subtly interweaves in technology, Tchai Kim's eloquent designs referencing Korean hanbok, and Grace Wales Bonner who explores hybridity and cross-cultural influences with references to the 18th-century dandy, her own Jamaican heritage and African textiles techniques.

Sustainability and ecological concerns were very real for students as nature is fighting a seemingly uncontrollable sea of waste plastics, synthetic fabrics and harmful toxic waste. The rise of Extinction Rebellion climate protests and Fashion Revolution, and the use of the hashtag #WhoMadeMyClothes, are developments that have helped make students more politically and socially engaged, and more aware of the consequences of fast fashion for the environment and for human exploitation.

Connections were made with the 'Fashioned from Nature' exhibition at the V&A in 2018, and in the eco disaster presentation at the Japanese Pavilion at the Venice Biennale of 2017. For example, as exhibited at 'Fashioned from Nature', Diana Scherer's ground-breaking work growing fabric from oats using a digital template inspired eco-focused projects within the studio. On our annual student trip to Amsterdam, we visited exhibitions including the Fashion Cities Africa at the Tropenmuseum, and Fashion for Good which

Figure 13.7 Final Major Project: Louisa Muir Little re-visits pattern magic and origami to create an inventive garment referencing the surface tensions between nature and architecture using handmade felt and calico.

Figure 13.8 Final Major Project: Lizzie Lovell explores Fashion Cities Africa using traditional and experimental textiles through weave and embroidery inspired by wabi-sabi.

Figure 13.9 Final Major Project, 'Beneath the Layers': Rob Wignall exploring personal family history juxtaposing dramatic pattern and textures using digital printing, draping and Pattern Magic.

Figure 13.10 Final Major Project: Jess Loxton here exploring the 'No Sew' laser cutting techniques utilising waste fabric for an inventive sustainable conclusion.

focused on sustainability. Such experiences provided valuable research opportunities into global contemporary design and experimental textile techniques for students.

As aspects of their research and material development, students often returned to Pattern Magic, wabi-sabi and ma within their final projects. Introducing students to such concepts with depth and sensitivity encouraged them to experiment in more dynamic ways and to explore wider perspectives beyond their own borders in ways that I hope will promote better cross-cultural understanding in the future.

Conclusion

To conclude, students address concerns around the environment, migration, society and gender. Their designs move beyond Eurocentric and ethnocentric discourses within fashion, and begin to explore cultural hybrids. In essence, they are laying the foundations for an alternative future. Outcomes are more politically, socially and ethically engaged through the students' own questioning and re-framing of issues deemed 'global'. These projects prepare the students for degree-level study and enhance their critical and creative understanding. They encourage risk taking and broaden perspectives.

Notes

1. Andrew Bolton, *Rei Kawakubo Comme des Garçons: Art of the In-Between* (New York: Metropolitan Museum of Art, 2017) 10.

2. Yohji Yamamoto and Wim Wenders, *Yohji Yamamoto* (New York: Rizzoli, 2014) 21.

3. Wim Wenders, *Notebooks on Cities and Clothes* (documentary film), Axiom Films, 1989.

4. Rei Kawakubo quoted in Bolton, *Rei Kawakubo Comme des Garçons*, 12.

5. Sanae Shimizu and NHK, Eds. *Unlimited Comme des Garcons* (Tokyo: Heibonsha, 2005).

6. ibid.

7. Aurélie Samuel, *Yves Saint Laurent: Dreams of the Orient* (London: Thames and Hudson, 2019) 43.

8. Junichiro Tanizaki, *In Praise of Shadows* (Sedgwick, MN: Leetes Islands Books, 1977) 36.

9. Kenko Yoshida, *Essays on Idleness*, trans. George Bailey Sampson (New York: Cosimo Classics, 2009) 36.

10. Tomoko Nakamichi, *Pattern Magic* (London: Laurence King Publishing, 2010), *Pattern Magic 2* (London: Laurence King Publishing, 2011) and *Pattern Magic 3* (London: Laurence King Publishing, 2016).

11. Wenders, *Notebooks on Cities and Clothes*.

12. Akiko Fukai, 'Foreword'. In Yuki Morishima, Rie Nii, Cynthia Amneus and Akiko Fukai, Eds. *Kimono Refashioned Japans Impact on International Fashion* (San Francisco, CA: Asian Art Museum, 2018) 3.

AFTERWORD

Sarah CHEANG, Erica DE GREEF and TAKAGI Yoko

Postcolonial and decolonial thinking are critical interventions in the writing of history. The discussions raised in this book have implications for all thinkers, practitioners, students and teachers. These discussions range from participatory research to historical revisions and close re-readings of fashion objects that offer new or alternative approaches to understandings of fashion as an inclusive and far-reaching phenomenon. For students and academics, this edited collection presents an original set of texts that diversifies and extends the conversation on the socio-cultural and political significance of fashion, especially in dialogue with other critical work on decolonization, indigeneity and redress. Furthermore, the various chapters allow for inclusive and more nuanced understandings of diverse fashion systems, shifting problematic perceptions and confronting persistent issues of exclusion and absence. This is essential to decolonizing fashion education and related design curricula, in both the Global North and the Global South, where they have been dominated by Eurocentric pedagogies and ontologies in the realm of fashion studies. It is our hope that students and academics, as well as already established designers and researchers, may find in these chapters a more inclusive range of narratives and conceptual/aesthetic positions that will support their own individual practices with greater sensitivity or empowerment no matter what background they are from, and that they feel seen and heard, and better equipped to effect change for a fairer fashion system in the future.

If we were to use the geographic units of the continent, this collection of essays could claim to have included mention of all regions of the globe (North America, Central/South America, Europe, Africa, Asia, the Pacific). However, the meaning of 'global' within 'fashion globalization' does not lie in the encyclopaedic idea that all parts of the world are involved in some way. Indeed, the terms that could be used to make such a claim would contain endless exclusions and elisions, and also many assumptions about what fashion is. Therefore, new critical approaches need to work very clearly with the inconsistencies, possibilities and impossibilities of cultures, ideas, objects and fashions as 'global' phenomena. In planning this book, we considered also notions of a culturally politicised deglobalization. However, in the process of working with the authors in this volume, it became evident that our project was engaged not so much with rethinking globalization as 'deglobalization', but rather with the consequences of 'decentring' of fashion from the limitations of Eurocentric/Euro-facing fashion centres. From an initial re-centring of fashion in the two-day seminar that was held in Japan, our discussions about diverse, overlooked, erased and even disavowed sites of fashion histories, contemporary developments and fashion futures have led from a re-centred to a multi-centred understanding of the fashion world. In knowing and addressing the fashion world as multi-centred, we begin to acknowledge diversity and welcome viewpoints that are different, even oppositional.

Working with scholars and thinkers for example, from sub-Saharan Africa, who have been underrepresented in Anglophone fashion studies, we make no claim to have 'decolonized' fashion studies. Rather, we seek to draw the readers' attention to the global dynamics involved when listening to, giving space to, and acknowledging the agency and voices of thinkers and makers from the Global South within English-language fashion studies. Furthermore, this collection makes clear the power of interactions between fashion practice and theory as a continuum of globally distributed knowledge production, where embodied practices in the self-fashioning of identities are felt and interwoven in the daily experiences of identity and belonging. Embodied knowledge is acknowledged as witnessing fashion in forms of sense-making, or performances of belonging or resistance, or as sites of memory or memory practices and the reclamation of histories.

In shaping the future of fashion studies, one of the strongest roles for decolonial approaches currently lies in supporting a new capacity for hearing a greater diversity of voices, and thinking openly about what this means for how fashion is understood. Decolonial approaches draw attention to the importance of attending to the conditions of fashion knowledge as well at the content of fashion histories and discourses. The revised vocabularies and active listening required, and capacities for more equal inter-disciplinary and cross-cultural communication and alliances, will all be paramount in shaping this powerful and socially relevant terrain.

INDEX

Index

Index

Index

Index

Index

Index